GERHARD BERGER

Patrick Stephens Limited, an imprint of Haynes Publishing, has published authoritative, quality books for more than a quarter of a century. During that time the company has established a reputation as one of the world's leading publishers of books on aviation, maritime, motor cycle, car, motorsport and railway subjects. Readers or authors with suggestions for books they would like to see published are invited to write to: The Editorial Director, Patrick Stephens Limited, Sparkford, Nr Yeovil, Somerset, BA22 7JJ.

GERHARD BERGER

The Human Face of Formula 1

Second edition

CHRISTOPHER HILTON

Patrick Stephens Limited

First published in 1993
2nd edition 1995

British Library Cataloguing-in-Publication Data:
A catalogue record for this book
is available from the British Library.

ISBN 1 85260 515 4

Library of Congress catalog card no. 94 73830

Patrick Stephens Limited is an imprint of Haynes Publishing,
Sparkford, Nr Yeovil, Somerset BA22 7JJ.

Typset by G&M, Raunds, Northamptonshire
Printed in Great Britain by
Butler & Tanner Ltd, London and Frome

Contents

Foreword
by Ayrton Senna

There are a lot of good things to say about Gerhard. He arrived at McLaren from Ferrari at a time when I had just got out of a highly unpleasant relationship with (Alain) Prost and then (Jean-Marie) Balestre. *My head was in my feet* — a Brazilian expression which means thoroughly out of sorts. I knew I could still drive a racing car but my mind was shattered, and I was eager to get back at them (Prost and Balestre) at the time. I was very hurt and had become a very aggressive person.

Gerhard arrived and in one of our first conversations I made a point of saying to him, 'Look, I had an extremely bad relationship with my last team-mate and I have no intention of repeating it. It only brought me harm and I do not want to go through a similar experience again. I know that it is not relevant to you, it has nothing to do with you, but I have to say this to you because I think we should try to have a professional and honest relationship from the beginning. We will both get some good out of it. We have to do our best to make this relationship work out well'.

He told me he had also had a bad relationship with Mansell and I remember him saying to me, 'You wouldn't believe how difficult it is to get on with Mansell'. More than ever, we both realized how important it was to work hard, to do our best to build up a good atmosphere in the team and between the two of us.

And it carried on like that. Of course, we had our misunderstandings, but the first time it happened, Imola 1990, we had a talk and sorted it out. At the start he pushed me aside, and I was furious. After the race I called him for a chat and asked what had happened. He hesitated a bit and I said that I agreed he had had a better start, but afterwards he had missed a gear and I had recovered ground. We were side by side when he pushed me aside.

We talked for a while and he admitted that it was not a thing to do, and that he would not have liked it if I had done it to him. There, it was clear to me that he was a good guy. Our chat was honest and sincere and I could tell he had only made a mistake — simple as that, like all of us sometimes make.

After it we started to build an excellent relationship. Obviously at the beginning I helped him a lot; I put much more into the relationship than I got out of it. I knew the team, how it worked, I knew the car and the engine deeply. To help was just the way it had to be and I never tried to hide anything from him. I did my best in an open way and he used my suggestions, followed my advice sometimes.

As time went by he learnt about the car, engine and everything and started to help in the car set-up and its development. Because we had worked together in a clean and honest way — and I had helped him in the beginning — he could feel relaxed about putting things in, too.

It was like that throughout the three years we worked together, and because we had such a good thing going as racing drivers we ended up having a great relationship off the track as well. He would come to my beach house in Angra do Reis before the Brazilian Grand Prix and we had a wonderful time. I would come and stay on his boat in Sardinia or Ibiza during some breaks between Grands Prix, and we became very good friends.

Of course, under pressure we fought hard. We both wanted to win. But it was done in a very open way, honest. For me — and I believe for him as well — managing to have such a good relationship was a great achievement. We proved that even though we were team-mates and in theory each other's 'direct enemy', we could do it. We proved that if you have a good attitude and good manners, professionally and personally, it is possible to do it even in such an environment as Formula 1.

You know, we had had bad relationships in our previous teams with our previous team-mates and even so we managed to come out of it, after three years, as very good friends. We were under big pressures, went through bad problems, racing fights and so on and we managed it well. I know I am repeating myself, but I honestly think it was an exceptional experience. I am glad I was fortunate enough to have it.

Acknowledgements

I sincerely thank many people who have given their time and their insights, particularly Gerhard Berger himself. Don't fall into the trap of trying to interview him; pose a question then sit back and enjoy yourself. He vibrates with good humour, can be outrageously funny, and the next instant he's serious, thoughtful, candid in the most innocent, disarming way. ('Ask what you like,' he said, 'because I want it to be a good book.' If it isn't that's my fault, not his). Berger's father Hans very kindly gave invaluable family background and a discreet glimpse or two of young Gerhard. Eric Silbermann, who looks after Berger's publicity, helped enormously in several directions at once, not least handling follow-up questions and doing it with the proper sensibilities.

Ayrton Senna had the kindness to provide the foreword and talk candidly of his time with Berger, some of it hilarious. Because of his extremely close friendship with Berger, I have decided to leave the foreword exactly as it was written for the first edition of this book. It stands, I hope, as a fitting memory to that friendship. Senna, incidentally, was a formidable opponent in the matter of practical jokes, as you'll see. I pay tribute to Betise Assumpcao, Senna's PR lady, for arranging the lovely — and heartfelt — words Senna gave.

Because of the breadth and scope of Berger's career, truly a lot of people did give their time and insights or pointed me in the right direction. They are (in no particular order): Derek Warwick, Johnny Herbert, Alistair McQueen, John Nielsen, Tony Jardine of Jardine PR, Manfred Schiechtl, Gerhard Kuntschik of the *Salzburger Nachrichten*, James Weaver, Gunter Schmid, Robin and Martin Brundle, Charley Lamm and Patricia Baduria of the Schnitzer team, Jeff Hutchinson, Elvira Ruocco of Alfa Romeo, Ian Brown and Silvie

Shannon of FISA, Pierluigi Martini, Hans Peter Brock of Sauber, Karl Wendlinger (Jr), Mark Blundell, Johnny Dumfries, Tommy Byrne, Agnes Carlier of Philip Morris, Cathy Muller, Roberto Ravaglia; Jackie Oliver, John Wickham and Alan Rees of Footwork; Manfred Hahn of Formel-3-Vereinigung; Les Thacker; Ann Bradshaw of Williams, Amanda Cothill and Andrew Marriott of CSS; Michele Alboreto; Thierry Boutsen; Laura Giglio for translations, Nadia Pavignani of Ducati, Rossella Amadesi of Red One, Dave Price; Colin Wilson of the RAC, Stan Piecha of *The Sun*, Pino Allievi of *La Gazzetta dello Sport*, James Hunt, Murray Walker and Stuart Cabb of the BBC; Rory Byrne of Benetton, Peter Collins and John Miles of Team Lotus, Maurice Hamilton of *The Observer*, Josef Kaufmann, Helmut Marko, Dieter Stappert, Pino Trivellato, Hans Stuck; Ron Dennis, Jo Ramirez, Norman Howell and Peter Stayner of McLaren International; Martin Donnelly; John Barnard of Ferrari, John Blunsden, Professor Sid Watkins.

Gabriella Strauss of BMW and Monica Meroni of Scuderia Italia became active helpers, organizing and finding and interpreting, and the book would have been seriously diminished without their efforts. Particular salutations to them and to Victoria Flack of Jardine PR who turned a lot of Italian into English perfectly and at the speed of a Formula 1 car.

I must also offer my sincere thanks to the *Autosport* team, because the magazine covers motor racing in all its guises so comprehensively and you can't properly reconstruct a driver's career without it. I am in debt to Simon Taylor, the deputy chairman, for permission to quote from *Autosport*, to Nigel Roebuck, the Grand Prix editor, for active assistance — background and foreground information and reflections — to Joe Saward (now *F 1 News*) who covered Berger's early forays, and to Quentin Spurring for a delicious anecdote.

I've consulted and drawn from *Motoring News* (and thanks to Executive Editor David Tremayne for permission to quote from it, and for such ready co-operation in opening his notebooks), Marlboro's *Grand Prix Guide*, Berger's autobiography *Grenzbereich* (with Dieter Stappert; Verlag Orac, Vienna), *Jochen Rindt* by Heinz Pruller (William Kimber), *To Hell and Back* by Niki Lauda (Stanley Paul) and *Colin Chapman, The Man and his Cars* by Jabby Crombac (Patrick Stephens Ltd). I'm grateful to Random House UK Limited for permission to quote Alain Prost's thoughts about the Portuguese Grand Prix, 1987, from *Life in the Fast Lane* by Prost and Jean-Louis Moncet (also published by Stanley Paul). The fire regulations are quoted from the FIA Yearbook 1993.

The main weight of the photographs have been provided by the International Press Agency/Pan Images, Geneva, and particular thanks to Jad Sherif for his care in their selection. David Mills of

Grand Prix Sportique kindly provided the superb Alan Fearnley study of Monza 1988. Charley Lamm of the Schnitzer team dug out some evocative Touring Car moments. Les Thacker (via Johnny Dumfries) lent a couple of nice moments in European Formula 3. Elvira Ruocco of Alfa Romeo produced (all unknowing) a delightful picture of a race Berger wasn't in! Pino Trivellato provided the naughty picture (it's so cheeky you can't miss it) and was chuckling when he handed it over . . .

One corner, two lives

The lean, tousle-haired Austrian famous for his wit and his smile levered himself from the Ferrari's cockpit and marched the short distance to the protective sanctuary of the motorhome. When he got there he felt his whole body shaking. He'd seen bad things before, but his body had never started shaking.

It had been, just brief moments ago, only a gentle early spring afternoon — hot and dry — spread all across the garden of Italy, the Romagna district. This warmth embraced the Autodromo Enzo e Dino Ferrari, a circuit set beside the gentility of the town of Imola. Gerhard Berger waited to go out as the second qualifying session for the San Marino Grand Prix unfolded. The team clipped a little television monitor onto the cockpit so that he could see what the others were doing out on the circuit. The clocks ticked to 1.18 pm. It was Saturday 30 April 1994.

He had every reason to watch the television pictures and no reason not to watch them. Another qualifying session, that's all. True, the Brazilian driver of a Jordan car, Rubens Barrichello, had had a mighty crash on the Friday when his car speared into the wire fencing above the tyre wall at a corner near the pits, but Barrichello suffered no more than minor injuries. The world had been like this for 12 years, two years before Berger eased himself into a Formula 1 car for the first time: comparatively safe, the cars so strong they were themselves protective sanctuaries. True, Berger had suffered a 'moment' on that Friday when he had a puncture at real speed, but so what? Just a puncture, no further consequences.

Now, out there on the circuit, the Simtek of fellow Austrian Roland Ratzenberger was trying for a fast lap, and although the Simtek could not be described as fast in the Grand Prix context all Grand Prix cars are fast. Berger would take a particular interest in

Ratzenberger. At 32, Ratzenberger had been around for a long time, but had only just reached Formula 1 and, by a paradox, he and Berger did not know each other particularly well. While Berger had been in Formula 1 since 1984, Ratzenberger drove elsewhere. By a second paradox, Ratzenberger followed Berger into the BMW team when — because of Formula 1 commitments — Berger could no longer indulge in a bit of Touring Car combat.

By a third paradox, shortly before the San Marino Grand Prix Ratzenberger was doing his daily jog at Monaco, where he had an apartment, and he passed Berger's boat moored in the harbour. Berger bade him come aboard and they talked for a while.

'I started to get to know him better then. On the boat we talked a little bit about his team,' Berger says. 'It was a day to remember more and more. I liked him very much.'

You can easily imagine the conversation, easy and natural and unbuttoned. Roland Ratzenberger was a nice, polite man and some have described him as gentle. Gerhard Berger has never permitted the fame and the fortune to alter any of his essential characteristics in any way. If you want a chat, he's your boy, and if you're vulnerable to a practical joke (like throwing your expensive shoes from the boat into the harbour) so much the better.

Now, the clocks ticking to 1.18 pm, Ratzenberger took the Simtek urgently through the corner called Tamburello and on into the Villeneuve curve just before the left-spoon of the corner called Tosa, fastest part of the circuit. The car left the track at 200 mph and struck a concrete wall with terrible force, savaging it. The medical team arrived and, Berger says, 'I could see them starting to work on his heart and I knew the guy was dead' — meaning dead or so badly injured he could not recover.

'I saw the accident in re-play and I sensed how bad it could be. I was completely shocked. Of course in our job you have to be prepared to see situations like this, but as it was another Austrian driver, a personal contact, it was worse. I know you shouldn't make a distinction between a driver you know and a driver you don't know, but it affects you in a different way. I got out of the car and I felt sick.' Berger walked to the motorhome and began shaking.

Ratzenberger, clinically alive, was taken to the track's medical centre and then by helicopter to the Maggiore Hospital in the town of Bologna some 19 miles (35 km) away. Eight minutes after his arrival there the finality was officially announced. No driver had died at a Grand Prix meeting since Ricardo Paletti at Montreal, Sunday 13 June 1982.

Berger sat in the motorhome and spent some 10 minutes allowing the shaking to subside and 'I didn't know what to do'. During those 10 minutes he asked himself the question that could not be avoided. He knew that there could be no temporary solution, no fending it off to buy some time. Either he must abandon his career at this instant and walk away never to return, or he must get back in the car and continue. He thought as calmly and clinically as he could and answered the question to himself alone. *I still love to drive racing cars even if there is the risk.* Therefore, in the logic of it, he needed to get back in the car immediately. 'I decided on my way forward and I stayed on it. If I was going to race the next day there was no reason not to practice now.'

In the week that followed, he would know many emotions, much emptiness, many inner conflicts about the decision. After all, as a poet once wrote, *in a minute there is time for visions and revisions that a minute will reverse.* Berger did not alter his decision.

He is no fool and the question he answered is not one that ordinary people ever confront. He reasoned as a racing driver would, balancing his own mortality against the passion of what he adored doing; and he drew his balance. Some chose not to go out onto the Imola circuit again when the session resumed. Under the logic, Berger did. It was in no sense insensitive.

'I knew already before I went out that the situation was critical, but it was not going to make any difference to Roland whether I drove or not. From the moment I took the decision, I told myself to concentrate on the job. It was a difficult situation and it was very hard. There was no pressure from the team on me to get back into the car. Jean Todt (the team manager) said, "Gerhard, if you want to drive, drive; if you don't want to, don't. If you do, just drive as quick as you want."'

Just before the crash, Ayrton Senna — close friend of Berger and his team-mate at Marlboro McLaren for three years — had set fastest time, 1 minute 22.430 seconds. Berger drove strongly, searching for pole position and briefly held it with 1:22.226. At one point he skittered over kerbing and then, making a final effort, ran out of fuel. He was third.

Among those who remained in the pits after Ratzenberger's crash was Senna, already extremely distressed about Barrichello, a fellow Brazilian. All are agreed that under the weight of Ratzenberger's death Senna did not want to race in the Grand Prix on the morrow — 1 May — but in the end he reasoned as a racing driver would, drew his balance and raced.

The San Marino Grand Prix began as so many others have, with a start-line crash, so that the pace car — a saloon — emerged to take the racers slowly round until the wreckage was cleared. The order as they circled obediently behind this pace car: Senna in the Rothmans Williams Renault, Michael Schumacher in the Benetton Ford, Berger in the Ferrari. After five laps the pace car peeled off, releasing the racers. Senna and Schumacher dug power so quickly that Berger fell some way back. They travelled safely through the left of

Tamburello and its brief run-off area screened by a concrete perimeter wall.

A fleeting memory, perhaps, passing through. Precisely here on 23 April 1989 Berger survived the most horrific of crashes, the one so etched from hell that you can't forget it. His Ferrari snapped out of control and beat itself to pieces along the wall before a firestorm from the fuel engulfed it. Berger recovered with minor burns, itself an authentic miracle. Later, 'I asked the circuit people if the wall could be moved back, please, and they told me no, it couldn't, because there was a river behind it. I was a bloody idiot. I said, "OK I understand".'

It was the way the world was.

They completed the lap and moved across the start-finish line into lap seven, Schumacher hustling Senna — an ordinary, everyday racing arrangement of men and machines duelling for the lead. They moved towards Tamburello.

A thought: between Tamburello on lap three, 23 April 1989 and this 1 May 1994, Berger had driven 79 races and Senna 80. Cumulatively that meant Berger covered some 3,530 laps and Senna 3,555. A rough estimate of the total number of corners, curves and chicanes they passed safely through in those races: Berger 30,368, Senna 37,297. Even narrowing this, between 23 April 1989 and 1 May 1994, lap six, Berger had passed safely through Tamburello 178 times and Senna 230 in races — and that does not include repetitively passing through in test sessions, qualifying, race day warm-ups.

In one sense — if it can be put in such a way — Tamburello had returned to being just another corner despite Berger's firestorm there, and now they travelled into it again. The clocks ticked towards 2.17 pm and the totals ought to have clicked to Berger 179, Senna 231, passing safely through. At Tamburello Senna's Williams went essentially straight on, skimming the run-off area. He left the track at 190 mph and, the concrete wall that Berger had hit so long ago rearing at him, Senna dragged the speed down to 136 mph in the 0.9 of a second before he hit the wall. The Williams rebounded off it, scattering debris, rebounded — rotating — onto the rim of the track, but its centrifugal force rotated it back to the run-off area where it came to rest. Like Ratzenberger only yesterday, Ayrton Senna was no more than clinically alive.

Berger: 'You know, after my heavy accidents at Monza and Estoril in 1993 I went home to think about things. And I said to myself, it is like you have a cheque book and you write them out, one after another, to the angels. And then one day you have an empty book and you cannot give them out again. I tried to push away these effects. At Imola, I went off at Rivazza (a horseshoe left-left) on Friday because I had a puncture. I was lucky. Then came Roland's accident, which was the same as the one I had in 1989. A wing. Then came Ayrton's accident. I took my speed up to 260 km/h and I felt nothing wrong with

14

the car. Then I saw that the front suspension was broken. I had hit some debris from Ayrton's car and if I didn't stop maybe the suspension breaks. Maybe in Tamburello . . .'

As Berger had rounded Tamburello he had been faced with this: to his right Senna's rotating car on the rim of the track; immediately in front of him Senna's right front wheel, wrenched off; beyond that a severed chunk of bodywork; beyond that at least four small shards of debris more or less evenly spaced across the width of the track.

Berger stopped because the whole race was stopped. At the most pragmatic level, there would be time to repair the suspension.

Senna was flown by helicopter direct to the Maggiore Hospital, rumours, contradictions and mistaken information about his condition everywhere. Somehow that made it worse.

At the re-start Berger took the lead, Schumacher bustled and overtook him. After 16 laps Berger stopped. 'I was ahead of Schumacher and everything was good, but twice the car felt strange at the rear and I saw sparks and I got afraid. I came into the pits and the mechanics couldn't see anything. Maybe they thought I was dreaming it. I went out again. When I stopped, Jean Todt could see in my face that I didn't want to do it any more and he told me to get out of the car. We found out three days later that we had a rear damper problem.'

Berger journeyed to the Maggiore Hospital and was ushered in to the room where Senna lay. The crash had been so physically destructive that Senna's relatives were not permitted to see him. Berger, measuring his words with great care, says 'I saw him at six o'clock that evening. He had no chance any more, but he was on a life support machine and his heart was still beating. He was alive. Ayrton and I had known each other since Formula 3 days and we started to get closer in Formula 1 when I worked with him for three years at McLaren. I went to the hospital because I wanted to see him again. I saw him and then I went home.' There was nothing else he could do.

Senna died, or rather was officially pronounced dead, some 40 minutes later. By then Berger had taken a helicopter from the hospital to Bologna airport.

'We landed near my plane, which was next to his. Even though I'd just left him it hit me hard. Monday was a very strange day for me. Very empty. I felt Formula 1 was far away. For the first time, I thought it wasn't so important to me. I felt very far away from *myself* and it was the first time that I had ever felt this. What was I going to do with my future? Of course I sat down and wondered but I didn't speak with anyone about stopping except a little with my parents. I was surprised at all the speculation.'

Berger did not alter his decision.

He spent a couple of days isolated on the boat in Monte Carlo, not answering the telephone, and flew to Sao Paulo to attend Senna's funeral on the Thursday. 'For me, it was as if Ayrton had organized it himself. The whole thing was on a bigger scale than you could imagine — a million and a half people in the streets, hundreds of soldiers everywhere, military aircraft overhead, helicopters. It was like the funeral of an American President. For a moment I thought, "He's up there watching, and he's going to be so upset if one person moves the wrong way at the wrong moment". The organization was unbelievable — as I say, like he had done it himself. Ayrton's parents were amazing. Usually, people go to funerals in black clothes, but his mother wore white and I thought that was nice. And his father was in front of the coffin hurting terribly but at the same time obviously so proud. It seemed to me the same as when you've lost someone in war, this mixture of grief and pride. That day was unforgettable.'

Berger was among those who bore the coffin with Emerson Fittipaldi, Alain Prost, Christian Fittipaldi, Derek Warwick and Rubens Barrichello. Johnny Herbert attended and so did Thierry Boutsen, one of Senna's earliest friends in Formula 1. After the funeral Herbert and Berger flew to Brussels; and from there in Berger's plane to Salzburg to be at Ratzenberger's funeral on the Friday.

'I knew that physically it was possible to be at both funerals,' Herbert says, 'because I'd booked my flights. I flew to Sao Paulo from London and then from Sao Paulo to Brussels. I could have taken the normal flight from Brussels to Salzburg but Gerhard had said he had his own plane so I went along with him. When I'd set off from London I didn't know about his plane. I think I found that out in Brazil.

'It was a Lear Jet, I suppose eight seats, and he flew it. As a pilot he was all right. He didn't talk much, that was one thing I found. It was the way he was at the time, probably, but I have found that quite a lot with him, anyway. People talk about "funny Gerhard", but I've never actually seen that myself. It's always been, like, straightforward. We spoke a little bit on the plane but not much. I kept trying, four or five times, but those situations are always awkward. I think Gerhard was emptied, I think he was upset. He'd had a good relationship with Ayrton.'

Austrian journalist Gerhard Kuntschik was at Salzburg airport 'helping Burkhardt Hummel (of him more later) organize transport for the mourners. I spoke to Gerhard. It was as if he was empty inside, as if he couldn't think about anything. He was very calm and silent, no look on his face at all like usual. He didn't speak much, he was completely different. I could see it all hurt him very much. Roland had even got Senna interested in him because Senna thought he was a guy to look out for. Roland made a lot of friends in his few weeks in Formula 1.'

The service at Salzburg's central crematorium, in the shadow of the famous castle — the Festung Hohensalzburg, a 12th-century fortress some 500 feet above the town — was private. From Formula 1, apart from Berger and Herbert, came Heinz-Harald Frentzen, Karl Wendlinger, David Brabham, Jan Lammers and Max Mosley, the President of the governing body — the FIA — but there were also Touring Car drivers and Austrian rally drivers. The service lasted half an hour.

'Max and I met after Roland's funeral,' Berger says. 'He is not somebody who tries to put a wall between himself and the drivers, between the FIA and the drivers. I talked to him, but not enough. We love to drive, but we need people to look after the day-to-day problems that are coming. We need a group to work on safety. I believe that Max is open to helping about safety.'

Berger was due to do a test session the following week — the week before Monaco — but didn't feel ready to get into a racing car again yet. Rumours circulated that he might never be ready again and the notification that he'd called a Press Conference heightened that. By definition people (except politicians) don't ordinarily announce Press Conferences to say they have nothing to announce.

Meanwhile, Todt said 'I speak to him all the time and as far as I can tell you everything remains normal. He has said nothing to me about retiring.' Ferrari press relations manager Giancarlo Baccini added that 'Gerhard will definitely race. He will be holding a Press Conference in Monte Carlo on Wednesday when he will be explaining his feelings and future plans.'

This took place at the Hermitage Hotel. Berger broadened it from a simple statement that he would continue to a baring of the soul. 'I will try to explain my feelings. When you're young, obviously you want to race a lot, it's your life. You have accidents, you see accidents, maybe you see people die, but it doesn't affect you so much; but when you're older you feel completely different. This is a critical point for me. You realise there are other aspects of life which are very important.

'In racing you always have a kind of risk. We saw it in Imola. If you look deep, you see it every day when you sit in the car. It is not so much the circuits or the drivers that are dangerous: 80 per cent of the time there is a technical reason why you go off. I wrote a list of accidents on a piece of paper and I was surprised how very, very often technical failure was the reason; and it applied to teams with high budgets and teams with low budgets. Formula 1 is so technically complicated that you always have failures, so you have to be prepared to take risks, but let's say I have lost a bit of faith in technology.

'Last week it was very hard for me to say I will keep racing, but I will go on again. I will try to put it out of my mind. If the risk frightens me too much, I stop. It's like a circus where you are up on the tightrope: if you keep looking up you are OK, but if you look down you are going to fall.

'After the accidents nearly everyone tried to go in front of television cameras and tried to give opinions. All the discussions about Imola being crazy not to have tyres (a protective tyre wall) at Tamburello. Well, I don't want tyres there. It's a 300 km/h corner. Maybe they would have helped Ayrton, maybe they wouldn't have helped me in 1989. Maybe it could have been worse. Everyone has an idea, to try to be popular, to be the clever one, but it doesn't work like this. Formula 1 needs to have all sides — the organizers, the technicians, the drivers, the commercial people — because it is so complex.

'My decision to continue is not something that just comes from the head' — meaning emotions were involved as well as the logic — 'and one day I would like to sit down with my children and say "I was World Champion". I've had wins and pole positions and fastest laps. I don't have so much to prove. The question to myself all week was *why take the risk*? The other side is *what of the rest of my life?*'

He spoke also of driving at Monte Carlo. 'I tell you, you think it looks spectacular, but it looks spectacular from the inside, too! You can see it in the lap times. And the lap times don't come from Loews (the hairpin), they come from around Tabac (the left onto the harbour), from the swimming pool section, around the Casino (in the square up the hill). And jeez, it's unbelievably quick now. Unbelievably late braking — just quick! It's all fine if you get it right, exciting. After a lap like that, you're sitting there, you are proud of yourself, you feel good about it, good with yourself — but around these corners here, Formula 1 is quick!'

I was curious to know why Berger called this Press Conference. A simple one-paragraph Press Release would have sufficed. 'The thing was that after the accidents at Imola all the journalists wanted to talk to me and I didn't go to the telephone because I didn't want to talk with them at this moment. If I went to Monte Carlo and I didn't talk with them all on the Wednesday, I'd spend my whole weekend with them following me asking me to speak and I wouldn't have been able to do any work. The other thing was that I had to make the situation clear because there was so much speculation.'

In the morning untimed session the day after the Press Conference, 25-year-old Wendlinger in a Sauber crashed heavily at the harbour-front chicane. Wendlinger was taken to Nice hospital in a coma: this same Wendlinger who had accompanied Berger to races as a kid, this same Wendlinger whose father Berger had raced, this same Wendlinger who had been at Ratzenberger's funeral. Berger visited him in hospital and that only fuelled the speculation again.

Berger did not alter his decision.

He qualified fourth on the Thursday and improved to third in the final session. Some good judges estimate that what he did in those two sessions is, taking everything into consideration, some of the bravest driving they've ever seen.

He would need time to bare his soul about the exact circumstances that led him to continue the career and time to discuss his relationship with Senna. Of the former, he told me at season's end — specifically in London in December: 'I did not seriously consider stopping after Ayrton's accident, but I did after Ratzenberger's accident. Suddenly I was very *disappointed* about everything' — disappointed carrying not the ordinary English definition but, and I'm feeling for the nuance of it, something much stronger: a great disillusion that the illusion of safety had been so crudely battered and at such cost.

'This sounds a bit strange, but I had some problems with myself after Ratzenberger's accident — more than that of Ayrton, yes, because after I decided to drive on after Ratzenberger's accident, what difference did Ayrton's accident make (to the fundamental decision)? Both were racing drivers and both are in the same category. One was more a colleague, the other was a close friend, but after Ratzenberger I decided on my way forward and I stayed on it.'

Berger's relationship with Senna was much more delicate and had a distinct undertone. Berger was getting five requests a day for interviews to talk about Senna, and he knew people would be trying to make money out of them. As a matter of principle, he refused them all. The BBC, however, was putting together a Tribute To Senna — due to be screened on New Year's Day — and approached him at a race near the end of the season. Yes, he said, he'd do it and for two reasons: he knew and trusted Murray Walker and the BBC was a non-commercial organisation.

There was a coincidence here. The day before I was due to meet Berger in London the BBC talked to me for the Tribute, and next day I explained this to Berger. Rather than talk about Senna again, he asked that I use the words he spoke for the Tribute because, I sensed, they were exactly what he wanted to say and exactly how he wanted to say it. Repetition would be futile and perhaps painful.

I'm indebted to Stuart Cabb of the BBC for sending me the whole interview and for Murray Walker for saying he was happy for me to use it. 'I approached the interview carefully,' Walker says, 'because it was about Senna and it was about death and you have to show care if you're asking a man to discuss that.' This is what Berger said.

Walker: What did you think of him before you were team-mates?
Berger: First, I don't know if anybody really knew him well except his family, but sure I was quite close to him. It didn't come because

I was a team-mate. The thing started much, much earlier — it had already started a little bit in Formula 3 — and, you know, you have a certain kind of people: you see them, you talk with them and immediately you feel a communication together. You feel some similar thinking, some similar way to do things, and that's what happened. I remember he was running for Dick Bennetts (of West Surrey Racing in Formula 3) and I'd talked with him about car set-ups.

Then he went into Formula 1 and I was still in Formula 3 so I met him in Monte Carlo (in 1984, Senna driving a Toleman, Berger driving an Alfa Romeo in the traditional F3 supporting race). We started to talk again. We got closer and closer and then I came into Formula 1 and we had some challenging races (from 1987). I was in a Ferrari, he was in a Lotus, but even if we were 'fighting' we always respected each other. Then, finally, we came into the same team and the friendship started to become closer — but, as I say, I think it started much, much earlier.

Walker: If you look at the two of you from the outside, he always seemed very, very serious and solemn and stern, and you're a happy-go-lucky, light-hearted person (Berger smiles). I would not have thought the two of you would get on together.

Berger: Yes, it was funny because everybody thought that, everybody thought we were going to have a big fight driving together, competing together. You say we were different, and I think that was exactly the point. Because we were different I learned a lot from him, but I could see he learned a lot from me, too. He learned, maybe, to see life in a different way. I remember when I arrived at McLaren he was so much focused on the job that it didn't go well. He was focused too much, and then when I arrived it didn't mean he had to work less, but he had to laugh, he had to enjoy it a bit more. He started to take this experience and he used it. Finally we were making jokes with each other, and he was getting into a similar direction to me. Maybe I was a bit worse than him (in the jokes), but at the end of the day we both laughed and we had a lot of fun together. We went round and really had a lot of fun.

Walker: Putting frogs in his bedroom and fish in his bedroom. Did he resent that? Was he angry about that sort of thing?

Berger (smile): First, I have to say we were all good friends. There was Josef the masseur, there was Ron Dennis, there was Lisa his wife, myself and Ayrton and we were a nice group. We always had a lot of fun. The way I used to make (practical) jokes didn't fit very well into Ayrton's measurements of how big jokes should be. For him, it was beyond normal thinking (laughs). He had to get used to it and it took him a year. In the beginning he just couldn't believe it, but then he caught up — and he was also quite good at these things.

Walker: You learned a lot from him as a driver. What sort of things?

Berger: I learned the opposite of what he learned from me. I learned to be more serious in some things, trying harder, working more on details and even thinking that everything in life is possible so long as you are convinced in your head that you can do it. As a driver we all know he was special. I mean, I didn't run with Jim Clark, I didn't run with Jochen Rindt and these guys, but, from the ten years that I have run, he was not one step, he was two steps better than anyone else.

Walker: When I remember him, I remember him as being absolutely fantastic in qualifying, I remember him as being absolutely fantastic in setting the car up and absolutely superb in cutting his way through traffic.

Berger: I think if he had a weakness he was not fantastic in setting his car up, but he was fantastic in driving whatever he got. At the end of the day he could put it together for him — so that he could drive it, he could do it — but I agree with all the other points. I had three years with him and, believe me, I was thinking day and night *how can I beat this guy?* Usually you find a weakness in your team-mate, and you start to work on this weakness to increase it and make you strong. With him I just didn't find anything. He was quick in qualifying, he was unbelievably quick in the races, consistently quick. He was quick in overtaking, he was quick in the rain, he was quick at street circuits, he was quick at quick circuits, so finally (grinning) I said *hell, how* am *I going to beat this guy?*

Walker: It must have been a combination of mental application and physical ability and experience.

Berger: His biggest strength was mental. He had a kind of concentration different to all of us. He could find in himself such a high concentration and sometimes it enabled him to do things and nobody could understand how he'd done them. As a racing driver, you have a car, you know the potential of the car, you know the competitors' cars, you know the potential of them. Of course you try to get as close as possible to them, but if a competitor has a car that is 2 seconds quicker — so obviously 2 seconds quicker that you can prove it in many ways — you respect that and you say "I have to improve my car to become similar and then I can beat him". For him, all these things didn't exist. Once the qualifying started he wanted to be quickest. He's in a Williams and it's not so good as the Benetton, but he does not think *I just cannot beat the other guy because he has a better car.* No. He went in and said *I want to be quickest, I have to be quickest and whatever happens I am going to be in first place* and he did it. It didn't matter what the conditions were, he just did it, and it's not by luck that somebody has over 60 pole positions.

Walker: But we all have less attractive sides to our personality, and I think of Senna as sometimes being too ruthless. I remember in 1989 in Brazil, at the start of the race he had a coming together with you, and then in 1990 with Alain Prost.

Berger: Yes, I mean, no question. If I were to criticise something about him, he was selfish. Even being close friends with him, sometimes it was impossible thinking about the selfishness that the guy had — but that was a part of his success, and that's why you respected it. Normally, if you have a friend and he is too selfish you don't want him as a friend — because if you have a friend you want to share things. But him you respected somehow because his success came a lot from that side of his character. It was funny because we knew each other so well and he knew I was criticising these things.

Let's say it was a phone call to me in Europe at five o'clock in the morning — because in Brazil it was the day and he didn't care if I was asleep or not — but if you called him and he was sleeping he didn't like it, you know. Anyway I'd pick up the phone say *ah, my friend Senna. What do you need today that you're phoning me at your own expense?* So we joked about it, but maybe that was the one weakness I could find in him. He had a good character, he was honest and he was very, very hard on other people, but he was also hard on himself.

Walker: Do you miss him as a friend?

Berger: Yes, yes, definitely. I don't miss him on the circuits because he just beat everybody and that's boring (smile, broadening to laughter), but no, no, I miss him a lot. He was my age, we got on well and in Formula 1 it's difficult to get friends. We even went on holiday together and, if you find somebody like him, it was fun and it was good and I'm missing the guy, no question.

Tamburello lay like an umbilical cord connecting 23 April 1989 and 1 May 1994. That early afternoon in 1989 had been gentle, as befits the garden of Italy. Long hours before, the sun had melted the wisps of mist that even in spring can cling to the wooded hills of Romagna, and now it warmed the circuit. The light cloud seemed static, not masking the sun but refracting it from a sky of glorious blue. The clocks ticked towards 2.30.

On the grid for this, the second round of the World Championship, mechanics fussed and fidgeted around each of the 26 cars and then melted towards the pits. The cars eased away on the parade lap, travelled in stately fashion around the 3 miles of the circuit at a pace dictated by Senna who held pole position in his Marlboro McLaren Honda. He brought them back to the grid and took his place on the right, Prost — also Marlboro McLaren Honda — drawing up alongside but slightly behind, the traditional stagger giving pole man the initial advantage. Nigel Mansell in a blood-red

Ferrari felt his way to his position behind Senna, Riccardo Patrese in a Williams Renault felt his way to his position behind Prost.

The other Ferrari, driven by Gerhard Berger, came slowly, slowly. An optical illusion suggested it came reluctantly, but that conclusion would have been entirely false, because of all places on earth Berger wanted to be *here*. He nosed it into position behind Mansell.

He wore a tee-shirt beneath his three-layer driving overalls. For a reason he wasn't quite sure about, he'd had the overalls made for the first race of the season, Brazil. Prior to that he'd always worn two layers. He didn't have his oxygen supply connected to his helmet 'because a lot of drivers, including me, never bothered'. He accepted this might be foolish, but he never felt he'd need it, and he could cite the statistic that in his 69 Grands Prix before he hadn't.

Around the circuit 20 observation posts with 20 post chiefs and 20 deputies stood ready, just in case; 69 incident marshals and 80 flag marshals stood ready, just in case; 178 fire marshals, members of a private company called Red One, stood poised with portable fire extinguishers every 300 metres of the circuit, just in case. Some 50 metres beyond Tamburello three of these marshals positioned themselves behind the armco, but near a small opening in it on to the track. They were Gabriele Vivoli, a 35-year-old metal worker, Paolo Verdi, a 41-year-old potter, and Bruno Miniati, 46.

Some sage once made the curious observation that everybody would be famous for 15 minutes, but he didn't envisage that you could be famous for 15 seconds and, when people found out who you were, famous for years afterwards. The three marshals were childhood friends and in a crisis each knew how the other would react, as they'd reacted two years before when, in qualifying, Nelson Piquet had crashed savagely at Tamburello and they'd doused a fire in his Williams. They'd come to be known as the Angels of Imola. At a vantage point not far from the pits, an Alfasud stood motionless. A former driver, Mario Casoni, held the wheel. Professor Sid Watkins, Formula 1's resident doctor, and Dr Domenico Salcito waited in it, just in case.

The precautions that gentle early afternoon were the same as for all Grands Prix, set out with clarity by the Fédération Internationale de l'Automobile, which governed motor sport and these days is known as the FIA.

'First intervention. Within 15 seconds of an incident liable to produce a fire, at any point on the circuit, at least two firefighters with portable extinguishers should have reached the scene and be capable of intervening with adequate means to clear the cockpit of the car within 30 seconds of the accident. The purpose of the First Intervention is to establish the necessary conditions for saving the driver.

'Second Intervention. Not later than 30 seconds after the accident a mobile appliance should be at the scene with means to completely extinguish the fire.

'It cannot be stressed too strongly that the First and Second Interventions must be fully integrated, as the value of portable extinguishers on the First Intervention is extremely limited.'

Precautions, of course, prudent and practised, although there had been no serious fire in Formula 1 since 1982. Stronger car construction and self-sealing tanks had, as it seemed, passed fires into memory. The tanks, made to strict FISA standards, were based on military helicopter technology. Shoot a bullet through one and it seals again — the helicopter does not come down.

The tail of the grid nudged into their places and settled. As always, the twin columns had a fearsome fascination: absolutely motionless until the red light goes to green, then total motion. The red blinked on, remained for three seconds, blinked to green, the engines already grunting to a grumble to a yearn to a shriek.

Senna and Prost dug power quickly, Mansell marginally slower so that a gap already stretched, Berger trying to press his car inside Mansell. He'd always been a quick-draw gunslinger at the start of races, intuitive balance and reflex and outright bravery. Like all gifted racers he saw, anticipated or created space within the total motion.

Mansell covered the move and that left Patrese free to explore the outside so that, into Tamburello, Senna led, then Prost, then Mansell, then Patrese, then Berger still searching for an opening, but as so often happens at Imola the order solidified, the five leading cars essentially equidistant. Berger completed the opening lap in 1 minute 41.567 seconds. Holding fifth, he completed the second lap in 1 minute 34.498 seconds, Senna and Prost now stretching the equidistance. He completed the third lap in 1 minute 33.319 seconds, the rhythm becoming quicker as the tyres warmed and the fuel load began to lighten a little. He was finding his running pace.

He flowed across the line to begin lap four, Patrese about four cars' length in front, Boutsen in the other Williams Renault about four cars' length behind. He accelerated smoothly and easily, hurrying in an unhurried sort of way towards Tamburello, that great carving curve of a left, wire mesh fencing and stooping trees on its inner, the grassy run-off on its outer before the wall.

The clocks ticked towards 2.38.

Mansell hugged the inside, the traditional line, and passed round. Patrese, following the same line, passed round. As Patrese gained the apex of the corner Berger went directly ahead off the circuit, the Ferrari bounding over kerbing and gouging dust from the grass. His speed: up towards 190 mph.

Distorted images. He'd remember entering Tamburello 'flat out, full speed, then something snapped at the front of the car and it went completely out of control. I tried to brake a little. I was heading straight for the wall. I thought "My God, this is going to be the big one." He took his hands off the steering wheel and folded them across his chest. He tried to make himself small in the cockpit, literally withdrawing into himself, part preparation, part hiding. From the kerb to the wall: 1.5 seconds.

The Ferrari left a wake of dust and, as it struck the wall, gouged a dust storm burying the whole car. He'd remember striking the wall, remember bits of the car wrenched off and scattered in some eye of a storm, cascading, dismembered, *but the angle of impact against the wall* dissipated the impact. If the Ferrari had met it absolutely head on — the crash everyone fears — the driver surely would not, could not, have survived. Without the dissipation, however slight, the shock-waves can be totally destructive, hammer-hammer-hammering back and breaking whatever they meet. And that was another umbilical cord to 1 May 1994. Senna hadn't had enough dissipation.

The angle flung the Ferrari away, rotating, thrashing. It shed wheels, shed more debris as it slithered across the grass, this centrifugal force drawing it to the wall again, spinning. The wall embraced it, wouldn't release it. The dust, wreathing itself into an elaborate pattern, hung harder than any mist.

The Ferrari spun a final time.

The three fire marshals 50 metres away remembered it in a communal distortion of images. 'We saw a vehicle flash like a meteor and shatter against the barrier. We moved together without saying a word. A nod from under the fire helmet was enough. We didn't even know whose car it was — and we were Ferrari supporters.' Verdi the potter remembered that 'the car passed nearby and suddenly I realised it was a Ferrari, but with all the smoke you couldn't see anything. Dead or alive? You don't know.' They came through the opening running so hard that they felt they 'had wings, the 6 kg portable extinguishers already in our hands.'

A spectator leaned over the wall fluttering his blood-red Ferrari flag. He hadn't had time to react, to withdraw it. He wasn't quick on the draw. When he did retract the flag it flapped like a broken wing and dipped away into the anonymity of the crowd. A deep, deep cry reverberated from this crowd at Tamburello.

The Ferrari came to absolute rest and what remained of its rear faced a giant white advertising hoarding, the white illuminating everything like a sight-screen. The Ferrari burst into an orange halo of fire that licked from it consuming the grass, this fire sucking into a bonfire reaching 3 metres, 4 metres above it. The flames burnished the carcass of the car, branded it, biting deep into it, and the flames on the grass rose, licked back towards it.

Another racing car passed in the foreground hugging the traditional line round Tamburello safe as you like, and it was a fleeting, blurred, anonymous car, just one of the 26. Which car? Nobody would remember that. Perhaps Herbert in a Benetton, perhaps not. Then another car passed, then another, a race going on.

In the Ferrari pit a mechanic, watching a TV monitor in absolute horror, made a noise like a moan. 'I don't understand, I don't understand.' John Barnard, the Ferrari's designer, 'took one look at the monitor and I saw the ball of flame go up. I turned away. That was it. I had a very strong relationship with Gerhard, I felt he was a personal friend as well as a member of the team. If he had been seriously hurt or even worse — if the worst had happened — I would probably have stopped motor racing. I suppose I'd been quite lucky in my career in racing, not just Formula 1, with only a few accidents to the cars I'd designed, and the drivers had all walked away. That was one I thought, "No. If this is really it, I don't want to know any more."

The fire began to consume what remained of the carcass, and the carcass had become a spectre, a couple of wheels hanging on one side, no wheels on the other, its shape shorn and shortened. Of the fire Berger would remember nothing. He was unconscious.

In the BBC commentary box Murray Walker thought Berger was dead. 'It's very difficult to know how to treat it when you're talking live. You can't say anything that approaches the lighthearted in any way and you can't be funereal.' Walker's voice, on air and live, betrayed his anguish.

'And, oh heavens above, this is dreadful, this is the . . . there are no words that can add to this appalling picture . . . and thank heavens there is a fire tender on the spot immediately.'

The tender, an Alfa Romeo and called by an English name, 'Fast Car', came in a rush and arrived in 13 seconds — at almost precisely the instant the first of the fire marshals on foot began firing his extinguisher. Some say that began at 14 seconds, some say at 15. He tucked his left shoulder against the heat and went into the bonfire still firing. He vanished within it.

The communal memory: 'We began to inundate the car at the base of the flames. We knew very well the power of the fluid in the extinguishers, Halon 24-02 (the chemical most widely used in motor sport), and that it can extinguish fires in 6 seconds. Berger did not move. We feared it was already too late. The flame colouring of the grass showed clearly that petrol was burning. There was a danger that the whole thing would explode, but you don't have time to think about that. We had to act fast or we'd have been caught in the centre of the explosion, too. That many litres of fuel. . .'

Verdi explains: 'It is one thing to extinguish a fire during training when you know there's only a dummy in the cockpit, it is a totally different matter when you're in there trying to save a human being from burning to death. During training we learn techniques of self-control so we can confront any situation, but it is very difficult to stay in complete control of yourself when that human being is there in front of you.'

The flame turned to black, an industrial black, a chemical black. The second foot marshal, firing from the hip, skirted the carcass pouring his extinguisher against the flames that hovered around the cockpit. The third poured his extinguisher into the base of the carcass, spraying the last of the flames that hovered there. From the arrival of the Alfa Romeo to the complete extinguishment: 23 seconds. The Angels removed the steering wheel and sliced through Berger's safety belts with the special small orange cutters they carried in their pockets.

'Then Berger moved,' Verdi says.

At the instant red flags were waved on the pit straight, the Alfasud bearing Professor Watkins and Dr Salcito set off hard. It didn't wait for communications, just went. At Tamburello Salcito 'dived from the Fast Car and hurled myself towards Berger. His crash helmet had been scorched and so had his gloves and part of his overalls. There was a terrible smell of petrol all around him. Fortunately the seat belts had already been cut open by the fire marshals, so we could immediately remove Berger from the cockpit.'

Watkins and two of the fire marshals — 'one each end and me in the middle' — carried Berger clear of the fuel-sodden grass.

Ordinarily fire marshals didn't touch accident victims — the medical team did that — but this was in no sense ordinary.

'Berger was in shock and agitated,' Miniati says. 'We had him stretched out on the ground and we were in shock.'

'He was in a state of psychomotor agitation (moving convulsively) and we were not able to hold him down,' Dr Salcito says. 'He would not let himself be helped.' Professor Watkins remembers that 'I lifted his visor. He was unconscious, his eyes were shut but his face was pink, not blue.'

The bodywork still smouldered.

Distorted images. Berger wondered 'Am I on holiday? Yes, I'm on holiday. No, I'm not on holiday.' He would remember someone trying to put a tube into his mouth, would remember how much that frightened him because it would suffocate him, choke him. A calm and measured English voice instructed him not to move, saying, 'You've had an accident'.

Watkins says that 'he opened his eyes and I was starting to stick an air tube into his mouth. He began to resist that and then he began to get very restless, so I straddled him across his chest. He wanted to get up and run away from the scene. I was saying "Gerhard, you've had an accident". His eyes did open and you could see his vision clearing. Consciousness began to come back and then recognition. He said "Professor", and I said "Just lie still, we're fixing you up".'

Salcito would remember 'we had to lie on top of him to hold him to the ground and cut the strap of his crash helmet, then we had to cut a sleeve from his overalls to find a vein in his arm to begin anti-shock therapy.' Watkins would remember 'we cut his uniform because he was soaked in fuel, put a drip up.' Miniati would remember 'an ambulance arrived all in a few seconds.'

Berger would remember how difficult a racing helmet is to remove, he'd remember wondering if he still had it on. He didn't know. 'So I've had an accident. But where?' He didn't know. He gazed from within his subconscious at his hands, and the flesh looked raw. 'Where have my driving gloves gone?' He didn't know that either.

In the Press Room, Stan Piecha of *The Sun* remembers that 'to start with everybody just sort of sat there and watched the television screen. It was only the seventh race I'd covered and I couldn't believe what I was seeing, I couldn't believe that any human being could ever walk out of anything like that. I thought "This is the first obituary I'll write".'

Nobody would be writing obituaries. They'd be writing about Angels and miracles and describing how Formula 1 had hauled itself from the primitive era of the 1960s to guarding the sanctity of human life very closely. Every detail you have read so far is, I hope, in no sense ghoulish, but rather a celebration of the sanctity and how it was achieved.

Dr Salcito expresses that. 'Another doctor arrived with a resuscitator in precisely 27 seconds. The level of co-ordination of the emergency services worked to perfection, just as the fire marshals did.' There'd have been almost a complete generation of portly, elderly Formula 1 drivers from the 1950s and 1960s around to watch the San Marino Grand Prix if they'd had this, but they hadn't.

And deep down we all knew that Gerhard Berger had been lucky beyond belief; that you needed luck as well as the emergency services. Deep down we all knew that one day a conjunction of circumstances would arise — the law of averages alone decreed it — when the luck would simply run out. We did not know, and could not have known, that it would not happen for five years and then, within two days, would happen twice: the first time claiming a different Austrian — Roland Ratzenberger — at the corner after Tamburello, the second time claiming Berger's friend — Ayrton Senna — at the same wall at Tamburello.

It is a great truth that before this moment on 23 April 1989, on this once gentle early afternoon, Gerhard Berger was well known within the confines of Grand Prix racing but not really a presence beyond them. It is also true that before this moment only three Austrian sportsmen had ever been famous beyond the confines of their particular sport.

The first, Jochen Rindt, died at Monza in 1970 qualifying for the Italian Grand Prix, his Lotus breaking out of control, thrashing itself into a run-off area, churning a dust storm. The aftermath is too macabre to dwell on, too invasive — someone coming back with a driving shoe and let's leave it at that, never mind the witnesses who went to the medial centre and what they saw there. Berger remembers it as a television event, something very remote. How else would a 12-year-old regard it, accept it?

'These were the days,' Berger says, 'when the big Formula 1 fever started in Austria and everybody was watching the races, and I was watching the races. I wasn't too interested because I wanted to drive myself, but still Rindt was the guy we watched. I was at home when I saw the accident.'

The second, Franz Klammer, a downhiller as Berger wished to be, won the Winter Olympic gold medal at Innsbruck on 5 February 1976. Wearing a golden racing suit, Klammer went number 15 on a mountain called the Patscherkofel and reached the absolute limit of what a man can do, leaning at seemingly impossible angles, the skis jud-jud-juddering. He skimmed over the finishing line and churned to a halt, arms upraised. He didn't look at the big decimal point scoreboard and didn't have to. He knew no other human being could have done it quicker. He was right.

A memory of Klammer at that instant: strong and handsome, intoxicated, fulfilled; but you need the context. Winter sports — equipment, flights, holidays — represented Austria's biggest industry. Here was the perfect advertisement for it on every television screen in the world. As someone noted cynically, Austrian commercial life had been saved. Franz Klammer's brother watched from a wheelchair, but on television, not on the Patscherkofel. He'd been a downhiller, too, paralysed now after a crash — to use a term that unites the downhillers and the motor racers.

Klammer had covered 3,302 yards (3,019 metres) in 1 minute 45.73 seconds. He beat Bernhard Russi of Switzerland, who did 1 minute 46.06 seconds. These are the sort of statistics you live with in motor racing too, and are another unification, the fractions you can't imagine but which prove everything. Did Klammer, there on the sun-kissed glistening slope of the finishing area, think of his brother? It's not the sort of question you ask, and nobody did.

Gerhard Berger saw it as a television event, something very remote from him, although happening not far down the road from the small township of Worgl where he lived. How else would an anonymous 17-year-old regard it, accept it? No other way.

'I was still at school when Klammer won,' Berger says. 'I remember it in the same way I remember some of Rindt's wins. I remember Niki's crash the same way. (We'll come to Niki Lauda, the third on the list, in just a moment.) I wasn't close to all these things, I was a boy who liked to do things myself. I didn't care about the others, I never worried about the others.'

On 1 August 1976 Lauda pressed his Ferrari round the fabled and feared Nurburgring circuit in Germany. All in a moment it broke out of control, beat against a barrier and bounced, burst into flames. He'd be saved by other drivers — a fire marshal in a tee-shirt didn't venture near — and live the rest of his life with a seared face, an ear that bore the traces of the fire, eyelids reconstructed. They took him to hospital in a helicopter, gave him the Last Rites. Of his crash he would remember nothing. Lauda himself, reflecting upon the death of Jim Clark in 1968 — when Lauda was 19 — felt no 'sense of drama, no feeling of awesome tragedy'. It wasn't so much a television event then as remote, news from another planet. Among many ironies Berger would scarcely know Lauda at all when he reached Formula 1, but came to know him well and respect him a great deal.

But now, when the past has been so forcibly forged into unity with the present and perhaps the future, as Berger sat in the cockpit of a Ferrari and gazed at the raw meat of his hands, he had become the fourth. The sun still loomed above the light clouds. From his subconscious an idea formed: he'd been trying to overtake Patrese, that's what must have happened. His body hurt and he thought 'It's the burns'. In the cockpit he'd moved around a bit, calmed, explained to whoever was listening where it hurt, but that must have been reflexes, the deepest primeval urge to re-establish normality, to survive by becoming normal again. He would have no memory of doing this. In the most dreadful extremes, people grip what they know, and that is normality. Next he remembered the ambulance, remembered thinking 'that's it, my career's over now, you don't play around with life', remembered thinking he hoped his daughter Christina hadn't been watching at home on television.

The race was stopped towards 2.43. Due processes had had to be enacted, cars flagged down and slowed, and actually it must have been earlier than 2.43 when the cars started slowing. Very sophisticated devices keep times to three decimal places every lap that every driver does, but when cars break wild what do times matter anyway? Olivetti/Longines, with all their sensors and computers, recorded Berger's third lap as 1 minute 33.319 seconds, as we have seen. Of his fourth lap they record nothing.

Peter Collins, managing the Benetton team that in a sense had nurtured Berger three seasons before, remembers that when the accident took place red flags were waved and everybody stopped on the grid when they came round, stopped at the start-finish line. Herbert, driving for Benetton, got out and said 'Not good, no chance, no chance'.

'I was talking to Johnny and it must have been a few minutes afterwards. Someone pointed to an ambulance and said "Hey, there goes Berger", but someone else said "No, no, he's just gone past in another ambulance joking and waving", and apparently he had.' It was what people wanted to believe and what Berger would surely have done if he could: joked and waved.

The ambulance arrived at the track's medical centre at 2.52. There 'all his clothes were taken off,' Watkins says. 'When you squeezed them, petrol ran out. We washed him down with saline.' The chief medical officer, Dr Giovanni Piana, examined him and diagnosed his breathing as normal; he hadn't inhaled fumes. X-rays and bodyscans showed a broken left rib, the left shoulder-blade fractured. He had second-degree burns to one hand and burns to the other.

Mansell returned to the Ferrari pit, head bowed, looking, as someone observed, 'like a hunchback. He walks back and forth with his right hand through his hair, he brushes it behind his ear and shakes his head.' In the pit Mansell found 'an incredibly emotional atmosphere. Anybody who had seen the accident — whether at the circuit or on television around the world — must have feared for Gerhard's life. Everyone in the team was obviously upset and half of them were in tears.'

Mansell walked with his hands behind his back to his own car, bent over the right rear wheel, ran his left hand over it. He leaned against the bodywork, stood again and kicked a tyre. The mechanics were silent.

The BBC, which, as Walker says, 'isn't in the business of showing pictures of people milling around, went, I think, to some other sporting event, and of course we didn't know Berger's condition.' (As a matter of policy the BBC does not show fatalities, but whatever its outcome Berger's crash happened live, offering them no opportunity for judgement or editing.) James Hunt, much lamented and then the BBC's resident expert who formed a formidable double act with Walker, set off to find Mansell with such urgency that, Walker says, 'he might have had a rocket up him'.

Mansell had to 'break into' the medical centre 'after I'd been physically slung out. So I knew he was alive, that his injuries were nothing like as bad as we'd thought. I was able to talk to him.' Watkins remembers Mansell saying in the medical centre, 'What the hell happened?' Watkins replied, 'He's in there, go and ask him, but he doesn't know either.'

Mansell 'walked back to the pits in a kind of dream — people were talking to me but I didn't really see or hear them. There was no one in the garage so I went to the motorhome and on the way James Hunt stopped me and said there was no way I should drive. I remember hearing the conversation and nodding to him, nothing more.'

At 3 pm Berger's father Johann (known as Hans) emerged from the medical centre, face reddened, and said, 'My son is lucid, my son recognised me. We're taking him back to Austria.' Five minutes later a chaplain confirmed it. 'Berger is saved.'

Piecha, accelerating under the impetus of a very big story, remembers 'everybody rushing around, some to the medical centre. We found out that Berger was alive, they'd wrapped him in tinfoil, which apparently is the standard procedure. Ferrari closed their pits, pulled the shutters down. I spoke to Mansell and he was extremely upset. In fact, James Hunt went to Mansell and told him not to go out at the restart because the same could happen to him.'

Hunt would keep no memory of talking to Mansell or indeed leaving his commentary position, and to be absolutely fair to him he'd been actively involved in motor racing for 20 years, had seen plenty of crashes — including some of his own — so that what might have been a notable encounter to you or me, meeting Mansell in such circumstances, was to him another encounter. Certainly Walker remembers Hunt returning to the commentary position and saying 'words to the effect of "I've told Mansell he'd be a bloody fool if he goes into the restart"'.

At 3.20 loudspeakers relayed three words. 'Berger is saved.'

In the motorhome Mansell couldn't bring himself to listen to the conversation darting to and fro. Should he take the restart? Mansell judged that if he did not it would have a direct bearing on the standing of John Barnard and adversely affect the team for a long time. He reasoned as a racing driver would, drew his balance. He'd drive. He did not judge it particularly brave, although he conceded that if another driver had taken the same decision in similar circumstances he'd have thought him 'stupid'. He reasoned, also, that at least he'd be alert to any potential problems, his senses heightened.

'There was a lot of jabbering and talking going on in the Ferrari pit,' Barnard says. 'Nigel came over, looked at me hard, face to face and eye to eye, and said, "John, if you tell me it is OK to get back in the car, I will get back in the car and I will go for it." I said, "Nigel, as far as I know everything is fine. I don't know of any problems" — because we didn't know what had happened. Could have been a puncture, could have been Gerhard making a mistake. Basically I said, "You just be careful, drive sensibly, stay off the kerbs."

'It was a hell of a moment for me. Such a decision is difficult because you really don't know what happened and you're not going to find out before you make the decision. If you say "I'm worried, don't drive", for evermore you have a problem because you have instilled uncertainty into the driver — and Nigel *needed* to get back in and drive because it shook him as much as anybody else. He's driving the thing, he needs to have confidence to get back in and think "I am all right".'

A few moments after the loudspeaker announcement the race restarted, Berger still in the medical centre. Mansell moved into fifth place. 'It wasn't easy to get back in the car, not at all, but I can assure you I treated that corner with so much respect — in fact afterwards I always made sure I was in exactly the right place and my whole body was one major sensor in that corner, feeling for any change in car reaction at all, because it's a horrendous corner.'

At 3.40, Mansell going round and round, the ambulance left the medical centre for the Maggiore Hospital, Hans Berger accompanying his son. They ferried him gently on a stretcher-trolley from the ambulance, the tinfoil still covering him, his head cast back, his eyes closed, a belt round his waist keeping him in place. Someone hovered over him holding a drip high in a right hand. At one moment careful hands had to tilt the stretcher to get it through a door. The faces gathered around it all understood, mute, the same thing: gently. Some say he'd regained full consciousness, some aren't so sure. During the journey Berger had begun to reconsider his decision to retire . . .

Shortly after the ambulance arrived in Bologna, Mansell stopped on lap 24 — gearbox — the way it goes in some races.

'Because I had carried Berger,' Watkins says, 'the fuel had soaked into my uniform from my waist downwards. I sat through the restarted race in the Alfasud in this uncomfortable condition, the fuel burning my balls off . . .'

Hans Berger gave a brief interview outside the hospital. Someone observed him as a 'big, tall, blond gentleman'. No, he said, he hadn't seen the accident because he'd been near the Ferrari pit. Now, he said embracing everything, *sehr gut, sehr gut* (very good, very good).

Berger's entourage thought it would be best for him to spend at least a night in the hospital. An air ambulance had been ordered from Innsbruck to transport him to the clinic there and the entourage telephoned to stop it taking off. A Dr Cancellieri said at Bologna that 'it left regardless'.

It rose and angled over the mountains whose contours Berger knew so well, peaks and slate-grey rock faces and crevices where the snow always snuggled, and pines that ran up to the tree-line feeding off so little soil; a monumental splendour far removed from mortality. The air ambulance turned almost directly south, still rising. The entourage still said *stay the night, go to Innsbruck tomorrow*. The regulations insisted that Berger could only leave the Maggiore Hospital if he discharged himself, which involved signing a legal document. He signed.

They wheeled him out of the hospital on another trolley, took him to Bologna airport and now he wore a white hospital tunic, a belt still holding him in place, head still cast back. They'd laid a plain blanket over his knees, but his knees were in the jack-knife position so that the blanket hung over them like an Alp. At 8.10 the air ambulance took off from Bologna for Innsbruck.

That evening, too, a bold journalistic notion stirred in the mind of Stan Piecha. He'd go to the clinic and interview Berger. 'I did a follow-up story (to appear on the Tuesday, the race report of course appearing next morning, Monday) on the lines of everybody felt that Berger had been pushing a bit too hard because of Mansell coming into the team, and Berger had something to prove. I filed that late on the Sunday night just in case I couldn't get Berger. I spoke to my office and they said *give it a shot*, so photographer Roger Parker and myself left early on the Monday morning after finding out that Berger had been transferred from Bologna to Innsbruck.

'We drove to Bologna and got another hire car, one we could leave in Innsbruck, because the one we had needed to be returned to Bologna. We got to Innsbruck about four o'clock, found the clinic. I went to the chap on the gate and said "I've come to see Gerhard Berger", and he said "Yes, he's over in the tower there, but I'm not sure which room he's in". We parked the car and walked over, spoke to the receptionist and she said yes. I believe it was the second floor.

'We went up there and Berger's personal masseur was outside the room. I explained who we were and asked would it be possible to see Gerhard? He said, "Well, at the moment he's resting and he'll be resting for at least another hour, but after that it will be fine." This was almost unbelievable. Before I joined *The Sun* I'd been a news reporter and it was always difficult to get into a ward in England. I thought we'd cracked it. The only thing was the time going on, and we had the question of getting the pictures to London. We went for a coffee, then back to the clinic, and about an hour and a half after we'd first arrived we were invited in. He looked remarkable because there was nothing wrong with him apart from his hands, and he sat up in bed.

'In fact, I was there when he saw the video — they brought a video in of the crash and it was the first time he had seen it. Apparently he wanted to see the video because he couldn't remember what had happened. After the impact he couldn't really remember anything. They put the video on and I was trying to concentrate on looking at the video and his face at the same time. His eyes were transfixed by the television screen and when the Ferrari actually exploded in a ball of fire he put his hands up to his eyes trying to stop himself looking, but he said he felt that he had to face that.

After the video stopped, he said "Well, that really was a big one".

'It struck me that he couldn't believe how he got out of it. Although he didn't say it, I'm sure he felt "Well, nothing worse can ever happen to me so basically I've got nothing to fear for the rest of my career. The cars are now so safe that if I can survive that I can survive anything." He didn't need to keep on — he had his own haulage business — but the fact was he enjoyed racing and when you look at him now he's certainly as daft as ever, isn't he? He did say it had flashed through his mind that this is not worth it any more, but even now, the next day in the clinic, he was already talking about, "Yes, I want to get back, it's the one thing that I'm good at". I would have thought we were in there about half an hour and he talked extremely well. Roger Parker did the pictures. I finished my interview and a local photographer turned up. He let us use his wire machine.'

And that was 24 April 1989, the day after. In the first edition of this book, I added here what I called 'Necessary post-scripts' to try and complete the background to the crash. The first edition appeared, of course, long before 1 May 1994. In view of that, some of the post-scripts are hauntingly ironic — and perhaps irony is the wrong word, anyway; perhaps it should be something a great deal stronger. Whatever, I reproduce the post-scripts as they were written because it was the way the world was:

'The rules state that in the event of a fire the First Intervention should be made by two firefighters with portable extinguishers, but different circuits have different methods. Imola is a track well equipped with fast vehicles so it's possible that the vehicle will get there before the men on foot,' a FISA safety official said.

'The number of fire marshals varies from circuit to circuit, but there should be extinguishers every 300 metres. The FISA inspector can recommend more people or less people, or tell them where to put the Fast Cars. In the majority of cases, the fire marshals tend to be locals, although I understand in Italy they come from a private enterprise and they are professionals who fight fires in other domains as well. In Britain they tend to be volunteers who are specially trained for motor racing. The times of the First and Second Interventions, incidentally, are an objective rather than a stipulation because clearly you can't guarantee them.

'Drivers are in fact very well protected for up to about a minute by the equipment they have. The breathing apparatus is optional and they tend not to use it. They have enough oxygen inside the helmet, assuming that the helmet is a proper fit and stays on the driver's head — of course, Niki Lauda's didn't because it wasn't the right fit.

'The foot soldiers usually have a powder or light water. The powder is a quick knock down and there's usually also another product that blankets a fire and keeps it out. On the trackside powder is more usual. The light water has an additive and is released as foam, which prevents oxygen getting on to the scene, because if you put a fire out and it's still hot it might spark back again.

'If Gerhard Berger had had a similar accident 20 years before, he would have been in really serious trouble. Ten years before he would have been in trouble from the impact: the car wouldn't have stood up to it in the same way, and the fire would have been bigger. Probably there would have been all sorts of problems.

'The fuel tanks are made to an FIA-homologated formula which is based on the stuff used in military helicopters. The technology is similar. If you get a bullet through the tank it doesn't bring it down — but there are limits. If the tank is torn open — by a piece of the chassis, as seems to have happened in Berger's case — it can't re-seal. However, the tanks put up with great impacts and in almost every incident are fairly rupture-proof under pressure. The connections will rip off and the tanks be self-sealing. That is why these fires are relatively rare.

'The amount of energy removed at the first impact, because Berger struck the wall at an angle, is enormous and an absolute life-saver. The worst example is David Purley at Silverstone and he was practically at 90 degrees. (Purley went off during qualifying for the 1977 British Grand Prix and his Lec-Ford car hit a barrier, reducing its speed from 108 mph to 0 in 26 inches. The G-force has been calculated at 179.8.) You couldn't get a worse accident than that and live. That was because the car absorbed so much of the impact. He took the G-loading but it was for a tiny, tiny time space. More and more people are realising that the human body can withstand the most astonishing loadings as long as they are only for an infinitesimal time — very, very short.'

Red One, the company that provides the fire marshals for Imola, knows its business. Based near Bologna and sponsored by CEA, who make extinguishers, it has 254 employees, some professionals, some part-time. They can he hired for a variety of jobs, for example protecting against fire in theatres and cinemas. Red One conducts rigorous training schools and spends whole days practising — including, of course, on cars.

'From time to time we go on specialist courses arranged by CEA in Castenaso near Bologna,' Paolo Verdi says. 'We try out new equipment and practise putting out fires that have been lit intentionally. Physical strength is important, but it is courage that counts. When we find ourselves in dramatic situations at race tracks we experience emotions you can't describe, but these fade into the background when they're compared to the effectiveness our interventions can have for another human being's life. Even our families, who understand this, accept the risks that our work involves.'

While Professor Watkins sat poised in the Alfasud all through the re-started race 'I contemplated the slow erosion of my private parts by the fuel. I came to the conclusion that we should seek another material that was impervious to petrol but allows you to sweat. I asked Mike Theobold of Advanced Safety at Work, and after a long search he found one, but it only came in khaki — I think from the Israeli army. None of the drivers would wear it. We've got round that by having it coloured to the driver's taste. However, very few of them have taken it up because it's quite stiff, but if you wear it enough it does become supple. I've been wearing one now for two years.'

Professor Watkins asked for something else. 'Berger's burns were because the leather of his gloves conducted the heat through the material of the gloves — they had a leather seam. Now the leather doesn't protrude from the material.'

'The accident really started,' Barnard says, 'because Gerhard was going over the kerb in the chicane and riding on the front wing, and ultimately that was the bit that broke. The upward force Gerhard was pulling into the front wing from the endplate going over the kerb did the damage. For whatever reason, Nigel wasn't using the kerbs as much, so it didn't apply to him.

'The wing broke at the inboard end, went under the suspension and sort of slid along. It wasn't the aerodynamic loading that broke it, it was the fact that when you short-cut the chicane by going smack, smack over the kerbs there, the endplate is effectively lifting half the car.' (Endplates are placed in front of the front wings to guide the air flowing at the car. If you ride high up and over kerbing the air goes underneath the endplates and they do lift the car, something they're not designed for.)

'It was just after the start of the race, full of fuel, so it was a very sobering thing. In design and construction we don't cut corners, but after something like that you double-check everything. It really prints itself on your mind. We don't compromise, but in designing racing cars you are always looking for the limit: the limit of performance, the limit of road-holding, reliability, everything. Unless you are on that limit you're not light enough, quick enough, whatever, and it's a very difficult balance to achieve.

'I have to say that the rules and regulations governing the increased crash testing and static testing that we have to do have really improved things. These rules make people achieve standards that are way above what you actually need to build a racing car and make it go fast. That is the way it has developed and it is good.

'However, if you sit down and try to work out what you are going to stress to what loads, you can almost never imagine certain situations. You think, OK, if the bloke makes a mistake, goes over the kerb, it's hard luck, something might break at some point.' In other words, it is impossible to guarantee every part of every car in situations you simply cannot foresee.

'We had a failure on Mansell's car at Monaco. Anything like that and everybody was twitchy (only two weeks after Imola). Mansell came over and said "That bloody thing failed and I never hit anything". I had a look and there was some white on the tyres. What had happened was that he'd touched a barrier maybe three-quarters of a lap before, buckled the wishbone and it had gone back straight. Only when it finds a high point on the circuit does it actually break.

'After a bit of gentle questioning he says, yes, he is touching the barrier, but for Nigel that is the normal way round Monaco. He said "I often lean on the barriers round there". I just said "Oh well". I didn't really know what to say. You could have tried to tell him not to touch the barriers, even though he's only leaning on them, but it is a different load case and one that you can't allow for. It's the same as Williams, who've had failures this year (1993). How long have they run those cars with those parts? A long time. Suddenly you come to Monaco, bingo, you have a problem.' Hill's rear wishbone failed and Williams thought Prost had a crack in his.

And here are two necessary post-scripts, joining the umbilical cord.

The first is from 1989. Berger missed Monaco so soon after Imola but drove in Mexico on 28 May, a testament to the Angels who saved him, to the technology of the car, and a testament to the man himself. At Monaco he watched qualifying from his apartment balcony with Michele Alboreto (Tyrrell) and they wondered what those drivers down there were doing going round and round sweating like crazy. At Mexico someone unthinkingly shook his hand. Berger winced and said something very funny . . .

The second is from my interview in December 1994. We'd been talking about the rush for safety in many guises since the deaths of Senna and Ratzenberger.

'I think everybody — the FIA, Max — did a great job over the year. They did a lot. Of course, you can always do more, but the big key to it now is to keep going, not to back off again. I think for next year we want to make it stable (rather than having to react to events) and the FIA has set everything right to have a stable approach — in fact, over the next few years. They've set up this Safety Committee, they've spent a lot of money and developed safety stuff. I think it's great and I think it's going to be all right for us. Corners like Tamburello you can't have (in their present form) any more. All those types like Tamburello are going to be out.'

Question: the impossible irony (alas, that word again) is that your crash there should have told the world something straight away, shouldn't it?

'Yes, but we all know this.'

But we all saw it.

'"Forget it, it's gone" (was the attitude.) They didn't do anything and that was a big mistake and now, since we're talking about it again, it was so wrong because then we saw Senna's accident and I thought *that's it, now let's really do something. Let's not just* think *about it, let's not think* if this *or* if that. *Forget that kind of thinking. We have to* do *something.*'

And don't drive if they don't?

'Right.'

As an old Italian proverb says: When you have burned yourself, even lukewarm water frightens you.

There was a dimension about researching the first edition of this book that took me by surprise. I'd envisaged a straightforward biography of value in itself, a career worthy of being recorded chapter and verse, but I hadn't anticipated the areas it would move into, and sometimes in the narrative I've allowed those areas to expand, although they might not seem strictly relevant. They are. If you're held within the enclave of motor racing — a small, incestuous enclave — every shift of movement, of personnel, of mechanical advantage holds the most direct relevance. And even if, like Berger, you start out a nice guy (as all are agreed) and end up a nice guy (as all are agreed), the questing, thrusting self-interest of the enclave opens up sharp corners, tensions broached among others, massive money in play, iron egos who want it very badly, multi-national companies looking for a return on their dollars. The story of a driver's career is not only what he did but what happened around him.

For example, you'd imagine that everyone in Formula 1 would know each other because it's so tightly knit, and you may be surprised how little Berger knew of other drivers when he joined them or they joined him, something equally true for designers and mechanics. They're all locked into their very own enclaves within the enclave.

The surprising dimension is that Gerhard Berger did not ever engineer any unseemly advantage, and, of the rich cast of characters he knew, he remains — even after the great tumult of Ferrari-Mansell-McLaren-Senna-Ferrari, even after Imola 1994 — as he was before, a good friend to many and enemy to none. He also remains dangerous social company because whoever you are he'll be hatching a devilish plot or two, or three. You know, plastering a photograph of a topless woman on to your passport photograph . . .

or throwing your passport into a swimming pool to see if it will float . . . or confiscating it altogether, secreting it somewhere and not giving it back . . . or (literally) Warwick's Ghost. We'll be meeting frogs placed in Senna's bed and a marble bust placed in Senna's bed and rancid Mexican fish placed *everywhere*.

In too, too many ways Formula 1 is a grim tale of captives in the enclave, convicts in an open prison who imagine they are entirely free but have to report and account for themselves *all* the time. It is oft-times portrayed with every symbol that comes to mind as representing success, and it's understandable. With the amount of money mixed with that amount of hype and danger, the portrayal is too seductive.

Behind it each driver makes his balance. Nobody forces you to get into the cars. Berger's balance was, and surely is, quite unlike that of the others. He went into the enclave because he wanted to, but he always knew where the exit lay, just over there a footstep or two away. If his story means more than the obvious — another driver's tale — it is that you can remain entirely normal, can earn and bank the massive money, win races and yet accept no compromise about who you are and what you are.

That's what took me by surprise.

Did I forget to mention the snakes? Senna found some of the frogs in his bed. (Only 16 of 26. Who was counting? Senna was). Then, just when he calculated he'd rid himself of this Biblical plague, Berger suggested he go back up and look for the missing ten *and the snakes*. There were no snakes, but that's the whole point. Would you take the chance? Did Senna? That's the point. (For the location of this and more examples, I'm afraid you'll have to wait until Chapter 11).

And there he was, the tall, lean Austrian, grinning like an urchin, a driver who had moved inside and outside the enclave for a decade and, in the words of Kipling, could 'walk with kings, nor lose the common touch'; a man who knew grief, expressed it, surmounted it and never forgot that life was still for living.

That took me by surprise, too. Not that he did all that, but that anybody — tennis player, footballer, athlete, downhiller and particularly motor racing driver at the very summit of Formula 1 — could still do it.

2

In the foothills

'My childhood was happy. I was always the same, plenty of practical jokes.'

Worgl, a town of 9,000 inhabitants in the Tyrol region almost exactly mid-way between Munich and Innsbruck, lies in a valley on the river Inn and is framed against a mighty backdrop. The Alps rise all around in gigantic ripples of rock to the snow-clad peaks of two mountains, Grossglockner (3,798 m) and Grossvenediger (3,674m). The resort of Kitzbuhel, where the beautiful people as well as the downhill ski racers go, nestles into the ripples of rock and a pleasant road winds from Worgl up to it.

Worgl is a typical Austrian compromise between workplace and playground. It has industry, which isn't allowed to be intrusive. The old town centre remains as quaint as a pastel-shaded painting. In winter, fairy lights hang in necklaces across the streets, softening the shadows from the overhanging gables where snow lies in thick wedges. A slender and graceful church spire looms. In summer you might hear a band pumping oompah music all round the park, or find yourself in one of the three pools at the swimming park where children cascade down the 165 ft (50 m) water slide. Walking the hills round Worgl can be both healthy and peaceful, and many visitors favour it. This is heartland Austria.

In the evenings, winter or summer, you will surely find yourself in one of the 38 cafés and restaurants, perhaps even in Gerhard Berger's favourite, the City-Pub on Speckbacherstrasse just up from the railway station. (If you're going, it seats 41, doesn't offer a billiard table — to have and have not is considered worthy of mention in Worgl — and is closed on Sundays.)

Austrians are industrious and the country's prosperity does not depend on tourism alone. Dieter Stappert, himself an Austrian who

41

would play a pivotal role in Berger's career, describes Berger's father as a 'typical stubborn hard-working Austrian businessman. Old Hans is the kind of man who'll have the family in the car ready to go on holiday, the phone will ring, he'll go in and answer it, tell the family something has come up and he'll join them on the holiday later. When he does finally get there he'll leave early to get back to the business.'

The family came from the Unterinntal area in the Lower Inn valley and were of farming stock. Hans, however, worked for a transport company ending up in their offices handling contacts with clients. He decided to begin in haulage by himself and in 1960 bought a single truck. Such people are the backbone of communities and he built ferociously on that single truck, creating literally a going concern which grew and grew. This led, inevitably perhaps, to a paradox. He could easily have financed his son's first tentative movements into motor racing, but Hans Berger regarded it as dangerous, almost frivolous, *and it cost money*. This violated the habits of his lifetime.

Gerhard was born to Hans and Olga Berger on 27 August 1959, four days after the Portuguese Grand Prix which Stirling Moss (Cooper Climax) won from Masten Gregory. A driver called Graham Hill crashed on lap 6, a driver called Jack Brabham had an accident on lap 24, a driver called Bruce McLaren dropped out with clutch problems on lap 39. Such a race would have meant nothing whatsoever to Hans Berger, even assuming he'd heard of it. The notion that his infant son would drive for the McLaren team and against the sons of Hill and Brabham would not have seemed fanciful so much as a waste of time; and time was money.

So Hans built and built, and created the successful company. He fully intended that in due course Berger should follow him into it. At each pressure point early in Berger's career Hans applied the logic of the businessman and didn't like what the comparison told him. Hans believed in the family motto: work, save, invest; and the motto did not cover throwing buckets of Austrian schillings at strange little vehicles which went round strange places. It covered large vehicles which moved cargo from A to B. Olga was evidently a typical *hausfrau*, rearing and bringing up a family. People introduced to her naturally called her Frau Berger without ever wondering about her Christian name.

In time, Gerhard would drive for a team called Schnitzer in the European Touring Car Championship and the man running that team, Charley Lamm, says, 'Hans Berger has a sense of humour. He likes to sit in a pub and talk and laugh. Gerhard brought an additional element to that because he *needs* humour, he needs fun to be a part of his life. I think if in the evening his father finds a casual environment he's content, but Gerhard *needs* to be the person he is, you know what I mean. However, I think he has a lot of his father in him. Formula 1 is also about earning money and Gerhard always declined having a manager. He'd work out what he wanted and how he wanted it. He has the talent of his father in this way.'

Worgl was a good place to grow up, not large enough to have the anonymity of a city, not small enough to be cramped and inhibiting. By nature rather than design Berger did not intend to be inhibited and remains precisely so today.

When he was three or four he began making conscious decisions about what he wanted to do — not go to kindergarten but mess around with vehicles. He knew that when his father was supposed to drive him to kindergarten he'd be concentrating on the business and if Berger hid in the back of the car and stayed perfectly silent his father would forget and drive straight to the office. Once there Berger would sneak out and explore the wide variety of machinery there.

It's uncanny, surveying the most successful drivers of the present age and the ages before it, how many were drawn to this very, very early. Jim Clark, brought up on a farm, knew all about the workings of tractors, how to drive them and how to make them *drift*; Jackie Stewart spent his formative years at a filling and service station, Ayrton Senna raced karts when virtually a toddler, Nigel Mansell ploughed a friend's ancient Austin 7 around fields when he was so small he couldn't see out of the window. Alain Prost came to it later, karting entirely for fun while on holiday in the south of France in his teens, but thereafter motor sport consumed his life very quickly, almost as if he needed to make up for lost time.

I don't believe you can read too much into this because an uncounted and uncountable number of kids must have tinkered and ridden and driven and grown out of it rather than into it. I do believe that the earlier you start the more you understand and the more of an advantage you hold. You have stored knowledge to draw on, a sympathy with the rhythms of motion.

Berger had his first major accident at the age of three when he fell off the fridge and cut himself below the eye, but don't read too much into that, either. All normal little boys have major accidents.

His sister Claudia, three years younger, remembers him as a 'daredevil' who lost his temper a lot and threw tantrums. He wasn't content with crying, evidently. He bawled his head off until the whole house echoed with it. Hans, more circumspect, remembers that 'as a child Gerhard was intelligent, extremely creative and already very independent. He had a mind of his own and was strong willed.' Did that include being strong willed against Hans (as happens with children)? Hans laughs and doesn't commit himself either way.

Claudia and Gerhard understood the art of parental manipulation. They weren't given regular pocket-money so Claudia would go to the haulage offices, nestle on her father's lap and extract 50 schillings — say a couple of pounds — from him, and she and Gerhard would share it.

Naturally Berger skied. They all can and do. If Worgl itself down there in the valley isn't ski country it is a conduit, not just to Kitzbuhel but also to a dozen other runs all over the gigantic ripples of rock. Every Tyrolean lad with red blood in his veins wants to be a downhiller and if, dear reader, you're a flatlander you might have difficulty envisaging the absolute potency of this. It's the equivalent of every red-blooded lad in Manchester wanting to be a footballer. In and around the Alps downhillers are genuine folk heroes and an Austrian ski official once told me that Klammer was more famous than the country's president. The official was not joking.

Moreover, Austrians are traditionally good at all forms of Alpine ski racing but particularly the downhill. To a small country which doesn't win much in any other sport except motor racing, it's them beating the world, it's heroic and breathtaking surges down the mountain, it's Olympic medals and World Championships. And the downhillers are close to racing drivers because both disciplines demand genuine courage, speed of reaction, balance, strength, and finesse when the world is flowing past you very quickly indeed. The tensions, even the mannerisms, before a downhill are similar to those before a Grand Prix, and both families would recognize their similarities instantly. It's surely no coincidence that Berger knows the ski racers and once invited them, including Klammer, to the Austrian Grand Prix, where a good time was had by all.

The practical jokes started early. If Gerhard and Claudia were locked in their bedrooms for some misdemeanour they'd climb down and set off. Hans was astonished that children could actually do that, although in winter their footsteps in the snow betrayed everything. They'd play a game called Dead Man, one of them lying motionless in the snow and when a car stopped thinking something terrible must have happened the Dead Man rose and legged it. As Berger says, 'I was always the same, plenty of practical jokes.' They'd hang on to the backs of passing cars (moving slowly in the snow, of course) and get a tow, skating along. Even with tender years Berger knew enough not to get near the exhaust pipes. Hans scolded him but secretly thought, 'At least my son is made of The Right Stuff.'

'It was quite funny,' Berger says. 'When I was a small guy there were two or three people in Worgl who used to compete in small Austrian races. After school, when everyone else went off to do their homework, I would go off to the workshops to see how the racing cars were built.' (Of this, more later.)

At secondary school he became involved in the usual fights and although he wasn't the strongest — a small, slight lad — he knew how to run.

He didn't show tremendous academic potential at school and didn't care much for homework. At 13 he had his first motorized transport, a bicycle with a little put-put engine and Hans only bought him that because Berger had broken his foot and had to get to school. Soon enough Berger tuned the engine so that it went faster than his chums' mopeds. Shortly after, he began to drive a car — Hans's 3 litre BMW — to the petrol pump. He drove a truck, as co-driver on a run to Verona in Italy.

In time there would inevitably be crashes on mopeds and motor bikes, and at least one in a car which struck a tree. Since Berger did not yet have a licence the local police were less than impressed and made deep noises of disapproval, suggesting that he'd never be *allowed* a licence. Definitely The Right Stuff for a Formula 1 driver. He got a Kawasaki and set off to do some *mountain* races. 'Oh, it was crazy, you know. Looking back, far more dangerous than racing cars.'

At commercial college Berger had a girlfriend some years older who owned an Alfa Romeo. When she drove him to the college in it the teachers, pedalling away on bikes, were less than impressed and made deep noises . . .

In time he'd grow to 6 ft 1 in (185 cm), a physical disadvantage in racing car cockpits. In time, too, there would be a steady girlfriend and a daughter, Christina, born in 1979.

'Gerhard became an apprentice in the family business', Hans says, 'first as a mechanic then doing the sort of things I had started with, on the client contact side, managing orders. For a few months he drove a truck himself.' Berger was punctual, worked hard and never played the boss's son. In 1979 Hans bought a small trucking company, Europtrans, put it in Gerhard's name, and put him in charge of it, although he also put a lady called Helga in there to handle it moment by moment. When Berger became a full-time driver and could no longer run the company it reverted to his father. No matter. Between them they'd built this into another going concern which today has 45 trucks and 125 employees.

When Berger reached German Formula 3 in 1982, he drove for a man called Josef Kaufmann and Kaufmann came to learn how it began. 'Gerhard was then head of a company called Europtrans, a bankrupt company his father bought and gave him along with some starting capital. Hans said to him, "OK, now you have three trucks and five employees".' Hans did not interfere in the running of this company and appreciated that Berger wasn't too proud to ask for advice.

Hans built and Berger built upon what Hans had built, accepting the responsibility of running a company and of having employees whose futures depend on you getting it right. Through the laughter and the jokes, of which there will be a great deal, please remember that.

3

Through the looking glass

'We had two racing drivers in the village where I lived. The most famous was Franz Albert, who won quite a lot in Austria, and the other was Frank Convalexius, a bike dealer who loved to race and was good in Austrian conditions. They built their own cars and sometimes Franz Albert even had a Formula 1 car there — a March. I was a schoolboy and interested in cars, so I used to look through their windows to see what they were doing. I couldn't go in, but because I looked so often sometimes they would let me in to have a closer look. My big thing was always racing but they didn't take me seriously because I was a small boy,' Berger says, exploring the start of it.

'One day when I'd reached the age of 18 I happened to be looking into the workshop of Frank Convalexius and he joked with me. "Why don't you race?" I said I couldn't because I was a mechanic learning my trade, I didn't have any money and my parents wouldn't want me to race, anyway. He said, "You can take my Ford Escort." I thought there must be something wrong here, but I said, "That would be fine, that would be nice." So he said, "I'll lend it to you for one race," I said, "Yes, fine."

'I thought to myself this is going to cost a lot of money, but he hadn't mentioned about the price. I played a sort of game with him. He gave me the date when there was a race at Zeltweg (the Osterreichring, home of the Austrian Grand Prix). The date came nearer and nearer and I still waited for the price. I didn't want to ask. Then he said, "OK, the race is next weekend." I told my parents I was going to school, but I didn't. Instead Frank and I went to Zeltweg and on the way there he said, "This race will cost such-and-such an amount," and I said, "That's fine, but I'll tell you one thing. I am so happy just to go to the circuit and watch the race" — I'd never seen a race before. "Drive the car yourself," I said, "because I don't have any money. I'll just watch and we'll still be friends. There won't be any problems between us."

'What I didn't know was that Frank had already told his friends, "Ah, this stupid Berger is going to buy my racing car." Frank wanted to sell it, he knew my father had money, and he had a plan: he'd put a big engine in it. I'd look good compared to the others, I'd buy it and he'd have sold it! The trouble was he'd already told everybody the car was sold to me. Now he'd got to tell them the car wasn't. He said, "OK, we'll take two risks. I'm going to take one, you're going to take the other. My risk is that you pay nothing for the race, your risk is that if you crash the car you pay a lot." I said, "OK, let's do this."

'It was the full Grand Prix circuit at Zeltweg and after practice Frank put our times away so other people couldn't see them — it was impossible to do the time I'd done! Of course the engine was supposed to be 1300 cc, but in reality Frank had put in a 1600. With this big engine I was quicker than everyone else. I didn't crash in the race, I won it, and *then* I found out about the engine. Frank otherwise was very fair. He said, "Listen, you shouldn't buy the Escort, you should keep going and try Formula Ford, you should try whatever cars you can because I think you have the talent to do something more," and he said it after this one race.

'For me it had been a big moment on the Zeltweg circuit, completely different to anything I'd known before. The noise in a racing car is so great you can get afraid about it. Everything's quiet in a normal car and suddenly you have a gearbox which is really loud.

'Afterwards I didn't say anything, but unfortunately I was in the newspaper and my father read it. That's how he found out I hadn't been at school but winning Zeltweg! He said he'd cancel all my money if I ever got into a racing car again.'

This matter of racing without mentioning it to your parents is almost a mandatory passage into the sport and one taken by, among others, Clark, whose parents learnt because some relative happened entirely by chance to be at his debut, Nelson Piquet who changed his name so his mother wouldn't know, and Lauda, who first raced two days after he promised his parents he wouldn't. Rindt began by racing a moped after he persuaded the local policeman he was 16, not 15, *and the moped belonged to the policeman.*

'I asked myself what I was going to do. I'd either have no money and race or have money and not race. I decided I'd wait and see what happened, and what happened was that I waited half a year and I said to myself I wanted to race whatever it took. I had some money because I was working. I bought an Alfasud which had crashed and been rebuilt and everybody said the car was finished because it was so 'soft' — flexing too much. The guy who owned it always ran in midfield, anyway. (As we'll see in a moment, Alfasuds contested a fiercely fought championship of their own.)

'The car was only cheap but I said, "OK, let's go for that one," because I didn't have much, money. I could stiffen it up and strengthen it and when I did it was good straight away. I went to the first race, Vallelunga in the Europe Cup, and there were 90 Alfasuds there. You had four sessions of pre-qualifying and I was sixth after the first day. I couldn't believe it, *they* couldn't believe it.

'In my qualifying session I asked Frank who was quick and he gave me the name of an Italian. I waited and just followed him — if I saw his brake light I hesitated a little bit then braked, so he was quickest and I was second quickest.' Berger was baulked in the race.

Alfa Romeo produced a drivers' guide, a page to each and in race number order. There's a picture of Berger's car — number 64 — and *BERGER WORGL* in a strip across the windscreen. Below, his details are carefully set out:

Born: Worgl 27/8/1959.
Address: Innsbruckerstrasse 43.
Profession: Mechanic.
Marital status: Single.
Concessionaire: Alfa Romeo Ascher Tirol.
Tuner: Egger Fritz.
Blood group: O.

and next to it was a head and shoulders portrait of a youthful, smiling Berger. The caption, *'He began racing in 1979 with a Ford Escort Group 5. In 1980 he moved to an Alfasud Group 2.'*

Just in case you're nursing the notion that Alfasuds were jolly little romps, consider that the 4-cylinder engines gave 1489 cc and the maximum speed was fixed at 155 mph (249 km/h). The cars had Weber carburettors and Lockheed brakes.

'I did one season of Alfasud and the only thing I didn't like was the front-wheel drive because I'd been used to rear-wheel drive. The season was a very good one from the point of view of the atmosphere — almost like a big dream. We slept in tents, had plenty of barbecues and so on (and he won a race at Dijon).

'I drove against Karl Wendlinger, the father! The son (Karl Jr) always travelled with me when I drove against his father, because, you know, if you're young you prefer to be with younger people. He was around 12 and now of course (1993) I'm driving against him in Formula 1.

'There was a bit of an Austrian mafia based around a racing school. They'd watched me in the Alfasuds at Zeltweg (where he also won) and said I was very good but "Alfasud is nothing compared to real racing in Formula Ford 1600 and Formula 3 and you really have a lot still to learn". It upset me a great deal because

Alfasuds weren't nothing, it was a European championship, all the Italians in there, Roberto Sigala who did Group C as well — good guys in there.'

The race at Zeltweg supported the Grand Prix. BMW were in their first season in Formula 1 (with Brabham) and the competitions manager, Dieter Stappert, stayed at a hotel up at the top of the circuit so that from his balcony he could enjoy the full panorama of the circuit. Stappert, incidentally, is Austrian and from the Tyrol. He says, 'I saw a green Alfasud driven by an Austrian who was mixing it with all the Italians — very rare to have a foreigner doing that. Alfasud was normally an *Italian* championship. He was in the middle of the bunch sideways all the time and he went on to win. I didn't remember the name, but I did remember he came from the Tyrol, too.'

Berger, meanwhile, 'said to myself, "Let's try a Formula Ford. Where can I get one, race one?" So I find a guy to rent me a Formula Ford 1600. I'd been in a go-kart in Rimini on holiday years before, but I'd never been in a single-seater.'

The telephone rang at a workshop just outside Bitburg, a hamlet deep into the countryside of the Rheinland-Pfalz area of (then) West Germany. Bitburg is just north of Luxembourg and handy for circuits like Spa, the Nurburgring and Hockenheim. Josef Kaufmann, an experienced racing driver who ran his own small team, lifted the receiver. 'The man said his name was Gerhard Berger. I didn't know him at all. He asked me if he could do a Super Vee race, because I'd had a Super Vee for many years and I'd raced it myself. I asked "Who are you? What have you done before? How old are you?" He said he was 21 and had never raced a single-seater though he'd been in Alfasuds.

'Because he had no Formula 3 experience I asked if he wanted to do some testing before he went into a race. He said, "No, no, I want to race. I don't want to test." I asked him where he came from and he said Worgl. I didn't know where that was, so he said it was near Kufstein, which I did know through Karl Wendlinger who I'd raced years before. I said, "OK, it is possible to do it. Just give me your phone number and I'll call you back in a day or two." Then I rang Wendlinger because I wanted to know, who is this Gerhard Berger? Wendlinger asked why I wanted to know. I explained that Gerhard had rung and was keen to do a race. Wendlinger said, "Gerhard is a nice, man, he's very, very good but we don't know how good."

'I phoned Gerhard and told him about an end-of-season race on the club circuit at Hockenheim. We agreed how much he had to pay, although I did it very cheaply because the German Formula 3 Championship had finished and this was an ordinary race. My brother, who is my chief mechanic, and I went to Hockenheim and I saw him for the first time. He looked extremely young, bushy hair, smiling. I told him that before we started the official practice we *had* to test. That could be done on the Friday in a session which lasted one or two hours.

'The weather was terrible, raining, raining. My brother said, "You really want to give him the car? Don't. I'm sure he'll destroy it." I said, "Well, we have to do something because we've come here specially for him and he's come here specially for us." I then told Gerhard, "Be careful, it's difficult in the wet." He started slowly and began to go quicker and quicker, and after 50 laps wasn't far away from a normal good time, only two or three seconds, which is nothing for a beginner. He did not spin once and said he was happy how the car had gone. I could not believe that he was so quick, you know.

'The official practice and the race were on the Saturday, weather dry, and of course he'd not driven the car with slick tyres. We started the official practice and he was good, although I have to say most of the top drivers weren't there. He did the whole practice session, no crash, no damage, nothing, and in the race he was good, too — fourth, solid lap times. After the race I felt relief because the car was still in one piece. We decided we'd try to get together for 1982.'

Moreover Berger dabbled briefly in Austrian Formula Ford 1600, doing one race at Zeltweg. 'I went round in my first practice and we'd had a carburettor problem in the Alfasud. If the car was wrong the engine didn't get fuel during cornering. I had exactly the same on the Formula Ford. I felt it and with the experience from the Alfasud I went into the pits and said to the mechanics, "The carburettor doesn't work properly! We'll have to change it." I was already fastest or second fastest. I remember the mechanic saying, "How quickly will you go when the car is working properly?" I jumped the start of the race and got a penalty which made me third, but I won after a big, big fight with the leading Austrians. Afterwards the guy from the Austrian mafia came and said, "Sorry about what I said about Alfasuds, you have to keep going." I said, "Yes, but I don't think I should stay in Austrian Formula Ford 1600".'

Moving into the first days of 1982 Berger took part in the Alfa Romeo Alitalia Ice Trophy, an event which had been running since 1977, on nailed Pirelli tyres. This year is would be held over four races, Serre Chevalier (France), St Johann (Austrian), Grainau (Germany) and Cortina d'Ampezzo (Italy). The official guide announced that 'drivers will be allowed to become familiar with the iced tracks during proper training sessions. Their lap times will be used to determine their starting order in the race. The winning driver will receive an Alfa Romeo Sprint prepared to take part in the European Trophy for a total value of 15,000,000 Lire (approximately £6,000).

The second driver will receive a Ducati 15 CV outboard motor' and so on down to fifth, a set of Pirelli P6 tyres.

Ninety-three entries came from Austria, Germany, France, Italy and one from Spain, Berger and Wendlinger among the 12 Austrians. The paradox is that Berger insists he didn't drive but *rode*. Alfa Romeo kindly sent me a selection of photographs from the Ice and Snow at St Johann and lively stuff it is, dodgem cars surging and bounding and bouncing round in a winter wonderland. A problem presented itself: Alfa Romeo couldn't identify which car Berger had been in, so I showed him the selection and he said, 'I wasn't in any of them, I rode a Ducati! The Ice and Snow was a great race. There was a guy who's name I can't remember always fighting with me (in the competitive sense), we had a big fight . . .'

Nadia Pavignani of Ducati sheds light upon this potential mystery, whose importance is not, of course, centred around such a relatively innocuous event but the fact that Berger *could* ride a Ducati competitively and fight with people while he was doing it. 'Although Alfa Romeo organized the event we had a race, too, because at the time there was an arrangement between us. Drivers and journalists could take part in our race on motor bikes and I remember well that Gerhard was very, very clever, he beat members of the Italian national ice team. I can't, however, remember where he finished — it could have been first or second — because the race wasn't really so important and it's a long time ago. I've been asked for photographs and it's a shame but we don't have any. It was really an Alfa Romeo meeting, you see, not ours. Gerhard was a very nice man and we became friends, which we remain. He still has a Ducati.'

There's another twist because Berger *did* drive his Alfasud in the Ice and Snow but the year before, and you can picture it: spectacular.

Josef Kaufmann's telephone rang again. 'It was in the winter time and Gerhard told me he'd like to do the German Formula 3 Championship. Austria didn't have one, I think, or if they did it was very small. The problem was to convince his father. I'd do it cheaply because I don't think Gerhard had enough money of his own to pay the full price, but I wanted him because I thought that this man with virtually no experience would be good.

'At the beginning of January he phoned and asked if I'd go and see his father to convince him. I drove down to Worgl and arrived about seven o'clock in the evening. Gerhard's father is a very busy man and Gerhard said, "Sorry, but we must wait a little bit because my father always works late." It was 10 o'clock before his father came. His father said hello, and I suddenly thought that Gerhard hadn't told him a thing about my visit! Gerhard said, "Now, explain to my father." *I* said, "Did you tell him?" and *he* said, "Yes, but . . ."

'Gerhard asked if I had some pictures to show his father and in fact I had a drawing of the new car, the 1982 model. I showed that to him and this is what we wanted to do. His father said, "What! You want to go into Formula 1?" He did not have any idea about racing. (To be fair to Hans Berger, a drawing of a racing car looks like a racing car, and if you don't know, the differences between F1 and F3 don't exactly hit you between the eyes.) "Formula 1, never," his father said, "because Gerhard is my only son and look at Niki Lauda. He is a very lucky man, but I don't want to see my son like that." I said, no it's not Formula 1, it's Formula 3, but it looks a bit like Formula 1. He asked what Formula 3 was. I explained and said I'd raced Formula Super Vee — which is nearly the same — and I'd already driven for 15 years. I said, "Look at me, I've never had an injury." But he said, "Formula 3 is going to cost me a lot of money."

'I thought, how can you convince a man like this? He doesn't want his son in Formula 1 because it's too dangerous, and he doesn't want his son in Formula 3 because it's too expensive. Then his father told me that Gerhard had a Kawasaki and Gerhard had done some hillclimbs with it. "Maybe we can do something but you must take the Kawasaki in trade and also his Alfasud." He showed me the Kawasaki, which was in the workshop, and it had slick tyres! It had been bought as a road bike but modified so that now it was no longer a road bike but it also wasn't a racer. I said I'd take the Alfasud. His father wanted me to take the Kawasaki as well, but not for the money, no, just so Gerhard couldn't ride it any more. "If I allow my son to race in Formula 3 he really must stop with this bike." He and Gerhard struck a deal: Gerhard would never touch the thing again. Gerhard said, "OK, it's all right, I won't."

'So Gerhard bought the Formula 3 car. He had a good relationship with Alfa Romeo — I think he had transported some of their road cars with his haulage company — and said he'd do the season with Alfa engines. He bought a Martini (a famed Formula 3 manufacturer) because I am the agent for Martini in Germany. I only charged him for servicing and the work my mechanics did. It was his father's money and Gerhard's, although I don't know how much each paid.'

Kaufmann returned to Bitburg and as the season neared his telephone rang again. Berger was bringing the engines so that he and Kaufmann could take them to Magny-Cours (the circuit in central France, now used for the Grand Prix) where Martini was. It also represented a chance to introduce Berger to Tico Martini. 'Gerhard said he'd start from Wörgl early in the morning so he'd be in Bitburg by late afternoon. You know when he arrived? Three o'clock in the morning. He'd come in an (expletive, expletive) old Volvo estate with two race engines laid in the back. I said, "God, how can you drive that?" I started the engine and all the lights came on, the water temperature was crazy. I said, "Sorry, but I really don't want to go all the way to Magny-Cours with a car like this." I had an Audi and we put one engine in it, Gerhard got in and fell asleep. He slept all the way down — all the way — and it must be 375 miles (600 km) from here.

'When we reached Magny-Cours Tico asked, "Who is this?" I said it was my new driver. Tico said, "What has he done before?" and I said nothing, nothing at all! Then on the way back he slept again all the way. I felt very tired so I drove extremely fast to keep myself awake. He woke up, looked out of the window, said "(expletive) I didn't tell them at home that I wouldn't be coming back alive," I said, "If you can do better . . ." He said, "Oh no," and immediately went back to sleep. We arrived at Bitburg about 10, 11 o'clock in the evening and he said "I have to take a hotel room because I'm so tired!" We found him a room and he slept until 10 the next morning. Then he go into the Volvo and drove home."

Berger's father had his own aeroplane and before Berger left Worgl with the engines Kaufmann wondered why he didn't ask his father simply to fly the engines. But, as Berger pointed out, his father missed runways and landed in fields with disconcerting frequency.

In German Formula 3, where Kaufmann would also drive, he'd met a Dane, John Nielsen, the man to beat. Nielsen, affable and thoughtful, had started karting as long ago as 1969 and single-seaters as long ago as 1974. 'I had the works VW Ralt', Nielsen says, 'and Gerhard was more or less running himself in the Martini. He was as he is today, a nice chap, you know, easy to talk to, easy to get on with. In 1982 he didn't do much.

'The next year he got better and better. He was very quick, no doubt about it but I think in those days he wasn't really serious about it. That's why his performances were up and down. Whether he thought in terms of progressing to Formula 1 some day I'm not sure. (Berger confirms that he didn't actually allow himself to think conclusively about Formula 1 until about three weeks before he first drove a Grand Prix car, mid-summer 1984, although along the way it was in his thoughts.) In fact, I don't think he thought about becoming a professional driver. Maybe people like me were too serious because we did think about that. Gerhard played practical jokes — he'd tell people who couldn't speak German very bad words to say . . .'

After such a brief career Berger found himself mingling with — in context — formidable drivers on the short circuit at the Nurburgring in the first German Formula 3 round which also happened to be a combined event embracing the second round of the European

Formula 3 Championship. Among an entry of 44 he'd find Nielsen but also the young, the ambitious and the fast: Alain Ferte, Philippe Alliot, Oscar Larrauri, Emanuelle Pirro, Didier Theys, Volker Weidler, Claudio Langes — the sort of drivers who might well, within two or three seasons, form the backbone of Formula 1.

In heat one Alliot took pole from Pirro (51.48 seconds against 51.60), then Nielsen and a delightful Italian called Roberto Ravaglia, Berger further back with 52.95. Larrauri went quickest from Ferte in heat two (51.15 against 51.32). Berger started from the eighth row for the 43-lap final which Larrauri won, Berger sixteenth, which is where you might have expected him to finish.

Nielsen, third at the Nurburgring, stormed the German Championship: front row of the grid at Hockenheim (Berger row five), fastest lap and victory. That's not the whole story of Hockenheim, however. Dr Helmut Marko, childhood friend of Rindt, former driver and now a team manager, watched Berger 'during the race and he did something which only a few drivers can do. He outbraked a guy into the Sachskurve (the horseshoe left within the stadium complex), was too late on the brakes but managed to keep the car straight. He went on to the grass and still he didn't lose control, still he tried to overtake the guy and that's what makes a racer, a real racer. From this moment on I saw there was a big talent.' In time they'd talk and lay plans for 1983.

Nielsen missed the next race, Salzburg, which allowed Kaufmann to take pole, Berger on the second row; it also allowed a driver called Bruno Eichmann to set fastest lap and win, Berger fourth. These are in a sense little races long ago, one season of domestic Formula 3 in one country, but because it was Berger's first season, and because by definition he knew so little about it, I propose to set it out round by round.

Nielsen came back for Wunstorf, took pole, set fastest lap, won. Berger started on the third row. Result: Nielsen 18 minutes 43.99 seconds; Eichmann 18 minutes 51.15 seconds; Berger 19 minutes 1.92 seconds.

'I thought', Berger says — governed by impatience as well as ambition, no doubt — 'let's try Formula Ford 2000. I went to Hockenheim and that was a really tough field, Ayrton Senna, Calvin Fish, Cor Euser.' Senna, driving a Van Diemen, took pole but 'cooked his clutch' on the line, Euser made a storming start, but as *Autosport* reported overdid things 'at the first chicane and launched himself into a series of rolls. Behind, there was carnage as drivers tried to take evasive action and the track was virtually blocked, leaving the organizers no option but to red flag the race.'

Berger is typical about it. 'I had a good start and after the first corner (the right-handed loop at the end of the start-finish straight) I was fourth, and I thought that's good. Then somebody jumped over my back wheel and I thought damn! But I really didn't want to give up so I thought I'd try and keep going. The brake pipe had broken and I went into the three cars in front of me — and there was a crash involving what seemed to be about 20 cars. I just couldn't believe what I was seeing. Cars were on top of other cars. I sat in mine under a barrier, nothing really left of the car, finished.

'I could hear people screaming. I thought it was all my fault. I saw them pulling Cor Euser out of his car and I thought, "Damn, he's got a broken leg — my fault." I didn't know he'd started the race with the leg broken because he'd done it the race before! Then a marshal ran up and started shouting — I couldn't see where — "It was his fault, it was his fault," but . . . he wasn't shouting towards me, he was shouting towards somebody else. I couldn't go to the restart because I only had the one car and it was in no condition. In fact I think only seven cars did go to the restart.'

Just to show how elusive progress can be, how close you may come and have it plucked away, here is the *Autosport* paragraph covering the restart. 'Ron Kluit took his Reynard into the lead and he began to edge out a slight advantage until picking up a puncture. Calvin Fish soon closed in on the ill-handling car and unwittingly nudged the Dutchman into a spin when Kluit got a little too sideways in front of him.

'The ensuing moment for Fish allowed Frank Bradley (Van Dieman) into the lead, albeit closely followed by a train of cars consisting of Fish, Rosso, Kristian Nissen, Max Busslinger, Ralf Rauh and Henrik Larsen. The Swiss, Busslinger, then spun off at the Sachskurve and Fish retook the lead until Rosso found a way past with two laps to go, going on to score his first 2000 victory.' Senna's team-mate at Rushen Green, Mike Mackonochie, finished 'a respectable eighth' which itself shows how elusive it can be. Senna wouldn't find it so, of course, and that's another paradox. The only Formula 1 team-mate he'd find with whom he could co-exist amicably (in the broad meaning of that term) would be the tall, lean Austrian who'd completed a fraction of the initial race under the barrier expecting to be blamed and fined and banished and heaven knows what else.

How elusive? Whatever happened to Kluit, Bradley, Rosso, Nissen, Busslinger, Rauh, Larsen, Mackonochie? Good men no doubt, ambitious men no doubt, and all of whom, presumably, had never heard of Berger nor had any particular reason to have heard of him.

At Erding in the German Formula 3 Berger qualified on the fourth row, Nielsen pole, of course, fastest lap, of course, winning of course, Berger fifth behind a driver called Baron Thomas von Lowis of Menar. Where is he today? Running the Bundesbank? (He was, evidently, an experienced F3 driver although not noted for speed.) After Erding, Kaufmann's phone rang:

Berger: 'Josef, that's it, I don't want to race any more.'

Kaufmann: 'Why, why?'

Berger: 'Well, look, I am not very good.'

Kaufmann: 'Why do you think that?'

Berger: 'Well, I don't like to always finish fourth, fifth, sixth. I think I am not good enough.'

Kaufmann: 'Not good enough? You're just a beginner. You can't expect to win after so few races.'

Berger: 'Well, I don't race any more, I stop.'

Kaufmann: 'You can't. I have my mechanics to pay.'

Berger: 'Don't worry. I'll give you the money.'

Kaufmann: 'If you really want to stop, I'll race your car.' (Kaufmann himself had a car he estimated as between one and two years old, and no sponsorship.)

Berger: 'No problem. If you want it just take it.'

So, Kaufman says, 'I went to the Nurburgring and I told everyone Gerhard was a nice man and a fantastic driver. I took his car, tested it and found it nearly undrivable. Because he was a beginner he didn't know much and certainly not enough to tell me the problems. The Martini had wings but he couldn't tell me about the settings. After a few laps I spotted all this and explained to the mechanics how bad the car was. I also said, "I don't really understand how he could finish fourth, fifth, sixth with a car like this." We worked nearly a whole day on the springs and so forth. John Nielsen was quickest but he had the works VW drive — the first year, incidentally, of VW coming in. After this testing I was only a tenth of a second slower than Nielsen. Quick, you see. That was the Thursday and the race was at the weekend, a round of the German Championship. I phone Gerhard in the evening.'

Kaufmann: 'Look, you really must come because the car was (expletive) before, now it's fantastic. I've found a very good setting and I did a time a tenth behind Nielsen.'

Berger: 'Aaah, don't tell me stories like that. I don't believe them.'

Kaufman: 'Gerhard, you really have to come, you must do the race.'

Berger: 'No. I've stopped. I'm not coming.'

Kaufmann went home to Bitburg only 30 miles (50 km) away, had a good night's rest and returned to the Nurburgring on the Friday. Berger had already arrived.

Kaufmann: 'Hello, Gerhard, what on earth are you doing here?'

Berger: 'I want to do the race.'

Kaufmann: 'No, no, I don't give you the car because *I* want to *win* it.'

'But you know I did give him the car,' Kaufmann says, 'and in official practice he was second, very close behind Nielsen. He was very happy and he said "Fantastic".' He'd qualified on the front row for the first time, Nielsen pole (51.93 seconds against 51.52 seconds). 'In the race', Kaufmann says, 'Nielsen led, then Gerhard, me third. First corner I don't know if Gerhard touched Nielsen or not but it was finished for Nielsen. Gerhard led, me behind, a driver called Franz Konrad — later Formula 3 champion who did a lot of Group C with Porsche — hard behind me. The race was 40 laps and Gerhard led for 20, then just after 20 laps at a slow corner Gerhard missed a gear. I could hear the engine *baaarp, baaarp*, but he had a big problem because he'd broken second gear. At that moment Konrad overtook me because I was thinking "What's happened to Gerhard?" He couldn't complete the race.

'So Konrad won and I came second. After the race I thought we would have a big problem with Gerhard but he was so happy. I asked him how he could be so happy and he said, "The race is not so important. I know now I have the car and I can win".' This is much easier to say than to do.

There would be a non-championship German Formula 3 race on the old, full Nurburgring and thereby hangs a tale, although you will have to wait until the next chapter for the pay-off. Kaufmann said to Berger that he should do the race because the Nurburgring was a unique and amazing circuit. To help Berger learn it, Eichmann drove him round in a Porsche turbo while Kaufmann followed in another road car.

Although Kaufmann knew the exact place where Lauda had crashed in 1976 he had no way of knowing if Eichmann knew, or indeed if Eichmann pointed it out as they passed; and anyway it's scarcely the sort of topic Kaufmann would have raised with a young driver, particularly after what Berger would say next. That was, 'No, I really don't like it, I won't do the race.' Kaufmann, said, 'Look, what happens if you reach European Formula 3 next season and one of the races is on the full circuit? You won't know it.' Berger said, 'No, there won't be, I'm sure.' Work had already begun on the 'new' circuit which accorded to modern safety standards and bore no resemblance to the old. Berger didn't do the race.

A pattern had been established in 1982 and it can be followed easily enough: round seven at Diepholz, Berger third row of the grid, tenth in the race; round eight at Zolder, second row of the grid, third; round nine at the Nurburgring, third row of the grid, fourth in the race. A sharper test was at hand, round 10 at Kassel-Calden in October, a combined European round again bringing back Larrauri, Pirro and Langes. If Berger wanted to measure his progress across the season here was the chance. He qualified on the eighth row again with the comparison Larrauri pole 1 minute 4.87 seconds, Berger 1 minute 6.67 seconds.

Autosport reported, 'Once the fog lifted the competitors found a changed track from previous years, with the addition of a particularly tight and bumpy first gear chicane which completely upset most teams' choice of gear ratios and wing settings. There was a certain amount of argument after practice when Jakob Bordoli argued that Jo Zeller had missed a chicane and Eichmann protested both the other Swiss drivers' times, but the organizers brushed aside allegations of inaccuracy in their timing.'

Pirro won from Zeller — Larrauri's engine let go on lap 20 of 37 — Berger ninth. Final German Formula 3 positions: Nielsen 140 points, Eichmann 110, Berger 83, Kaufmann 78.

Berger, reflecting on the season, says, 'Josef Kaufmann was my team chief in Formula 3 and he drove as well. He was aged 33 or something, a youngish guy and a very nice guy. We had a lot of fun, we went out until three in the morning with the girls and the next day we were racing. Everything really was nice.'

Kaufmann, reflecting on the season, says only, 'We had a very, very good time,' off the track and declined further elaboration except to say that I will have to use my imagination — and so will you. 'Practical jokes? Every time something happened, every time he had a new idea to do something crazy.' On the track, 'He told me he wanted to do Formula 3 because he wanted to get into Formula 1. He did not start for fun. At the beginning he said he could only spend two or three years in Formula 3 and if he wasn't in Formula 1 by then he'd have to stop because he had a company to run.

'The atmosphere surrounding the championship was better then than now. Ten years ago motor sport was different. Now everybody works very, very hard, everybody wants to win, everybody *has* to win because there's so much money in it. If you're not good one year, the next year it's finished for you. The standard was not at all bad, although now it's much better and German Formula 3 is one of the best in the world.

'In 1982 Gerhard never crashed the car, he had no accident at all and he was always quick. When he went to McLaren in 1990 I thought maybe he could go quicker than Senna because Senna started his career so early and Gerhard was really 21 when he started. Right from the beginning he'd get into the car, do a few laps and see how it was and then go very, very quick. In 1982 he learned a lot and it's not easy because when you're a newcomer you don't know any of the circuits and there is no chance to learn them before — no testing, you just go there, have half an hour of unofficial practice, then you have the session for the grid and really to go fast you do need to know the circuits. Don't forget some of the drivers had already done two or three years in Formula 3 so they knew.

'And our car was not very good because it was the first wing car that Martini built. Gerhard would have finished better if we'd had another car, but as it was he still came third in the championship. Nielsen had an excellent car, a lot of money, and it would have been very hard to beat him anyway. At the end of the season Gerhard told me he wanted to do European Formula 3 in 1983 and Helmut Marko had some Austrian sponsors. I'd never done European Formula 3, I always preferred to stay in the German Championship and I stayed.' Berger and Kaufmann remain friends.

'After the last race', Berger says, 'Dr Helmut Marko came to see me and asked what I planned for 1983. I told him I had decided to stop racing because I had no money, no sponsors and I had my haulage company to think about. He suggested we try and find some money together to try and run a team. Well, we found the money and we took on an ex-Mansilla 1982 spec Ralt RT3' (Enrique Mansilla, a Brazilian driver).

To have left motor sport to build the business would have been a natural course. The racing had been fun, he'd made friends and at least one sports commentator — possibly Heinz Pruller of ORF television and radio — concluded that, all in all, 'Berger makes a good impression, well brought up and educated, good manners. His driving is clean, he battles hard but fairly. He doesn't behave like a lout on the track and he doesn't have accidents either, only a few spins. He's not hard on machines and he's particularly good in the wet.'

How tempting to have treasured this little homily as the obituary to a career and then melted away, to have gone to wherever such as Kluit, Bradley, Rosso, Nissen, Busslinger, Rauh, Larsen and Mackonochie would go. Or in Berger's case to become a member of the bourgeoisie, the haulage company expanding and expanding, become a pillar of the community and move towards a middle-age spread, the way people do. He might say in conversation, 'I raced a bit once, you know, but, well, it was a young man's flight of fancy. You didn't know I raced? It's a long time ago.'

But Marko had seen, Marko understood what he had seen, and Marko began a campaign. So did Burkhardt Hummel, another Austrian, an entrepreneur and breathtaking finder of sponsorship. (One coup was to get a small Alpine record label who specialized in yodelling to sponsor a car, so that their name became visible all round Europe — but would that make you buy yodelling?)

Stappert occupied a clear position of importance as competitions manager of BMW. 'At the end of 1982 Burkhardt phoned me up and said "There is this Tyrolean racing driver and we need to help him." I asked who the driver was, Burkhardt said, "Gerhard Berger" but the name didn't mean anything to me. However, I said, "OK, we'll go and talk to him." A week later Marko phoned me up and said, "There is this young Tyrolean who is really quick and you'd better keep an eye on him." I said who? Marko said he'd been racing Alfasuds last year. Then I remembered I'd watched the Alfasud race from my balcony at the hotel at the Osterreichring. I asked Marko, "Was this the crazy guy who mixed it with all the Italians?" He said, yes, he was. I said, "Ok, we have a meeting'."

Marko confirms this. 'Yes I rang Hummel, the guy who organized sponsorship money. I rang Stappert and said that I had a crazy Tyrolean. I introduced Gerhard to people who were important at that stage. When I first met him he was the same as he is today. You could make an agreement with him verbally, you didn't need a contract.'

The campaign shifted gear. Hummel phoned Stappert again and, as Stappert says, 'We fixed a date to meet Gerhard at Worgl. We went to his favourite pub, The City-Pub, and Gerhard arrived in a Porsche Carrera! He had everything. I realized in the first 15, 20 minutes that the guy was well-educated, from a wealthy family, good looking. All the girls were after him — you could see that in the pub. So I asked myself: why does such a guy want to go motor racing? I really didn't think he was serious.

'I spent most of the evening trying to convince him that motor racing was the wrong way to go. I tried to explain to him that every year in every country there are 20 people who regard themselves as the next Niki Lauda, the next Fangio or whatever, which makes easily 2,000 in the world, and only the ones who are strong enough, strong-willed enough *and* take risks *and* survive — because there is a pretty good chance you will get killed — *might* make it. I said, "You've got everything, you've got money, you've got cars, you've got girls, so why bother?" He kept saying, "I want to drive and if you don't help me I'm going to do it anyway." That convinced me: he didn't want to give up.'

Stappert: 'What about your parents?'

Berger: 'Of course my parents hate it because my mother is in fear and my father wants me to work in the company.'

Stappert: 'Well, what are we going to do now?'

Berger: 'If you could talk to my father — you're well-respected in the area, you're Austrian and you have the job with BMW — maybe he'll listen.'

Stappert: 'OK, tomorrow we'll see your father.'

Before that fateful meeting Stappert questioned Hummel about what they should do and they agreed to persuade Marko to set up a team to contest the European Formula 3 Championship. 'We arrived. There was Gerhard's father and mother, and his father looked at me as if to say, "I don't want to talk to you." I explained to him who I was and that I thought his son had quite a talent. I also told him that to my deep astonishment and amazement he seemed to have a strong will. I said a choice must be made because there were two ways of doing it: either he's got to take it seriously, which he can't do if he's working at his company all day, or he keeps on working at his company and does the occasional race around the corner, so to speak. To do it seriously, you should give him two years to a large extent free of the company. After the two years we'll all see if he has the talent and we'll also see if he has the strong will he says he has. So far we can't judge. By then we will realize — and you will realize — if he has a future in motor sport. If he hasn't, he can always come back to the family business and just enjoy himself doing a couple of races.

'I'll never forget the expression on his father's face, and I knew that if there had been any way he could have killed me and got away with it he would have killed me then. He just didn't want to know. He just didn't want to hear of it. I don't think it was the possible danger so much as he thought it a waste of time. To the father it seemed obvious that by doing this his son would never make money. He thought it a nuisance and he was sure that two years out of the company would be time sacrificed.'

Spare a thought for Hans Berger and this parade of strangers who kept coming (and would keep coming) to his door to persuade him about flights of fancy. Stappert is persuasive. Hummel can sell fridges to eskimos effortlessly. Marko is the sort of man you'd entrust a son to. Gerhard Berger can be persuasive. Cumulatively they represented an irresistible force.

It was no contest.

Marko, a member of the Austrian mafia (no disrespect intended, you know what I mean), says pointedly, 'In Austria we don't have the industry to support motoring, we don't have manufacturing, so the Austrians have always made their way into motor sport in a different way, via Germany through personal contacts, being a nice guy and things like that.

'Gerhard spoke in a Tyrolean accent and me, from Graz (the other side of the country), I found it difficult to understand him. We had a meeting to discuss everything and he was, I think, two hours late. I started to educate him. If you're emerging from the Tyrol you have to get organized, you have to wear the right clothes, be punctual.' Marko advised Berger to learn English, the lingua franca of motor sport, and Hummel — who Berger describes as 'the eternal optimist' — suggested it wasn't a good idea tactically to draw up at potential sponsors in the Porsche Carrera. So instead Berger drove an old multi-coloured Audi. The Volvo estate would have done nicely but maybe it had finally breathed its last.

4

Game for a laugh

'In the winter time we got the racing calendar for European Formula 3,' Kaufmann says, his whole face enveloped in a grin, 'and there was the old, full Nurburgring first race. Gerhard phoned me and said, "I've just seen the calendar. I must come, we must go there and you must show me the circuit." I said nobody could go round because of the work going on to make the new circuit. So he came and for three days he walked the Nurburgring. Every day he did one or two laps on foot (and the circuit measured (14 miles/23 km). Then he came to see me in the evening at Bitburg. He took a pen and a piece of paper and made a drawing of the circuit. He said, "This corner I think I do in fourth gear, this one in fifth." I could not believe how he could remember it, not having driven it, and what he'd worked out was very good.

'Everybody arrived on the Thursday for the first practice on the Friday. What happened? Twenty centimetres of snow and they cancelled the meeting, so he never did drive the Nurburgring and he'd been out there for three days walking it . . .'

One way and another, European Formula 3 came at you strongly (snow permitting), Nielsen, Pirro, Ravaglia, Pascal Fabre whom Berger had already raced, and more: the studious-looking Italian Ivan Capelli who one day would find out all about the perils of driving for Ferrari (and thus create a vacancy Berger would fill), another Italian called Pierluigi Martini who one day would find out all about the perils of trying to stay in Formula 1, Tommy Byrne, a broth of an Irishman, French sportswoman Cathy Muller. Flying visits, literally, would be made by an American, Davy Jones, by Johnny Dumfries, a titled Briton who did not care to be addressed by his title, as well as James Weaver, Martin Brundle and very briefly by Senna.

'It was really great,' Muller says, 'because you had drivers from all over the place and a lot of laughter. Most slept in their trucks, all the trucks travelled together and if we had two or three days' "holiday" between races we'd socialize, swim, talk. Everybody helped everybody.

'Gerhard was really very nice, always very nice, always smiling, always doing jokes. I slept in my truck, my sister with me, and she'd cook and make tea for the other drivers. Many times in the mornings Gerhard came round with fresh bread which he'd bought and we'd have breakfast. Yes, nice. On the track we'd sometimes fight together, often a big fight but always correct, no tricks, no pushing each other off, and away from the track people were friendly — which you don't get in national championships.'

An inevitably sexist question to Cathy Muller, which must be dealt with to get it out of the way. Did the fact that you were a woman affect the attitude of the others to you as a driver? 'They respected me for what I was doing in the car. For me, above all, Gerhard was a big brother, kind, and he respected me as a driver, too. If today he happens to meet my sister at a Grand Prix he always asks "How's Cathy doing?" and it's as if time hasn't passed, he's still the big brother. That is superb because he hasn't become big-headed, not at all, he's natural, just himself, and that makes him a big man. There aren't many like that.'

Byrne, who also came around for breakfast, captures the era in a torrent of words. 'I tell you what, we probably had more best times than anybody else ever, the whole lot of us, that bunch of people who were driving then. We'd get the job done and then go out, Gerhard, Capelli, myself. We had water fights on roofs the whole time, but we were serious on the track. You'd run them off the track first chance you got. Gerhard was a fun guy, always playing practical jokes, always up to that kind of stuff — just the same as me, you know. We liked to have a good time but we could do a job on the track so we felt there was never any harm in any of it. If you can do the job why should people complain? But, you know, some people did.'

Weaver captures the era like this: 'It was a lot of fun, certainly for me, because you were travelling abroad, new circuits, new people, new languages, new food, new everything. Really it came as an enormous breath of fresh air after you'd been going to Silverstone, Brands, Thruxton, Thruxton, Thruxton for years. I didn't have much money . . .'

Ravaglia, from Venice, captures the era like this: 'In 1983 I was with the Trivellato team (more of them later) and Gerhard was with Helmut Marko's team. I knew Gerhard was — how can you say it? — not a rich man but he could spend some money on his motor racing, so I was little bit surprised because sometimes he slept in his truck. I arrived at one circuit very early in the morning and there he was asleep in it. For me Gerhard was a good driver because he had talent. Some drivers, for example, are good because they drive in Formula 3 for a long time and after four or five years they become better and better, but that first year Gerhard was able to do good races and good times even with a car which wasn't really good.'

Happy, innocent, make-do-and-mend days. Joe Saward, who'd cover the season for *Autosport*, remembers that Berger could often afford to stay in hotels, 'but at least half the field lived in transporters. For example I lived for a while in Gary Anderson's truck, then the Yokohama truck, then for a while in Eddie Jordan's truck.'

On a more sober note, Hans Berger emphasizes that whilst at first he did not accept his son as having a driving career, when he reached Formula 3 Hans 'made a decision to accept it. I fully stand by this decision and it has not changed since.'

The European Formula 3 Championship comprised 15 rounds plus the traditional Monaco race supporting the Grand Prix and stretched full across the season from Vallelunga, Italy, in March to Croix-en-Ternois, France, in October. Ralt cars provided the backbone, if you can put it like that, with essentially a choice of three engines, Alfa Romeo, Toyota and VW. Berger had Alfas from Trivellato.

'I ran him in a year-old Ralt,' Marko says, 'with an Alfa Nova engine. The whole operation was two mechanics — one English, one Austrian — and a low budget. Very soon a funny thing happened. The first race, Vallelunga, we found out that he didn't know anything about a car: what is oversteer, what is understeer, a spring. We didn't find out until after practice. We asked him things and he didn't know what we were talking about!'

'After Vallelunga', Stappert says, 'Marko phoned me up and said, "This guy is a lunatic, he's completely disorganized, he has no idea about a setting a car up. He's much worse than I was in my early days and I know how bad I was." I said, "What about the rest?" Marko replied, "He's exceptionally quick. What we have to do is convince him not to drive around the problems of the car but learn little by little".' (As an aside, the naturally talented can do what is termed 'drive around a problem' by adjusting to compensate for it. You can't, I can't. They can.)

Berger qualified third at the next race, Zolder, behind Byrne and Pirro. *Autosport* reported, 'The temperature had risen several degrees by the Saturday afternoon session and times were generally slower, although young Austrian Berger was one of the very few to improve his time.' He made 'a mess' of the start of the race but quickly overtook Fabre and next lap Martini. He set off after Nielsen and on lap 10 of 22 they had a 'coming together' at the chicane — 'Nielsen trying too late to shut the door on the charging Austrian. The Danish driver was out on the spot but Berger made it through and set off to chase Didier Theys.'

Nielsen remembers that 'Gerhard had missed the start but was quite quick coming up through the field. Just when he passed me he pulled over and pushed me into the armco. I felt so — how do you say? — angry. I didn't feel it was necessary.' Berger finished third.

After the race Nielsen 'ran across to him and we almost had a little fight, a physical fight. Somebody stopped me before I hit him. It was the heat of the moment where you just can't control yourself. I don't associate with violence and I don't think I'd ever done anything like that before. Up to then we'd been good friends and after that we were also good friends. We got over it quickly, no problem. We shook hands at the next race.'

Stappert, who'd been at the French Grand Prix at Paul Ricard, remembers that 'the Monday after the race I was flying back to Munich. I bought *L'Equipe* and they carried the top 10 results from Zolder. I read them in reverse order because I thought that with a bit of luck he might have been around seventh, eighth. When I reached fifth I was disappointed — he wouldn't have finished higher. Then *G. Berger, third*. This was hard to believe, a podium in only his second European Formula 3 race.'

At Magny-Cours Nielsen won, Berger sixth. He came home to the Osterreichring on 22 May and *Autosport* reported that 'Pirro dominated qualifying thanks to the advantage of heavy Michelin support to set a time a fraction quicker than the Austrian Burger (*sic*), who knows the Zeltweg track almost as well as the back of his hand, but not well enough to prevent him crashing towards the end of the first session, leaving plenty of work between sessions.' Byrne stormed the race after a bad start, moving past Pirro and Berger with two laps left to take the lead, Berger taking Pirro on the last lap for second place.

'Gerhard was as good as anybody,' Byrne remembers, 'if he had everything right. We didn't understand a lot of technical stuff in those days but I do know he had Michelins and I had Yokohamas, which put me at a disadvantage, but I always liked the Oster-reichring.'

Stappert recounts a naughty tale about the background to this race. The Trivellato team were running Pirro, and Berger had an engine problem. 'He went to the factory and the guy said "Go in there and take the third engine from the right" or whatever. Those were the days when things happened like that. There were five or six engines, but on one a label hung. *Pirro*. Gerhard and whoever was with him immediately thought "This must be the one", moved the label to another engine and took Pirro's. I don't think Trivellato realized until the following winter.'

The round at Silverstone attracted a vast entry, 39. Brundle and Senna had been arm-wrestling an epic Marlboro British Formula 3 Championship and now decided to see what they could do against the Europeans. Davy Jones decided he'd have a go, too, and his reflections on Senna are interesting, not least because of their future bearing.

'Senna proved in 1983 that he had all the natural ability in the world but he could also focus completely on what he was doing and hold his concentration on that. Nothing broke him away from it. I was only 18, becoming 19, and I had a lot to distract me. I don't think Senna had any distractions. Although I was as quick as Brundle and Senna, as a race progressed I might make a mistake, miss a gear change, but those guys, they wouldn't. Even at Formula 3 it was a very high level. For example the old Stowe corner you took flat out in fourth, you arrived in fifth, changed down, then flat. Well, Senna wasn't even lifting, he was flat in *fifth*, so I had to raise my whole level of getting the momentum out of the car. That's the only way you can go as quick as Senna and that's what I learnt in Formula 3 — to carry that momentum.'

Berger had not driven Silverstone before. Brundle took pole from Senna, Dumfries third, Berger twenty-first. Silverstone was not, and is not, easy to learn, and Ravaglia and Martini, among others, complained they hadn't had enough time to set up their cars properly. In the race who noticed Berger? Brundle led from Senna and Dumfries — 'Senna,' Dumfries says, 'put me on the grass going down to Stowe.'

Dumfries, meanwhile, broke the lap record and Senna lost control at Woodcote, shedding parts of the car. 'The weirdest thing put me out of the race,' Dumfries says. 'Senna had his accident and I ran over a big bit of the debris. It punched a dent up into the monocoque right underneath the pedal mounting bar. It bent the pedal bar and the throttle started sticking. That eventually put me out.' Brundle won, the British press proclaiming that Senna's reign of invincibility had been terminated, Byrne second, Berger thirteenth.

There's a nice story from Silverstone which Les Thacker of BP, and helper of Dumfries, still tells at dinner parties 'to show how normal Gerhard Berger is. We had the usual thing, the pit lane walkabout and spectators couldn't get near the cars — not like in the old days. We wheeled Johnny's car out so that at least the people on the walkabout would have something to look at. They even wanted to touch it, they wanted to be around the drivers. I'd had some postcards of Johnny done through BP and he was signing them. In no time a bloody great queue formed and spontaneously Gerhard joined the back of it.

'Without looking up Johnny asked each person who reached the head of the queue their name or who they wanted a postcard autographed for — "my son Sean", or whatever. Gerhard must have taken five or 10 minutes to reach him. Johnny, again without looking up, asked, "What's your name?" and Berger said, "Gerhard." Johnny did look up, his face wreathed in a smile, and he said, "You bastard!'" Thacker had anticipated the moment and held his camera ready. You can see the result in the section of illustrations.

At Knutstorp Berger qualified strongly, fourth, and as Saward wrote, 'Despite overnight rain Sunday morning was bright and sunny. The morning warm-up was eventful to say the least. Berger found himself without a clutch but this did not seem to worry the Austrian who jammed home the gears and flew to the second quickest time behind the omnipotent Nielsen.' In the race the omnipotent Nielsen won from Berger by 15 seconds. Many people noticed this drive by Berger, emphasized because he was in a small team. Such details can be important, significant, the real context of a race rather than the finishing order.

Then, in context, disappointment — only fourth in a Formula 3 race at the Osterreichring supporting the Grand Prix. Alistair McQueen, running the Eddie Jordan team, remembers the race well. 'Berger was a very much fancied runner. We had Martin Brundle and Allen Berg and Brundle cleared off into the distance, chased by Berg, both of them on Yokohamas. Berger was the first man on Michelins and he and Berg fought out second place before they tangled.' The battle lasted until the Boschkurve (a horseshoe right at the back of the circuit) on lap 8. They came across a backmarker, Berger evidently tried to take them both, he and Berg touched, and Berg went out.

'Gerhard was very much the joker in the pack, a very amiable person. That was the overall impression I formed: much the same mould as Keke Rosberg in terms of flamboyant style in the car and out of it,' McQueen says. 'Keke would always come up and have a chat. He portrayed the superstar but he didn't behave like one in terms of avoiding the crowd.'

Interestingly Brundle doesn't remember knowing anything about Berger, to him just another continental driver among so many who had scarcely set Silverstone ablaze when they'd raced there earlier. 'When we got to Austria we heard a bit of talk of him as the local hot shot', Brundle says. 'I didn't even know he'd been in German Formula 3 and at the Austrian meeting I never saw him. I was on pole, led the race from start to finish, and in fact Gerhard tripped over my team-mate Berg after they'd had a good scrap. Gerhard is one of those guys who kept getting better and better. At the time he'd not done much racing, had he?'

Stappert remembers the Osterreichring. 'Gerhard supposedly got a new engine and it never worked. He was running, I don't know, eighth or somewhere, mixing it with people he hadn't come across before, and this was the first race his father came to. His father couldn't believe how bad he was. His father knew he'd been on the podium before and thought he'd win this bloody race but Gerhard just couldn't get the engine to work. Old man Berger stood there in the pits watching the car and he said, "If he hasn't got the money to buy himself a good engine he'd better give it up because this is a joke," This is how he looked at it, like a businessman.'

Stappert remembers something else. Apart from Hans Berger, he found himself standing next to Bernie Ecclestone, who owned the Brabham team (which had BMW engines, of course). Clearly Stappert had not hesitated to tell Ecclestone of Berger's talent and promise. 'Gerhard was competing against some obscure Swiss guy for I suppose seventh place and they're going up the hill. The other guy obviously had a quicker car and Gerhard pushed him on to the grass. Bernie Ecclestone said, "And this is your friend?"'

Martini set off on a strong run, winning Nogaro and Jarama. There Berger suffered gearbox problems in qualifying but, *Autosport* reported, made 'a fantastic start to claim eighth place at the end of lap one and he looked very fast until his retirement with differential failure on lap six'.

That wasn't the whole story of Jarama . . .

'I threw him in the swimming pool, I pushed him in,' Byrne says. 'He had an adjoining room to me in the hotel, he climbed over the balcony into my room and he took everything out of my closet — I'd just got my laundry — and threw it down into the pool, everything: my clothes, my suit. You know the little kit you have for shaving? He opened that up and threw all that in item by item. People in the pool, old ladies and so on, were swimming around in my stuff. I mean, sure that was funny, but you know there's funny and there's funny. He once sewed the arms and legs of my overalls, I put them on at the last minute before a race and *that* was funny. It took me two weeks to find out who'd done it. But I didn't think throwing everything in the pool was funny.

'Shay, the Irish mechanic who worked for Eddie Jordan, was with me. Gerhard had a BMW — a free one! (Byrne remembers details like that.) He'd parked it beside the pool. He'd left the boot open and we found the tool-kit. That went in. We took the nuts off a wheel, we took the wheel off, we took the front lights off, the windscreen wipers off, the rear wheels off, everything out of the boot and threw it into the pool. I can guarantee you if there had been an ignition key we would have driven the car in.

'So now he's in the pool swimming round and diving to get his stuff out and we're trying to get my stuff out. The only reason I was upset was I'd just had all my clothes cleaned and I didn't have as much money as him. I was angry enough to have thrown his car in if I could have done.'

Berger remembers swimming around after nightfall among 'seats, everything you could get off the car, and then of course we had to leave the hotel. They didn't want us any more.'

Cathy Muller remembers 'everything floating in the pool, even a toothbrush!' She regarded it as ordinary, not remarkable. 'It was warm in Jarama and whenever we went somewhere warm you got a shower from Gerhard. He'd throw cold water over you and in the sun you dry quickly so it didn't matter, but once he did it when I was next to my racing car and he made the car very wet and the mechanics were screaming, they were really angry.'

'Jarama was famous for all kinds of things,' Saward says, 'but mainly for the water fights. These water fights in the paddock were horrendous. The local big shot would arrive and have a bucket of water tipped on his head. It was not possible to walk into the paddock and stay dry. Gerhard and Tommy were running up and down the roofs of the pits and if you stopped to have a chat with someone, next thing you know there's a bucket of water over you.'

Berger finished sixth at Imola and thereby hangs another tale. 'The last three laps were absolute mayhem between Claudio Langes and someone else, Capelli I think,' Saward says. 'They cut all the chicanes, they were all over the road, they nearly ran head on into the pit wall. Behind them came Gerhard and a guy called Franco Forini who briefly reached Formula 1. Gerhard overtook him on the last corner for sixth place. I saw this and it was absolutely brilliant. Forini had forgotten to look in his mirrors and Gerhard went *boooom* straight past him. I don't think anyone then — even Gerhard — expected him to go as far as he has. I certainly didn't. I thought he'd get to Formula 1 and potter about. I didn't envisage he'd be picked up by Ferrari and become a megastar. Don't ask me why. It just never entered my head. Mind you, moments like the one at Imola made you think.'

'He was always an aggressive driver, absolutely,' Byrne says. 'The problem is you have to get up the front to really show that aggression. He got let down with things like tyres. You have to be careful because in those days you had Michelin tyres and Michelin tyres. Not having the right Michelin tyres would bring anyone down and we all went through it.

'Did I feel Gerhard would make it into Formula 1? I gave up thinking about who makes it and who doesn't make it and who's the best driver and who's not the best driver. When I started racing I didn't think about anything like that. I said, "Well, I'll go into Formula 1 now because I'm the best driver in the world and I'll make some money out of it."

'I suppose if you'd asked me that question a year or two years later I might have been bitter because I wasn't in Formula 1 any more. I'd have said, "This guy doesn't deserve to have made it and that guy doesn't deserve to have made it" — Capelli or any of them — but it turns out, you know, they deserved to make it because they're there and I'm not. That's the difference.

'I just took it as it came along, I never thought ahead. I drove the car and it happened to come easy to me. Nobody was as good as me, nobody, right? It's always the same story. Nobody is as good as Senna — that's the way Senna thinks. Gerhard would think the same thing. Any driver who doesn't isn't going to be any good, anyway. What driver would ever admit there's another driver better? If you admit that you're wasting your time in the first place.' We're back to the elusive thing which can come and go away again and do that with indecent haste.

Martini won the European Formula 3 Championship with 66 points, Nielsen 62, Pirro, 52, Byrne 35, Theys 25, Berger and Brundle 18.

'Gerhard was an aggressive driver,' Martini says, 'and was — and is — a good friend. Even then, in 1983, he'd become a friend, always honest. Most drivers were friendly although of course you can have a good feeling with someone but not perhaps with everyone. He was very quick at Zeltweg and he did a good race in Sweden, but in other races it was very difficult for him.'

Pino Trivellato approached him to drive in the Macau Grand Prix on 20 November, the first time Berger would enjoy what you might call contemporary machinery, a Ralt Alfa Rome RT3. Significantly it was Ravaglia's car. Senna would be there and Brundle, Roberto Guerrero, Jones, Byrne, Muller.

'The bastard ruined my career, so he did, ruined my career,' Byrne says, although he's chuckling and snorting with affection when he says it. 'You remember that "Race of my Life" he did in *Autosport* two or three years ago? He mentioned Tommy Byrne more than he mentioned himself, all the partying over at Macau and everything. I laughed and I said to myself, "It's just as well I'm not racing in Europe any more, it really would have ruined my career." Yes, I laughed about it. You know you're not supposed to smile or have a good time, particularly when you get to Formula 1, but he still does and I did, too. It's not worth it if you can't smile. What's the point of having $20 million and being miserable?'

Autosport carried this 'Race of my Life' in May 1990 and since what Berger had to say about Macau, 1983, captures many facets of the man I quote it here extensively.

'For me it was a new experience. I didn't expect a lot of success there because it was a new circuit to me. I still had little experience in Formula 3 and I didn't know the Trivellato team. I didn't know anything. I just knew I wanted to drive the following year for the team. I remember when I went round the circuit I was in love with it from the first moment, it was really something that I liked. It didn't compare with another street circuit.

'I remember Hong Kong was really quite funny. I had a special radio for the helmet that I'd got in England and brought with me. Cathy Muller asked me, "Ah, where did you get that nice radio?" and I said, "I just bought it here. Very cheap." "Ah," she said, "I want one, too." So I said, "It's very easy. You go by taxi," and then I made a map. "You go right, left, right, left, right left, left, straight. Ten minutes with the taxi you will find it and there you will get it cheap."

'So off she and some other drivers went in a taxi, right, left . . . and came back five hours later, everybody upset, to find out that I'd bought the thing in England. That was the first good thing! Then I went in the evening with Jean-Louis Schlesser to the massage clubs, and had some fun there . . .'

(Muller remembers the incident, all right — the radio, not the massage parlour — and says, 'He was constantly playing tricks like that.')

'I remember it was the day before practice. Always I was the last one to turn in for the night and Tommy Byrne was always one of the last ones, too. It was already 3.30 am and I thought, "If someone sees me now I can't practise tomorrow!" I was just about to leave and I look round the corner in the disco and who was sitting there with three girls around him? It was Pirro, having some fun there, too!'

(Two other facets: Dark, unsubstantiated tales linger of Berger and Byrne throwing the skipper of the Macau ferry from Hong Kong overboard, you know, the way passengers do. Meanwhile Senna, who hadn't driven a street circuit before and had just flown in from Europe after testing the Brabham Formula 1 car, went quickest in qualifying, jet lag and all, from Guerrero, Brundle, Martini and Berger.)

Back to the 'Race of my Life': 'Practice was nice. I was going round but I didn't find the line. I wasn't quick and suddenly an orange car passed me. I'd never seen a car like this before, it was a Japanese car (a Hayashi-Toyota). It was so quick round the corners, it was sideways 2 mm from the wall, fantastic. I tried to follow him. I thought this Japanese guy is really pushing! Afterwards I looked on the list which car it was, and it was Eje Elgh, a Swede! My mechanics were laughing because I was speaking about a Japanese driver and he wasn't — but he really showed me the lines through here and from this moment on I was quick.'

The Grand Prix spread over two heats. In the warm-up before the first, which started at eight in the morning, Brundle went fastest and Berger brushed his left rear wheel against a wall: easy to do on a street circuit. Martini overslept and only arrived in time to complete a couple of laps. In the first heat Senna took the lead, Berger trying to stay with Guerrero — second — and it ended thus.

In the second heat Senna led again while further back Byrne, Berger and Jones jostled and struggled. Berger took Byrne on the straight on the third lap, but Jones attacked him and they passed and re-passed three times on the straight a couple of laps later.

'I was always a man who enjoyed new, challenging circuits,' Jones says. 'That's particularly true of circuits you really need to learn and when you're against people you've never raced before. Gerhard and I were having a very good dice. How did I now Gerhard was reliable enough not to do anything silly when we were passing and re-passing? You learn how to line people up very quickly, you get a feeling for people that have the experience and are in control of the situation — and equally for those who are driving over their heads. They go for it but they don't really know what is happening around them, what's surrounding them.

'One of the main reasons we swapped three times on the straight was that we were both confident in our race cars, both getting the most out of them. We chased each other, closed lap after lap, and I suppose we had a mutual feeling. David Hunt had a shunt down in turn one and they'd lifted his car with a crane above the circuit. Gerhard and I came through and I hit some oil Hunt must have dropped. It slid the rear end of my car and I tapped the guard rail quite hard. It knocked the rear wheel and when I turned into the next corner going up the hill the car spun completely round and that was the end of the race for me. It was unfortunate I slipped up because it would have been a successful race for me.

'In fact the Macau Grand Prix decided me — after racing Gerhard — that it would be a lot of fun to race against him again, and Pirro and Capelli and so on. I wanted more challenging circuits than Thruxton. I got to know Gerhard. A lot of people say we look alike so many took me for him, although I don't know if it happened to him in the same way. I thought of him as a friend and I'd be comfortable calling him up on the telephone to talk to him, or having a chat at a race track. I'd go up and say hello to him and he'd treat me just like a friend. I appreciated that. I tried to be like that, too.

'When you put your helmet on, put your race face on, you know, it's a totally different story because you are competing against each other. Once you take the helmet off afterwards you look back on it as a sort of a laugh because you enjoyed it. And he was certainly enjoying it, oh, absolutely. I had a lot of respect for him because not only did he race but he also managed a trucking company as well.'

The Macau Grand Prix finished overall Senna, Guerrero, Berger.

The 'Race of my Life' again: 'I was not far behind Guerrero in the second heat but I preferred to have a sure third place than to risk for second. So for me I was really happy because it was a great race and from then on people started to realize who I was. Everything was fine.

'In the evening I went to pick up some prize money and they gave me the quickest lap. I never did this lap, which got some extra money. I checked and it was Senna who did the quickest lap and we told them. In the evening there was a party and I spoke for the first time with Senna and with Dick Bennetts (running Senna this season) who I knew because I bought a Formula 3 car from him. On the Jumbo back Tommy Byrne was completely drunk. He cut a pillow and shook the feathers everywhere. It goes round and it looks like it's snowing in the plane. People were very upset! It was nicer those days, less pressure, much more fun.'

Trivellato offered him a drive in European Formula 3 for 1984 and BMW, via Stappert, offered him a drive in the European Touring Car Championship, a heady mix which he'd relish, every moment of it.

'I felt during the 1983 season,' Marko says, 'that he should go to a bigger team because he was so disorganized. He didn't know anything about the technical side and Trivellato had a proper engineer, an Englishman, although at that stage Gerhard couldn't speak English, not a word. It was important that Gerhard got out into the world. That was the right thing to do. We'd done our year with the very low budget and got quite good results. He showed speed although he made mistakes. For example he spun in the Sebring corner (at the Osterreichring). Nowadays it's fifth gear flat out but in the old days — with much less grip from the tyres, much less grip from the chassis — he tried it already in fifth, and spun of course.'

Pino Trivellato is a good man and true, bubbles with life and has plenty of experience. Years before, he'd run Riccardo Patrese who was then 'a boy with a difficult personality and we quarrelled a lot. He was introverted — Gerhard, no! Gerhard wasn't driving for a competitive team but I saw immediately his potential and he was quick. Mechanical problems kept stopping him. I spoke to him when he came to my factory to search out some spares and gears for his car. He was nice and simply said, "I'm trying to help the team." Our friendship began at that moment. I'd asked him if there was any possibility of his going to Macau and he became instantly interested, and said he'd like to do a Formula 3 season with us but he wanted to see what our team was like, so he looked at it. We drew up an agreement for Macau and after that race he was very, very satisfied, so we signed a contract for 1984.

'Ravaglia had been in the team for three years and between he and I, as Gerhard knew well, we had a good friendship. Gerhard is clever but also honest. He told me, "If Ravaglia is in the team, too, you have to prepare two cars and I want a well-prepared chassis for myself, but I promise I will find a job for Ravaglia." Gerhard knew Dieter Stappert well and convinced him to sign Ravaglia for the Touring Cars. Ravaglia was the happiest man in the world. With BMW he became a professional driver.'

Ravaglia says, 'I don't know the real reason why Trivellato took Gerhard but maybe he wanted to be the only one in the team. He introduced me to BMW and for that I say thanks. I partnered him in Touring Cars.'

Stappert phrases it thus. 'At the end of 1983 people began to accept that (a) Gerhard didn't understand anything about a racing car, (b) he was a madman, (c) he was very funny, and (d) he was incredibly quick. Those were the four components people realized. I took a lot of abuse over the winter, me Austrian, him Austrian, about getting him into Touring Cars, but I said, "Wait for the first testing, wait for the times." A lot of needles were stuck into me.'

In Touring Cars Berger would drive for the Schnitzer team, based in Bavaria. The team had begun competing in 1966 and, using BMW engines, had had their champions, among them Jacques Laffite and Rene Arnoux. Charley Lamm of Schnitzer says, 'Dieter Stappert really built up the BMW racing programme. He had a lot of ideas, a lot of vision, he persuaded BMW to make a 1.5 litre turbocharged engine, he wanted BMW to participate in Touring Cars. He asked Schnitzer to run and develop the programme together with BMW's motor sport division.

'We started in 1983, sponsorship was hard to get but we managed to run two cars at the first race, Monza, one for Hans Stuck, the other for Dieter Quester. Stappert said to Quester that BMW wanted to use a young Austrian as his co-driver and his name was Gerhard Berger. Quester said, "OK, he is young, he is my fellow countryman, but I don't want to be a driving instructor when I get into the European Touring Car Championship!" He refused to partner Gerhard and so Carlo Rosso (an Italian) came instead. In 1984 Stuck and Quester went in one car, which allowed Stappert to put two youngsters in the other — Gerhard and Ravaglia, who Gerhard had recommended to BMW.'

Meanwhile . . . 'When Gerhard joined BMW all of us did fitness training at St Moritz in February 1984, and it was one of the funniest weeks of my life,' says Stuck, former Formula 1 driver who during the season would find himself driving *his* BMW very hard against that of Berger. 'There was a very nice-looking barmaid working in the hotel and I was the first one to be successful with her. In my room I heard a very strange noise from the balcony, so I went out on to it to see what it was. When I got outside the barmaid closed the door behind me. Gerhard and others had made an arrangement that when I'd done the deed they'd make the noise and I'd be locked out. I stood completely naked at about -25°C. You can imagine how small *it* was! Luckily the room was only on the second floor and I climbed down. I found something to wrap around myself — can't remember what it was — and went through the lobby like that, back up to the room. They'd locked *that* door. It was really very, very funny. Gerhard and the others were laughing their behinds off. But I was outside and they were inside the bedroom . . .

'One of the fitness programmes consisted of 15 to 20 miles of cross-country skiing every day and Gerhard wasn't fast, always at the back. We used to ski to the foot of a glacier to a restaurant famous for its desserts. This particular day when we arrived Gerhard already sat there eating his second or third dessert; no pain, no sweat, and he'd arrived half an hour before. We said "How the hell did you manage this?" and he said, "I was the fastest today." We found out later what he'd done. He'd hired a horse-drawn sledge to take him up! The trainer wasn't very happy but it's typical of Gerhard. He always finds a way round a problem.'

We've heard many witnesses testify how matey European Formula 3 was but Dumfries chose to approach it from another direction in 1984. 'We didn't mix that much; Berger was always reasonably friendly but I don't think I was. I didn't want to be. I wasn't very interested in being, that was my deliberate decision.

'When you're living on top of one another and you haven't yet adopted a professional attitude in your career — namely separating what goes on when you're in the car and what goes on outside it — you have to put certain barriers up. I was inexperienced then. I suppose I thought it was the way to drive hard and in an uncompromising way. That might be impaired if you're getting friendly with the drivers around you. I didn't feel the same way at all after I'd done a year in Formula 1 later on because by then I had much more experience. After Formula 1 I could be perfectly friendly with people in the paddock and perfectly ruthless with them on the track because I'd established that situation, whereas in Formula 3 I hadn't clearly established that in my own head. It meant that I wasn't on the end of any of Gerhard's practical jokes.

'By the time of the first European round at Donington (on 25 March) I'd already done two rounds of the domestic British championship and won those so I was getting on to a roll. We had works VW backing so we did have very good engines — Judds — and in Europe we used Yokohama tyres, really good, the ones to have. The Michelins were also good and Berger had those, but John Nielsen got the best out of them.'

At the risk of belabouring what is obvious, tyres can be crucial. Jones 'joined the Eddie Jordan team in 1984, we did a test at Silverstone with Dunlop, very, very fast, and we chose to do the Dunlop tyre deal for the European series. It was a disaster. Half-way through we ended up switching to Yokohamas. The season was a disappointment to me because I felt it separated the talent too much: if you had Michelins you were automatically quick, you'd run at the front, the rest struggling against the Michelins. I tended to doubt I'd drive my hardest to be sixth or seventh on the grid where somebody who had Michelins would be third or fourth and he didn't deserve to be. I'd like to have been able to *race* Gerhard and Pirro and Capelli.'

At Donington Berger qualified third behind Dumfries and Jones, with Muller fourth. In the race, an extremely wet one, he suffered understeer and prudently accepted fourth place.

A week later he went to Monza for the opening round of the Touring Cars where he'd meet a completely different group of drivers, Tom Walkinshaw, Win Percy and Chuck Nicholson in Jaguars, Steve Soper and Jeff Allam in a Rover, Thomas Lindstrom in a Volvo.

'Stuck and Quester kept at some distance from Gerhard and Ravaglia,' Lamm says, 'because as senior drivers they really were in another league. Then Gerhard said, "I want to show Quester that I am not the one who needs driving lessons," and in first qualifying he beat Stuck's time. Nobody could understand it, imagine it, believe it. He did it with pure determination, he over-drove, he gave 120 per cent. I didn't want to watch what he was doing with the car and it may be that he couldn't have repeated the lap if he'd tried another 10 times — but he did it that once.'

Ravaglia says, 'Gerhard was not a difficult partner for me because we had a good relationship. That's normally difficult to find between two drivers handling the same car because invariably you have competition between them. Perhaps it was because I was now more or less making my career in Touring Cars and he in single-seaters heading towards Formula 1, so I wasn't trying to show I was better than him and he wasn't trying to show he was better than me. I feel there was competition, however, when Gerhard drove and Stuck drove the other car. Sometimes Gerhard would make mistakes because he wanted to be in front of Stuck, but to balance that it was our first year in Touring Cars. We had no experience of long-distance races, we had crashes and things.'

At Monza, Stappert says, 'With every lap that Gerhard did a needle which had been stuck into me came out, and people said, "Ah, you were right".' After challenging for the lead, Ravaglia spun off at the Lesmo curves and damaged the air cooler. 'If it hadn't been for that we would have won, and won all the races which came after that — which didn't clash with European Formula 3. Gerhard was the quickest BMW driver all the time and this made life easier for me.'

At Vallelunga a week later Berger and Ravaglia qualified fourth. In the race *Autosport* reported that 'with pit stops going on all around, the Wurthe Hartge BMW suddenly burst into flames in the pit lane. One of the Wurthe mechanics was seriously burned and the pit lane thrown into confusion with cars screaming in to refuel to find it full of fire marshals. Out on the track the action remained frantic with Berger being rather rudely punted into the sand by the Kellerners/Brancatelli car.'

Lamm says, 'Gerhard and Ravaglia understood each other very well and it became a wonderful co-operation. A lot of people were saying, "They're not newcomers, they are very, very quick, they can set the pace from Stuck and Quester".'

At Zolder in Formula 3, a race won by Briton Russell Spence from Dumfries, Berger came fourth. Dumfries says, 'Gerhard was always there or thereabouts. I don't know exactly what sort of equipment he had. He was being run by Pino Trivellato, a really nice guy, very experienced but quite a small effort compared to, let's say, the three guys who were beating him most regularly — myself, Nielsen and Capelli. Nielsen and I were works VW drivers, Capelli the works Martini driver and it is an advantage at that level.'

Berger came seventh at Magny-Cours, third at La Chatre and thereby hangs a tale or two which must be trawled from the recesses of memory, because they convulsed Formula 3 and assumed particular significance. Capelli won from Dumfries. 'That was the race, I think' Dumfries says, 'when Capelli's team (Coloni) started using the bent engine. I mean, he was absolutely uncatchable. La Chatre has a slow section and then a long straight. You'd hold him out the back and he'd pull away on the straight. I'm sure that Trivellato were on to them quite early. Trivellato protested Coloni. I remember Berger saying on several occasions he reckoned Coloni were running bent engines. I was non-committal, again reflecting my naivety.'

We have reached what Sherlock Holmes would undoubtedly have called The Affair of the Airbox, and we shall have to reach deep into it soon enough, physically and figuratively.

Pino Trivellato had had his suspicions since an Italian Formula 3 race at Imola. 'I became a spectator. I went to Tosa and Acque Minerali and Rivazza and took times. I noticed that at the Acque Minerali Capelli was slower than Gerhard but each lap Capelli gained a second, a second and a half. It was not possible that Capelli lost so much in the slow corners and had such an advantage elsewhere. It was a mystery.' Pino Trivellato does not resemble Sherlock Holmes in any way you can think of except one: if they had to, they'd investigate.

Berger won at the Osterreichring. 'I didn't do that race,' Dumfries says, 'but everybody knew Berger would win there because he was really quick all the way round. He blitzed everyone.' He did, taking pole a second quicker than Jones. At the start Jones attacked but on the loops of the circuit suddenly lost downforce and spun out. Berger ran nicely to the end, beating Langes. Trivellato judges this one of Berger's best two races of the season, coining a lovely phrase to capture it. 'Gerhard had a "gear" more than the others.'

Monaco, supporting the Grand Prix, of course, revealed much. Langes took pole from Nielsen, Capelli fourth, Ravaglia (making a rare appearance) fifth, Berger only tenth a place behind Weaver. 'In practice,' says Weaver, 'on my qualifying lap Johnny Dumfries decided to go into the pits and I literally drove straight over the top of him. It didn't do either car much good and later I rode up in the lift in one of the hotels with, I think Jonathan Palmer. Some of the Williams Formula 1 team happened to be in the lift, too, and one of them said, "How did Johnny get on?" and the other said, "A complete prat drove into him." They were talking about me.'

Weaver continues, 'Funnily enough I was hacking my way up the mountains to a restaurant at the back of Monaco, Gerhard coming down in his BMW. I remember him coming, you could see him round a hairpin, almost smell him before he reached you, brakes on fire. He screeched to a halt and had a chat about practice.'

'I hadn't been on pole,' Nielsen says. 'Langes beat me by one hundredth of a second, you know, and did it 10 seconds before practice ended so I was not too happy about that. Secondly, he took the lead. It was the year before they changed the chicane at the harbour to a first gear corner like it is now. Instead of lifting, as you usually did, I tried to go through flat. Not possible. I hit the kerb on the inside, flipped the car, and it flew across the track and hit the armco on the other side.'

Nielsen sat trapped for 18 more laps before they got him out. 'There was no pain when the car came to rest. I tried to get out but I couldn't.' He was taken to hospital with a damaged pelvis and two broken ribs. Capelli, hard on Nielsen when the accident happened, managed to avoid him. If he hadn't . . .

'Like any top driver,' says Weaver, 'Gerhard is very, very hard, but scrupulously fair. John had his accident, yellow flags waving, and he genuinely slowed down, which is very rare. I was right behind him. I'd like to think I didn't take advantage of his backing off. If the guy in front slows down for an accident you hold back for a bit, get a run at him and bounce him. Dead easy. We carried on racing when we were past it but I don't think I have ever raced against anybody of that level before who'd done that.

'To be honest, I don't think I would have slowed down as much as he did if I'd been in front of him, because you're running third at Monaco in a Formula 3 race and you think, well, everybody who matters is watching this. You know, he had the self-confidence to slow right down, then as soon as we were clear to leg it again. That impressed me. The guy is obviously an exceptionally nice chap and incredibly brave, naturally brave — he did a bit of skiing, didn't he?'

On lap 13 Langes hit the wall exiting Rascasse, Capelli leading Berger by 15 seconds. Weaver, hampered by mechanical problems, drifted fractionally back. Capelli won it comfortably enough by 14 seconds, Berger second, Weaver third.

Berger was third at the Nurburgring, a race won by Dumfries from Capelli. The Affair of the Airbox began to loom ever larger. 'It was,' Dumfries says, 'something I hadn't taken seriously but then thinking back to La Chatre and now the Nurburgring, I couldn't believe how quickly Capelli caught me. He started miles back, I won but he was really catching me *so* fast at the end.'

The grid at the (new) 'Ring: Dumfries and Berger on the front row, Capelli eighth quickest. Capelli worked through the traffic — he took Berger on the inside at the chicane and reeled in Dumfries who, in the last couple of laps, dug out a response and won by no more than a second and a half. Dumfries, ruminating these many years later, says team manager 'Dave Price used to say . . . Dave was sharp . . .'

Monza followed and the Affair exploded. *Autosport* reported that 'both sessions' — two heats of qualifying — 'saw the Italian contingent having fun and games, their interesting manoeuvres being noted down as ones *not* to try. The recovery trucks were certainly kept busy picking up the pieces. In one of the incidents, Berger had his progress checked by an errant Italian and was none too pleased.' The race? Capelli won from Berger.

'Monza was strange,' Dumfries says. 'I made a reasonable start, second to Capelli and I thought, OK this is no problem, I'll start pushing. Formula 3 is not like Formula 1 or sports cars or anything else, it's flat out the whole way. You stabilize your position on the first couple of corners and then you push *really* hard. I'd done one or two laps and someone spun off at the chicane — I hit the gravel and I was gone, history. People always go across the chicane at Monza and they can spread gravel. Anyway I was into the catch fencing, finished. Capelli went on to win, Berger second. Afterwards Trivellato protested the Coloni car.'

In scrutineering the Coloni was found to be 8.8 lb (4 kg) underweight and, *Autosport* reported, an 'illegal airbox was thought to give the car a 15 bhp advantage' adding that 'the irregularity of the airbox was proved to be quite deliberate'.

Dumfries, naivety falling away, explains: 'A vacuum test was carried out on the Coloni airbox. You create a vacuum in there so you establish whether air is leaking into it from anywhere except from where it should be. Coloni had a very elaborate thing: you had the airbox opening aperture but they'd welded a plate through the middle of the airbox with a one-way valve so air could only go in that way. They had a hole in the airbox so the air was coming in normally and also being sucked in from the hole while the car was running. The valve shut off really quickly and pulled the vacuum up really quickly, so the officials figured there must be something wrong with it. They cut it open and found out what it was.

'Capelli got slung out as a result and there were all sorts of things which went on between Trivellato and Coloni and the Italian Federation, and Trivellato kicked up a lot of stink and the Italian Federation became cheesed off about the whole thing. They felt it was bringing them into disrepute. I seem to remember there was a threat of Trivellato having their competition licence revoked unless they quietened down a bit. Capelli lost nine points at Monza but that was another bone of contention because everyone thought he should have had all his Championship points taken away.

'Coloni could have appealed the loss of the points but nobody in their right mind would appeal that. I didn't see that as an issue. They couldn't have got away with it. Capelli was going round saying that he never knew about it and he made a point of saying that to people. I think he approached Dave independently and said, "I'm sorry, I didn't know about it", but Dave didn't buy that at all. For me, it's impossible to comment on it. Only Capelli knows. Maybe you don't wonder, you see. There is a possibility that a driver wouldn't realize: you have works engines, you're going to have two or three horsepower more than your average driver, you think you're better than all the rest, you think your car is better set up, so it does make sense not to wonder.

'People used to think we were best. I figured we were getting the job done, we had really good set-ups, Dave modified the monocoques and we knew for sure we had stiffer cars, we had works engines — the two or three horsepower — and I was whipping everybody. As a driver you don't think in terms of illegality.'

Price says, 'Eddie Jordan always reckoned the airbox finished at the bottom of Lake Como because it suddenly vanished. And Coloni wouldn't give the trophy back! I remember Gerhard saying to me they'd kept it. Monza was unbelievable. They'd been doing it all year and we'd not realized. At Silverstone a Martini on Michelins was almost keeping up with us and that had never been known before. (Dumfries won in 28 minutes 16.57 seconds, Capelli third did 28 minutes 28.07 seconds.) Maybe no one would have noticed but Capelli started sixteenth on the grid and came up through the field.

'Johnny became the first Formula 3 driver to lap Monza in its then current configuration under 1 minute 50 seconds. Nobody had achieved that previously, not even Italians. Come the race, Capelli was going so quick Johnny couldn't believe it. I didn't think much of it, but Pino Trivellato must have heard something or had some kind of information because he protested it.'

Pino Trivellato says, 'Capelli said immediately he didn't know anything. There was a big scandal and it finished in a court of law. I hired a good barrister who understood sport and we won the suit, but for what? We lost the Championship and Coloni were punished for that race alone, not disqualified for the whole of the season. This was one of the reasons why I took the decision to abandon the motor racing world, because it was no longer as it had been in the past . . .'

Trivellato guards other memories of Monza. 'When Gerhard first joined us he wasn't so good as a test driver but he learned and often found good solutions to problems. Monza was peculiar, a race of two heats. In the first Gerhard came fourth and I asked him if he would like to change the set-up of the car. He said no, it was OK and in fact he finished well in the second heat. The important point is that he sensed it hadn't been the car.'

'I know at one stage Gerhard was down totally,' Byrne says. 'He was slipping out of it completely. The last year of Formula 3, I think, was terrible. He'd had enough of the whole lot. He said, "To hell with this" but he was also into the Touring Cars and it went from there, something happened with BMW so it's the luck of the draw.'

At Enna in Formula 3 he'd be third, at Mugello second and by now Gunter Schmid of the ATS Formula 1 team showed interest. Berger would have a 'test' in their car at Zandvoort two weeks after Mugello and one way and another he'd never be out of Formula 1 again all the way to here, so that while it's elusive for some, the coming and the going away with indecent haste, for others it's a natural, normal progression or, as someone said about Senna, a birthright.

Davy Jones reflects broadly on that. 'Gerhard didn't change during that year of 1984, oh no, no, no. Gerhard is a very good racer but he is also out to have fun, a prankster in his own way. The other good thing has been to see Gerhard go on and do as well as he had done in Formula 1. I feel happy that I did have some races against him, as I did against Senna and Brundle, it gives me confidence that if I was able to get into a Formula 1 situation I could do the same because I know what my ability was against them.

'It's been difficult because I'd love to be in Formula 1, absolutely, but you have to be in the right place at the right time with the right people. In 1983 I had the opportunity to test with Brabham — Pirro and Martini did, too, all on the same day — but I was only 19 years old at the time and I realized I was out of my league. Earlier this year (1993) I tested for Benetton but, you know, it's not an easy road to get to the top.

'Senna was always nice to me but so focused, he didn't care about anything except his racing, whereas Gerhard could relax away from the racing situation, but the two had the same mentality when they did get in the racing car. They would get into a rhythm in a race and it was very difficult to break it, they didn't make mistakes and they went fast. They were a couple of years older than me and their maturity helped them to be able to hold their concentration.'

Tommy Byrne reflects broadly, Byrne who penetrated Formula 1 briefly in 1982. 'Formula 1 is a terrible thing, it can really hurt, hurt you bad mentally and screw you up bad. There are a very few straight people in it. When I did drive in Formula 1 people have their own reasons why I didn't make it. The reason is I got into a Theodore and not a McLaren was nothing to do with saying, 'Niki who?' cracking a joke about Niki Lauda. That was no big deal.

'The luck of the draw is usually if you get into a bad car you stay in a bad car, if you get into a good car you stay in a good car and become a good driver. I came from a background in Ireland with absolutely no money and I made it all the way to Formula 1 with the help of some good friends. We didn't have a ranch in Brazil like Senna. I couldn't just retire from racing, quit, because I had a bad car. I didn't have a truck company in Austria to fall back on either. If I'd turned the Theodore Formula 1 drive down people would have said, "Who the hell does that cocky bastard think he is, not taking his chance?" Senna was able to sit back and say, "No, I don't want this one, I don't want that one" and that is exactly the difference. But you know what, I'm still happy.'

The irony remains that far from reclining at his executive desk at Worgl and considering the most tempting offers Berger got himself into an ATS, a car with as little future as the Theodore; a chance, and he took it.

Before we lock into the Formula 1 enclave (although with exits just over there a footstep or two away), an anecdote from Ravaglia. 'Oh I remember one time in 1984 we were at St Moritz (the dreaded BMW fitness training). Gerhard had an Audi, a really old car and every morning he drove from the hotel to a parking place, ice, a lot of snow. In the mornings Gerhard always liked to do some spins. Every day he spun and damaged a little bit of the car and every day he did the same accident and on the last day the car was finished. I don't think he could drive it home.' The point of the anecdote is that in 1984 Gerhard Berger remained exuberant, adoring the possibilities of motorized movement and not too concerned with the conclusions.

This was the man who fully intended to sample the (dubious) delights of the ATS at Zandvoort in a 'test' and the BMW in the European Touring Car Championship *on the same day*. The geographical fact that he'd be doing so in different countries was no more than another dimension to the great adventure. If you're young fit, talented and eager, what else would you do? Have a go and see what happens.

A lot happened.

5

A tall order

As midnight approached that Thursday in late July a strong, usually amiable German called Manfred Winkelhock lapped Spa with gathering urgency in a BMW. The second qualifying session for the eighth round of the European Touring Car Championship — a session traditionally held in the dark — moved towards its close. To run in the dark was prudent because Spa would last 24 hours and adjusting to the circuit in the day and the night necessary. If you'd been here before you could explore your car set-up, if you hadn't you could feel your way round, finding lines, braking points, learning to exercise your control over the circuit in the headlights or making sure, amidst so many shadowy pine trees and skimming curves, that it didn't control you. Spa was a lot of things but hellishly quick, and the 24-hour race a lot of things but hellishly important.

The Schnitzer team ran two cars, Winkelhock partnered with Ravaglia and Berger in one, Stuck, Quester and Weaver in the other.

Winkelhock lapped and lapped, and Berger tapped Saward of *Autosport* on the shoulder and said in his heavily accented English, 'You're coming to Zandvoort with me.' Saward, understandably mystified, wondered why. Berger said, 'I'm driving a Formula 1 car for the first time there.' Saward murmured 'So what?' 'No, no,' Berger insisted, 'you're coming.' Saward sensed Berger wanted a companion, the comfort of familiar company. To a driver, of course, the first examination of a Formula 1 car is a profound moment, measuring himself against the ultimate. To the journalist it's just another driver having a feel, the way they all have to do. Hence the *so what?*

Saward had arrived at the circuit late. He hadn't made a hotel booking and when he reached the town of Spa he panicked at the thought of having to sleep in the Press Room or wherever, and asked tentatively at the most expensive hotel if by any chance, sir, you have a room? Bruno Giacomelli, a driver, had just checked out and would Mr Saward like Mr Giacomelli's room? Mr Saward would. He contemplated an agreeable, perhaps tranquil weekend of good motor racing and good food, Belgian cuisine being unlorded outside Belgium but inside Belgium and inside Belgians a filling balance between French flair and German quantity. There are worse ways of eking out a crust than such a weekend.

Just before midnight Winkelhock struck the armco at La Radillion just up the hill from Eau Rouge at high speed, bending the suspension. He emerged unhurt and the BMW, according to contemporary accounts, emerged with less damage than might have been expected. The Ravaglia/Berger/Winkelhock partnership would start seventeenth, itself of no particular importance in an event spread over 24 hours.

The race would begin at 5.00 pm on Saturday, Friday being a day off. This allowed Berger to go to Zandvoort, have his feel and return in good time. Winkelhock (the ATS driver in the Grands Prix) would be going there, too. It's a curious quadrant of Europe, tight and neatly packed: south from Spa you're in Luxembourg, east you're in Germany, north you're in Holland and it's all smooth, open motorway to Holland, virtually no traffic. It is entirely possible to visit four countries within one hour — but Zandvoort, on the coast from Amsterdam, lay further, some 185 miles (298 km).

Lamm says, 'Gerhard could be released to go to Zandvoort and Stappert was right to do it this way. Gerhard always made it clear that he had higher ambitions and I knew he ought to reach the highest level of motor sport. He used his days with us in a good way, he enjoyed the competition and he also saw that you can show your talent in Touring Cars but he wanted to go where the best are. Maybe with another driver we'd have said, "Never mind Zandvoort, why aren't you concentrating on your job with us?" With Gerhard it was accepted he'd go.'

Saward recalls that they waited until qualifying had finished — and to see Winkelhock was all right. Then Berger tapped Saward on the shoulder again and said, 'OK, we go now.' Ravaglia remembers Berger and Saward saying, 'Don't worry, we'll be back by tomorrow evening.' That would be the Friday, giving them 24 hours to prepare for the 24-hour race.

Berger, Saward says, 'set off in his road BMW and drove up towards Holland. While we were still in Belgium we began to run out of petrol and neither of us had any local currency. We found a petrol station where they had one of those automatic pumps and we tried to make it work with whatever currency we did have. It wouldn't accept any of it, so we sat and a motorist came in and we offered him what would have been one of the best financial exchanges of all time to get enough Belgian francs to fill up the BMW. He thought we must be criminals and vanished. Eventually someone did agree to exchange some and I think we had to do it on a one-to-one basis, although I can't remember what currency we did use. Anyway, if you look at the worth of the Belgian franc it *was* one of the best financial exchanges of all time.

'We went to Schipol, Amsterdam's airport, to pick up Gerhard's mechanic who'd flown in earlier in the evening and was waiting for us. We went into Amsterdam and found a cheap hotel, the three of us in the same room. Next morning the car had been burgled, which amused Gerhard because, as he said, there was a spare set of keys in the glove compartment and they could have simply driven the car away. As it was they only took the radio. Then we went to Zandvoort.'

Berger would drive the ATS, the car of a small, frequently beleaguered team who since their foundation in 1977 had remained beleaguered. The season before, 1983, they'd secured BMW engines which Winkelhock drove. Across 1983 and thus far into 1984 Winkelhock had only completed six Grands Prix and not qualified for four.

Gunter Schmid ran ATS autocratically, sometimes convulsively. 'For a couple of years I'd been invited to the skiing at Kitzbuhel,' he says. 'Gerhard was always at my side saying, "I'm a young driver and I'm very good." At that time I wasn't very interested because he drove Formula 3 and some other stuff and I didn't know him.' Nor did Schmid know of The Plan which he'd be invited to carry out.

Stappert confesses candidly that, 'We started the whole operation of getting Gerhard into the Austrian Grand Prix of 1984 (in August) at Kitzbuhel at the Hahnenkamm in January.'

The Hahnenkamm, just up the winding road from Worgl, is like the Monaco Grand Prix, centre-piece of a skiing season, and gives one of the great spectacles of downhill as the racers cover the length of a soccer pitch in mid-air on the enormous slope towards the finishing line.

'This was a clearly defined, choreographed thing we wanted to achieve,' Stappert says. 'Jackie Oliver of the Arrows team (also Formula 1) was there, Gunter Schmid was there, we had lots of fun but we never talked about Formula 1.' — except, presumably, Berger himself: see above — 'We wanted to establish a human relationship, so that people would know Gerhard. We relied on the fact that in the first half of the season with Trivellato Gerhard would be one of the main contenders for the Championship and we'd have a chance of getting him into the Austrian Grand Prix.

'I would have preferred to persuade Arrows to run a third car because I really didn't want Gerhard to start his Formula 1 career with Schmid. I liked Schmid as a person, he could be a very nice guy, but I had scepticism about his abilities as a team manager. I thought, "ATS can't run one car. What happens when they try to run two?" At the beginning of July I thought that maybe we should take a chance and go for it.'

Schmid himself 'noticed Gerhard was driving harder, trying harder in European Formula 3, so I said, "OK, we'll try him. If he can find some money we'll run a second car for the Austrian Grand Prix." Up to then we'd only been running one car with Manfred in it. Manfred made a big noise, he was extremely upset about having a second driver around. Yes, Manfred made a big noise but in the end it didn't prove a problem.'

Pino Trivellato, contemplating the potentially uncomfortable balance between his world, European Formula 3, and the desires of a racer says, 'For any driver to pass from Formula 3 to Formula 1 is a dream come true and he cannot pass it up. I understood why he could not finish the season with us. The same thing had happened with Patrese. We were in the European Formula Two Championship and in the last two races could win it, but Patrese decided to go to Shadow in Formula 1. The same thing now happened, with Gerhard going to ATS.

'Gerhard knew that in his contract with us was a clause covering payment for the whole season. The team had a budget of 350 million lire (approximately £140,000) and Gerhard had to pay 100 million ($40,000) and if he didn't finish . . . well, to have Gerhard in the team was in a sense a big investment because he never destroyed cars like other drivers did. He broke very few parts of the car! We remained friends and when I was recovering from a heart operation Gerhard offered me his house so that I could relax.'

Meanwhile in Formula 1, Stappert judged that 'the relationship between Schmid and Winkelhock started very much to deteriorate. A lot of things went wrong, two tempers met, and they couldn't look each other in the eye. You could think it was going to fall apart. I felt, being a friend of Manfred's, that I couldn't put Gerhard in a second ATS because I'd be hurting Manfred, but on the other hand I was convinced Gerhard could be a big star. I thought, here I am BMW's competitions manger, there is a German-speaking guy, he's Austrian, and I should look after local talent.

'Should I let the opportunity pass by just for fear that if it went wrong people would blame me afterwards because he's Austrian? Nobody would have blamed me if he'd been Chinese, Brazilian, British, French, or whatever. It wasn't his fault he was Austrian, not my fault that *I* was Austrian, but he had such capabilities I thought I might as well do it. I spoke to Hummel. He said, "You talk to Paul Rosche (in charge of technical matters) to try to get the engine, I'll

talk to Schmid to try to get the car." The first th
"You are going to get yourself into a lot of tro'
ans." I went to the boss of BMW motor sport,
tion and said if we lent Gerhard two engines f
overhaul costs so we wouldn't lose any mon
Schmid's future because you could see the relaw
Winkelhock wasn't going to continue. He agreed.'

Schmid says, 'BMW gave us more engines for Gerhard, so we prepared the car and then we had a big surprise. Gerhard was too tall and couldn't fit in the car!'

To be fair to the memory of Winkelhock, killed in an accident at Mosport the following year, he feared not competition from Berger, but ATS dissipating whatever feeble strength it had, and Berger confirms this. 'Manfred was not afraid of me — he was an experienced Formula 1 driver. He said, "If ATS can't do one car, how are they going to do two?" He was right, yes. Eventually they did manage to prepare one car properly (hmm, almost), and it turned out to be mine! Manfred was a good guy and I had no problems with him.'

Thus The Plan brought Gerhard Berger to Zandvoort. Saward remembers that Friday there. 'We hung around and hung around and eventually Gerhard said, "We'll do some laps in my BMW." I think he'd only been to the circuit once before, in European Formula 3 in 1983. We did some laps and that was fine, then he started to go quicker and quicker, and it got hairy, and then it got really hairy. I sat there murmuring *hmm . . . oh . . . hmm.* In the evening we found another small hotel and then went out to dinner with Schmid, all very strange. We ate in two places! They decided that the food in the first one we tried was inedible so they sat and watched while I ate it, then we moved on to the second place.'

On the *Saturday*, Schmid says, 'We decided to change the monocoque. We took the back out to give Gerhard a little bit more space. He wasn't comfortable, but it did make the car drivable to him.'

Berger remembers this first taste of Formula 1 with these simple but extremely eloquent words. 'Oh, the power of the Formula 1 car was terrible, so much more than in Formula 3.' Schmid mirrors this precisely. 'Later on Gerhard told me, "When I was driving this car I really didn't know what was going on, I simply didn't have enough experience".'

Looking back Berger says, 'There was a problem because a cylinder head gasket broke, water went into the engine and the power was down so I couldn't really push the engine, but the car proved to be all right and I could drive some laps.'

Winkelhock had arrived to do some testing of his own. As the day melted, Saward became more and more concerned. Spa was due to start at 5.00 pm and there they were in Holland. 'I kept tap-

s Gerhard's helmet when he came into the pits and saying "Look your watch, look at your watch. We must leave, we must leave".'

If you want Formula 1 badly and suddenly there it is, simply walking away is no easy matter. You're exploring a new world and the temptation to have a few more laps, a few more laps, can be nothing less than overwhelming. Or as Berger himself puts it, 'This was my most important day in racing, yes, a Formula 1 car. I didn't really care about anything else.'

Schmid says, 'He was very enthusiastic, he had a strong feeling that he had to drive in Formula 1. It was the only thing he wanted at this time. He did everything to get a car. He even brought his own mechanic (the one who'd waited at Schipol) to see what we did, and the whole time Gerhard hung around the car looking carefully at what was going on.'

(It might all have been different. John Wickham ran Spirit, a small team just into Formula 1. He recalls, 'At the end of 1984 when Spirit were struggling, Bernie Ecclestone called us and said, "You should take this young man Berger, he's got lots of political support and can bring some money," but as it happened Gerhard went with ATS. I think it was Gordon Coppuck — the designer — who spoke to him. Anyway he must have thought ATS were a better bet, German team and so on.')

So: Saward fretted at Zandvoort and Ravaglia fretted at Spa. He'd have to take the first stint while Berger stole those precious more laps, more laps. Lamm looked at *his* watch with consternation. Winkelhock was at Zandvoort, too, don't forget.

'I was expecting Gerhard and Winkelhock to be at Spa,' Ravaglia says, 'and we had no explanation why they hadn't returned. I'd thought the ATS test was only on the Friday, not continuing into the Saturday.' Before the start Ravaglia paced the pits and said, 'This is going to be a very long race . . .'

At 5.07 pm the pace car peeled away, releasing 53 starters, Walkinshaw (Jaguar XJ-S) taking an immediate lead. Walkinshaw's car would subsequently set fastest lap with an average speed of 92.1 mph (148 km/h). Ravaglia drove steadily in midfield and Lamm continued to look at his watch. At around 6.30 the first tyre stops began. Ravaglia came in and Lamm announced, 'They're still not here! You're the only driver we've got. They must still be at Zandvoort.' Ravaglia moved back out.

At Zandvoort Berger suddenly said to Saward, 'Right, we're off.' They ran across the paddock to Berger's car and as they accelerated away Saward held the steering wheel while Berger undid his driving overalls and folded them down on to his lap so he wouldn't sweat. 'He drove the whole way back to Spa like that,' Saward says, 'and the journey was insane, completely insane, no traffic rules. On the motorway we overtook a car which already occupied the fast lane — we overtook between it and the central barrier. We weren't going at the BMW's maximum speed, so much as *averaging* its maximum speed.

'I'll swear we only stopped at one set of traffic lights. A car waited there, I can't remember what it was but a pretty souped-up sort of car, and the guy was gun-gun-gunning the engine preparing for the green. Of course I'm in the passenger seat so I've Gerhard on one side of me and this guy on the other. I looked at the guy and he looked at me. I leant back so he could glimpse Gerhard's racing overalls. This guy was so shocked we were about 50 yards down the road before he moved when the lights did change. Then in the country roads towards the circuit we got lost. That was something, that was.'

'Ravaglia became desperate,' Lamm says, 'because his second stint neared its end. We, I must say, were a little bit desperate, very nervous and maybe also a little bit angry with Gerhard.' Ravaglia remembers being 'really tired after the four hours'. He had reached the maximum he could drive continuously and pitted again. As Berger and Saward arrived in the paddock Berger braked hard, said, 'Here, you park the car', and ran towards the pits doing up his overalls. In fact, if you can phrase it this way, he arrived a few minutes early.

'We shouted at him,' Lamm says, 'and Gerhard asked, "What's the problem? I am here, it's a five-minute pit stop, what more do you want? There's no way I would have been too late, I'd never let you down. Don't worry." He's that type of man. Somehow you'd think he took things carelessly but no, he didn't. He was of a completely different character to the usual driver and he never saw the danger.'

Ravaglia, thankfully emerging from the car, said to Berger, 'I was afraid that after tasting Formula 1 you'd lost interest in Touring Cars and wouldn't come back at all.'

Saward, the car parked, moved to the pit and was mildly surprised to see Berger not yet in the car. He'd imagined Berger would vault straight in and roar away. Saward couldn't know of the planned five-minute stop. After the hurrying, no particular hurry.

Lamm says that 'Gerhard got into the car and that was it, away he went. You know, to be in Formula 1 you must handle in a certain way a situation which is putting pressure on you, and actually that's what he had done.'

Winkelhock returned, too, and the Schnitzer became the Schnitzer team again, rather than 'anyone present please drive the car'. After six hours they lay fifth but two laps down on the leader, Walkinshaw. Towards midnight a shower drenched the circuit, cars spinning here and there almost claiming, among others, Weaver who lost control at Eau Rouge but held the car before it went off.

Two Alfas collided injuring a marshal and the pace car came out. An hour later two pace cars were out, leading to a bizarre situation. Walkinshaw had pitted and rejoined and was immediately held behind one of the pace cars, while Alain Cudini (BMW and partnering Thiery Tassin and Danny Snobeck) — who'd taken the lead while Walkinshaw pitted — just escaped this pace car and travelled fast until he reached the second one much further round the course. And Spa measured 4.316 miles (6.946 km). In simple logistics it meant that Cudini lay a lot further on when the pace cars retreated.

At 12 hours Cudini led from Stuck/Quester/Weaver, Walkinshaw two laps behind, Berger seventh but five laps behind; and fog which had hovered in the trees descended like a cloak. 'It got so foggy,' Weaver says, 'they were frightened to send the pace car out because somebody would have driven straight over the top of it. A marshal did stand in the middle of the road waving a yellow flag and they put a torch behind him, but of course in the fog and at night you couldn't really see and a BMW hit him, threw him over the bonnet. That did slow the race.'

Eventually the two pace cars emerged again and remained out for 2 hours 20 minutes. At 8.30 that Sunday morning the fog lifted and Berger versus Weaver was a sight to behold. At 18 hours, however, the Berger car had gone, engine blown. Walkinshaw won what Weaver describes as a 'glorious race, really' — in pure racing terms, of course. The marshal, taken to hospital, was subsequently reported as saved.

'ATS had enough money as a team,' Schmid says, 'but we didn't pay Gerhard, he had to give us money. He was a young driver and that's usual with young drivers. He found some sponsorship with a company making fork-lift trucks, another company gave him some and taken together it would be enough to give him one Grand Prix.'

The appeal of making your début at your home Grand Prix is clear, not least because raising sponsorship becomes much easier. Rindt drove his first and only Grand Prix of 1964 in Austria, Lauda his first and only Grand Prix of 1971 in Austria.

'Five days before the race,' Stappert says, 'the whole deal nearly fell apart. It's almost impossible to keep secrets in Formula 1 and news that BMW were supplying Gerhard with engines and ATS had a car for him leaked out. Another driver wanted the drive. He had powerful friends and nearly got it. (The full story of this cannot be told for legal reasons, leading, as it does, into shark-infested waters. Sorry to be enigmatic.) In the end BMW decided that because they had promised Gerhard the engines they would keep faith with him, although it was close.'

The usual focus for the race is Zeltweg, the small town nearest to the Osterreichring. When Rindt made his début the focus was also

Zeltweg but the circuit at an airfield, so bumpy Formula 1 didn't return. Rindt, only 24, took care — as Pruller recounted in *The Story of a World Champion* — to stay as unobtrusive as he could, avoiding photographers who wanted him shaking hands with Clark and Graham Hill. Rindt, Pruller wrote in a lovely ripple of phrases, 'didn't yet feel like master in his own home but more like a guest in his own country'.

Berger faced no such problems. Lauda had locked himself into a fascinating, hypnotizing duel with his team-mate at Marlboro McLaren, Prost — entirely different sorts of men and approaching the race meetings in different ways. Prost tried to be fast all the time, Lauda paced himself, thinking and calculating, thinking and calculating. The foreground is well enough known and I've already covered it in the opening chapter, Lauda already twice World Champion and survivor of the fire at the Nurburgring in 1976, now in the third year of a comeback and regarded by everyone except himself as superhuman. Prost won the race before Austria from Lauda by 3.149 seconds, giving a points position of Prost 43½, Lauda 39.

Who would notice Berger or for that matter a young fellow-countryman, Jo Gartner, in a team as small and beleaguered as ATS, Osella? The crowd, all of Austria and a giant global television audience would be watching Lauda. In the far, far background Winkelhock made uncomplimentary noises about ATS, stirring rumours that he wouldn't be driving for them the following year. Who noticed or cared?

'I was ordered,' Stappert says, 'to tell Gerhard very clearly before the Austrian Grand Prix it would be a one-off deal, the engines would only be available for Austria. On the Wednesday evening, Hummel, Gerhard and myself went to a little place near Zeltweg to eat and I explained the situation and how close we'd come to the deal being called off. I said, "That's the way it is but we have to accept it and we're going to try." With all our excitement — which there was because Gerhard had a new toy, if I can put it like that — I suddenly felt 20 years younger. We had pressure because of being Austrian, the pressure of the race being in Austria, but I tell you Gerhard doesn't care about pressure, he can take all the pressure in the world.'

In the background Stappert and Marko had continued their campaign to give Berger the best. 'We knew,' Stappert says, 'that Schmid didn't have the manpower to look after the second car. I persuaded Paul Rosche to get one of his mechanics to take a week's holiday and he spent it at Zeltweg! There was another guy who had been with Gerhard in Formula 3 — he'd got tired of the constant travel and worked in an engine shop in Graz. He came out and looked after the car so Gerhard had two very good people.'

Marko says, 'I organized my old mechanic, Franz Bucher' — the man from Graz — 'and he prepared the car. He's one of the best in the business, he can work 24 hours a day and when he says a car is ready, it's ready. Everything was organized through the back door, you know.' To which Stappert adds, 'The Gunter Schmid car was basically then a good Formula 1 car, simple, without a lot of sophisticated stuff but a nice balance and it worked if it was looked after all right.'

A contemporary account says that during the Austrian Grand Prix meeting the ATS pit 'frequently became the scene of high comedy. It appeared the team could never get both cars working and on the track simultaneously.'

During the Friday morning untimed session Winkelhock did not manage a complete lap, hampered by a lack of fuel pressure and gearbox problems. 'In the first practice on the Friday morning,' Stappert says, 'Gerhard was twelfth, quite a sensation even with a BMW engine.' Winkelhock's problems persisted into the afternoon. Winkelhock, and we can only imagine his mounting frustration, perhaps mounting fury, watched helplessly as Berger progressively did this:

A warm-up lap then 1:34.484, cutting that immediately to 1:33.993. He pitted, went out again, did another warm-up lap, then 1:31.904 — five seconds off the leaders' pace, but that mattered nothing. A gaggle of cars were in the 1:31s, including the Ferrari of Arnoux. Berger handed the car to Winkelhock who had a brief thrust (if you can call it that), first lap 1:40.069, second 1:33.276, third slowing to 1:34.885.

'In the afternoon,' Stappert says, 'Gerhard had a problem with the gearbox and he fell back to eighteenth place, but I think if everything had gone well he'd have been eighth. I'll never forget the sight of him on his second or third flying lap coming round the right-hander before the pit lane straight, 2 in away from the guard rail, but you knew the guy had the car under control. Wonderful to see.'

On the Saturday Winkelhock's car suffered the fuel pressure and gearbox problems all over again — the team had no spare gearbox to change overnight. They gave Winkelhock the only working car to hand — Berger's — for the final qualifying session. He made three abortive runs before, summoning everything, he did 1:30.853, seventh row of the grid; then he made a final run which he aborted at the end of the warm-up lap. Berger didn't get into the car. Berger remembers, 'I was quick from the beginning on. I remember my first practice at Zeltweg. I had a bad engine in the car, it was just there so we could run. Next Paul Rosche brought a used Nelson Piquet BMW engine with a lot more horsepower but I didn't do a good lap with it. I didn't get another chance the next day because we had no gearbox, but I felt with that Piquet engine I could have been somewhere like the second or third row of the grid for the race.'

The world watched the front of that grid, Piquet pole with Prost alongside, then Elio de Angelis (Lotus) and Lauda. Berger's Friday time proved worth the tenth row, Gartner a row behind. 'Gerhard was destroyed, Hummel was destroyed,' Stappert says. 'I had a big argument with him. I said, "Don't look so bloody down. I hope nothing worse happens in your Formula 1 career — because you're starting from eighteenth place in your first race. There are a lot of bad things waiting for you. Eighteenth is OK."'

In race trim Berger took full advantage of the Sunday morning untimed session, covering 14 laps, one more than anybody else. During these he did 1:35.355, twelfth quickest. Winkelhock's gearbox, rebuilt, promptly gave way making him a spectator. I can't tell you what Winkelhock said because I doubt anyone dared go near him.

De Angelis stalled on the grid necessitating a restart. 'At the first start,' Stappert says, 'Gerhard went up the hill, Jo Gartner behind him, and I still think that Jo — not on purpose — hit him from behind. Gerhard's car went over a bump, got sideways, and came back into the path of Gartner. Gartner's car hit him with the left front wheel into Gerhard's right rear. Gerhard's car went *wham* at 125 mph (200 km/h). For a second, or a tenth of a second, I thought, "This is it. You forced the guy into Formula 1, he is going to hit the guardrail and if he's lucky he'll only break both his legs." I could see the headlines in the next day's newspapers. Somehow through a miracle Gerhard collected the car but his Formula 1 career very nearly finished then, 300 m after it started. Good guys have luck, you know, because good luck is a big percentage.'

The restart? 'We knew,' Stappert says, 'that the green light would come on after 4.3 seconds. Being Austrian you find these things out at your home Grand Prix. I told Nelson (Piquet, Brabham, with BMW engines, don't forget) and Gerhard, "Wait 4.3 and then you go." Piquet led from Prost, Lauda sixth.

'I had a bet with Jackie Oliver of the Arrows team,' Stappert says, 'that Gerhard would start in front of his cars and he said never! Of course I lost the bet. Before the race I said, as a joke, "You'd better push your guys to keep them ahead of Gerhard because we are going to beat you in this race." Oliver said if Gerhard completed just one lap in front of his two drivers he'd sign him there and then. And then of course after the first lap Gerhard was in front. Hummel and myself went with a little piece of blue paper and said, "Now you sign." Oliver said, "What is all this about?" Then he scribbled on the piece of paper, *This is to sign Gerhard Berger*. Fun, good fun.'

In the matter of self-control, of bending time to his will by waiting and calculating, Lauda was as good as they come and sliced past de Angelis on lap 2, Derek Warwick on lap 3 and settled behind Patrick Tambay's Renault. By then in that other world down the field Berger ran seventeenth. 'It was a good thing,' he would say, 'that I drove my first race in Austria because I knew the circuit very well and that helped a lot. The other thing was that it has long straights so I had time to think.' It's an honest and instructive comment, isn't it?

On lap 9 Lauda took Tambay for third, Prost attacking Piquet, Piquet pulling away, Prost attacking again. Steadily, stealthily Lauda came, picking up a fraction of a second this lap, a fraction the next, and after 20 of them the gap stood at 4.21 to Piquet, Prost of course in between them. By then they had lapped Berger, fifteenth.

On lap 28 de Angelis's engine blew towards the Boschkurve. Rather than park it and walk back he chugged on, fire belching from the back of the car laying oil. Senna noticed this — from where he happened to be on the circuit, perhaps far away, he could see it down the descending loops. Senna also saw in the moment that de Angelis wasn't one for a long walk and so knew to watch for any oil. To be able to see de Angelis limping back, however, depended on chance, on your angle of view.

Rounding the final loop feeding on to the start-finish straight, de Angelis just gone by the pits and no oil flags being waved, Piquet arrived and his Brabham slithered. He caught it. Prost had had gearbox problems and arrived at the oil with one hand holding the lever in fourth. He could not control the McLaren with his other hand alone as it spun and he pirouetted into the armco. Lauda stalked Piquet and on lap 40 sneaked through. It had been seven years since Lauda led the Austrian Grand Prix.

He had taken himself to within sight of nine points, Prost none.

Two laps after this Lauda heard a 'big bang' and thought instantaneously 'That's it,' probed around the gearbox and found second, third and fifth. No fourth proved a handicap at a track where you needed it a lot. Lauda's mind examined this problem. He deduced that Piquet couldn't know about the fourth gear, Piquet would anticipate he — Lauda — would crank the pace down towards the end of a race and anyway Lauda didn't 'give a damn' about how much he won a race by, only that he won it.

He decided that Piquet would be thinking, 'If I make a charge Lauda will respond, so why bother?' Lauda further deduced that Piquet's tyres would be in no condition for a charge. 'I can't recall,' Lauda subsequently confessed, 'ever cluttering my mind to that degree during a race.' It gave him a headache.

Lauda won by 23.525 seconds.

Berger came in three laps later, twelfth, a genuine achievement,

The trick photograph! Berger drove Alfasuds and was at the Ice and Snow shindig, but he wasn't in any of these . . .

Aspects of a racing life

The Trivellato team decided to practical joke the practical joker and sent this lady into the truck to introduce herself to a slumbering Berger – saying she was a fan.

Above *Please, Johnny Dumfries, may I have your autograph? The ploy that caught Dumfries out at Silverstone in European Formula 3 days.*

Below *A glint of sunlight at the Nurburgring. Dumfries won this European Formula 3 race in 1984, Berger was third.*

Above *Spa 1985, Berger going hard – hard as you can.*

Below *Team mates. Ravaglia imparting information, Berger listening intently.*

Above *Berger wins the (wet) Spa 24 hours in 1985.*

Below *The Schnitzer Touring Car years. Pensive . . .*

Above left *A celebrated victim of the Lung Test, Flavio Briatore of Benetton.*

Above right *The designer touched by genius who remained a Berger supporter. John Barnard and his wistful grin.*

Below *Zolder 1986 and Berger's last race in Touring Cars with the Schnitzer team. Berger has an arm draped round Charley Lamm (right).*

Above *The last moment at Zolder. Berger gets out and hands over to Roberto Ravaglia.*

Below *Spa Touring Car action, 1986. The Berger/Ravaglia car is on the right. It had led until two hours from the end of this 24 hour race but fell back to third after mechanical problems.*

Bottom *And this is the pit stop at Spa which cost the lead.*

Top *Touring Car victory at Misano in 1986 for Berger and Ravaglia.*
Above *Turning in, 1987, Berger's first year with Ferrari.*
Below *Straight line speed, 1987.*

Above *Close up, 1987.*

Below left *The face of 1987, taking the pressure.*

Below right *The warm-up at Detroit in 1987 was wet. The ghostly towers of the Renaissance Center loom as a backdrop.*

Above left *Well, is the pressure showing?*

Above right *Enzo Ferrari, Alboreto and Berger enjoying a joke in 1987.*

Below *The superb Alan Fearnley study of Monza in 1988, Berger leading Michele Alboreto into the first chicane, the race where they finished one-two in memory of Enzo Ferrari.*

Top *The year it might have gone better, 1988.*

Above *Control, poise, determination.*

Below *Just in case you forget how big those rear tyres are and the adhesion they give. Hell sucks, they say. So do these.*

Above left *The scales of justice being weighed? Not at Detroit in 1988 although he started from the front row.*

Above right *Part of it is knowing when – and how – to switch off. Berger in the pits, 1988.*

Below *Cramped, isn't it?*

Left *One of the moments of your life, victory at Monza in 1988: the day of raw emotion when so many strands came together.*

Middle left *The podium at Monza, Berger paying his tribute to Alboreto. Eddie Cheever (Arrows) looks exhausted.*

Bottom left *Berger testing the Ferrari at Jerez in 1989.*

Right *Phoenix 1989 and a strange place to take Formula 1 cars. He didn't finish – the alternator went on lap 61.*

Below *The stark, symmetrical beauty of a Formula 1 car, 1989, smooth, sensuous – and swift.*

Bottom *A study of poise in the wet.*

Above *In sun and shadow, but mostly shadow, 1989.*

Left *Happy birthday to you . . . Spa, August 1989. Berger is thirty.*

Above *The face of anxiety, 1989. Or maybe just concentrating . . .*

Right *The pit is not a peaceful place. Always there are topics to be chewed over, problems to be dissected, opinions to be considered.*

Above *A strong run at the end of 1989. Here – Portugal – Berger has beaten Alain Prost by 32.637 seconds.*

Below *A glimpse of the future. Berger has just finished behind Senna in the Spanish Grand Prix, the race after Portugal. In a month they'd be team-mates.*

Above *Life with Nigel Mansell was not necessarily easy at Ferrari in 1989. Here Mansell harries Senna in Portugal.*

Below *Berger and Mansell, a strong pairing.*

This spread *Berger's nightmarish accident in 1989 shocked the world.*

Berger fra le fiamme: milioni di spettatori hanno sofferto davanti alla Tv

Miracolo a Imola

24 aprile '89

Berger, la vita in pochi second'

Per l'austriaco miracolo
La macchina dei socco
funzionato alla perfezi
oscure le cause: secon
avrebbe perso l'ale
non conferma, ne
e nei filmati cer

L'USCITA DI PISTA

LO SCHIANTO

IL ROGO

Berger dall'inferno alla

Il fatto del gior

Ore 14,38: l'incidente
A 285 all'ora, la Ferrari va
dritta alla curva del Tambure'
Impatto tremendo e l'incen

Parlano gli angeli che lo hanno socc
«Smanacciava forte, come un epiletti

la Repubblica
25 aprile '89

Un intervento di chirurgia plastica sul pilota della Ferrari, uscito vivo dal rogo della sua vettura domenica a Imola

"Il mio viaggio all'inferno"

Berger sarà operato alle mani, salterà i prossimi gran premi

di CARLO MARINCOVICH

INNSBRUCK — "Ho pensato molto a Lauda, adesso so quello che ha provato e mi sembra così bello essere qui in buone condizioni. Povero Niki, ebbe la sfortuna di incappare in quel rogo in un'epoca in cui le macchine erano di alluminio e bruciavano come la carta. E anche la sfortuna di Imola e di Bologna, hanno fatto molto per me e vorrei fare chiaro che in questo ritorno improvviso a casa non c'è alcuna polemica, alcuna sfiducia."

Il tedesco, in inglese e un po' anche in italiano Gerhard Berger racconta la sua avventura nel reparto chirurgia plastica al terzo piano della clinica universitaria di Innsbruck. "Vi prego di estrar polemica: Domenica sera ho chiesto io di lasciare l'ospedale di Bologna e di essere trasferito in Austria per un motivo molto semplice: io vivo qui, ho i miei cari, posso spiegarmi meglio nella mia lingua. Volevo sentirmi con ja casa. Ringrazio i medici di Imola e di Bologna, hanno fatto molto per me e vorrei fare chiaro che in questo ritorno improvviso a casa non c'è alcuna polemica, alcuna sfiducia."

CORRIERE DELLA SERA
24 aprile '89

114

Left *Preparing for the Spanish Grand Prix in 1989, more than five months after the fire at Imola.*

Below *In 1989 Mansell did shave off his moustache – then grew it again.*

Top right *Space age technology and what seems to be a lunar base directly behind, 1989.*

Middle right *A new world entirely, Marlboro McLaren and Honda power in 1990.*

Bottom right *Testing time at McLaren. From left to right Allan McNish, Berger, Mark Blundell, Jonathan Palmer and Ayrton Senna.*

Left *Berger, pensive at Marlboro McLaren.*

Below *Tight, taut and twitchy but a nice hustle through. The problem: you always had to be tighter, tauter and twitchier than Senna at Marlboro McLaren.*

Bottom *Computer print-outs, facts and figures, numerals and graphs. Hey, is that what I was doing? Yes, it was.*

Above *The optical illusion the spectator rarely sees. A Formula 1 car looks stark and very mechanical until its bodyskin is clipped on. It doesn't take long and Berger won't have to wait long.*

Right *Now you see what I mean about what it looks like without the bodyskin . . .*

Below *The face of 1990, looking older now. Was it only four years before that he'd seemed so chubby (facially), so carefree?*

Left *Pedal power, keeping fit and no G-force to bother about.*

Below *Taking care of business.*

Bottom *Unlimited horizons, your own plane and the wide blue yonder, which will surely take you to the next Grand Prix race.*

Right *Berger really does play ice hockey.*

Below *A little training on the beach.*

Bottom *Speed, speed, speed – even on the water.*

Above left *Caressing the kerbing, 1991, on the way to becoming himself again, not a Senna clone.*

Above right *The distortion of the camera captures how prehensile a Formula 1 car really looks, a sort of superb scoop.*

Below *Steve Hallam, a good man and true, shares the computers' secrets with Berger, 1991.*

Above *The Marlboro McLaren Honda vintage 1992, the year Berger scored 49 points – only one less than the mighty Senna.*

Below *He always drove well in the wet, a strangely sensitive discipline which some have and some haven't got so much of.*

Above *Berger could make corners an adventure . . .*

Below *. . . like this.*

Above *In Brazil, contemplating the first race, or rather what happened after five laps of it - the engine failed.*

Above right *Eyes scanning the new season of 1994.*

Right *Saluting the crowd at Imola, but the weekend became sadder and sadder and sadder.*

Above *In the aftermath of Imola, Berger, Michael Schumacher and Niki Lauda talk safety and mean what they say. This is Spain.*

Right *Once he'd decided not to retire after Imola, Berger gave everything in the next race, Monaco. He finished third.*

Below *Traditional Berger preparations immediately before a race: chat, drink mineral water, relax. Jean Alesi, next to him, gives an interview. Hockenheim – and great things were coming.*

Above *Berger won and saluted the crowd as they saluted him. Ferrari's time in the wilderness was over.*

Right *Close your eyes, stand upright and think of Austria. Berger, at home on a podium.*

Below *Any Ferrari driver is a big driver if he's in a Ferrari and he's at Monza for the Italian Grand Prix. Berger signs and signs on the safe side of the paddock railings.*

Above left *The morning warm-up session at Monza ended like this, although Berger would have a further – and hilarious – encounter with an ambulance driver this same morning.*

Above right *Hey, old man, we did it! Nigel Mansell, who has just won the Australian Grand Prix, salutes Berger, second, as Berger salutes him.*

Below *At Monza he rode the kerbs, as he does, and finished a brave second to Damon Hill.*

175 miles (282 km) and lasting 1 hour 20 minutes. Berger treasured the straights to gather himself, Lauda, travelling a great deal faster, had the experience to be able to execute bluffs and double bluffs with a flawed car. As everybody says, it takes time to learn it, several years, but — and this is important — Berger had had gearbox troubles of his own.

'His second start,' Stappert says, 'wasn't so good, then the gearbox started to play up, but even then you could see the sort of driver he was. If you lose, I don't know, third and fifth gears your lap times become two or three seconds slower. After four or five laps Gerhard was nearly back up to standard. He adjusted to how to run like that. I'd had the needles stuck in me over Gerhard going into Touring Cars, then more needles with Formula 1. Again, with every lap Gerhard did a needle came out. Schmid hadn't had a finish for I don't know low long and everybody was happy. The BMW motor sport boss was there — impressed. He said, "I know that we said one race but I believe you now," and he added something I am really proud of: "Thank you for being stubborn enough to push the thing through even though he's Austrian like yourself".'

Schmid says that 'usually Manfred practised and qualified well. Ten times that season he put the car on the fourth or fifth row but we never finished a race. Gerhard did his first and finished, and Manfred was very upset again, he did not like this idea. In fact Gerhard's result was so good he found some more money, so he could spend it on doing another Grand Prix, Monza.'

Statistics are a useful tool if used with caution. During the Austrian Grand Prix the lap times showed Berger's immaturity at this level with a fastest of 1:36.914 and a slowest of 1:59.955, and endless fluctuations in between. Only twice during the whole race did he lap more or less consistently, and then for only three or four laps. Compare that with Senna's entire span, 1:34.348 and 1:37.206, or Prost's before his pirouette, 1:33.081 to 1:34.827. One of the astonishing abilities of the experienced Formula 1 driver is that he narrows the 3.692 miles (5.942 km) of a circuit like the Osterreichring to fractions — eye-blinks — and sustains them.

Two years on Berger would demonstrate how he had mastered it, too: across 68 laps of the difficult terrain of the Mexican Grand Prix in October 1986 his span ranged no further than 1:20.543 to 1:24.126, slowing at the end. Full through the middle of the race he ticked off 1:21, 1:22, like drum beats.

While he raised money Berger missed Holland on 26 August — where Prost beat Lauda — but went to Monza for the Italian Grand Prix on 9 September. 'For Winkelhock,' Stappert says, 'it got worse and worse and Manfred was the poor guy, his relationship with Schmid finished, no alternative any more — which means no future in Formula 1 any more. I felt sorry for him. Manfred could see his career in Formula 1 going away from him. Here was this young Austrian who, for whatever reason, had shown he was capable of getting to the end of a race. In Monza things got worse. Manfred had so many problems with the car, the team was over-pressured trying to run two cars, as we all could foresee, and Gerhard had these two guys looking after him. Poor Manfred was left out on his own. However much I felt sorry for him I couldn't help it. I realized I was going to get a good part of the blame (Winkelhock German, BMW German, ATS German, Schmid German), but I couldn't help that either.'

Qualifying was a rerun of Austria, albeit with variations. In the Friday morning session Winkelhock's suspension broke, flinging him out of the Ascari chicane and reshaping the car. That session Berger was forced into the pits with his undertray hanging loose. It meant that for qualifying ATS had only Berger's car and significantly he took first use of it: four runs, a total of 14 laps, and he got down to 1:33.161.

When Winkelhock took over, the gearbox developed a grumble and he struggled through a warm-up lap, struggled to 2:00.593 on his next and last lap because the gearbox growled *enough*. His time would keep him out of the race. Martini, next slowest and twenty-sixth, did 1:38.312.

On the Saturday morning, Winkelhock found that the gearbox on *his* car grumbled so he and Berger shared Berger's during second qualifying in the afternoon. They worked that car hard, Winkelhock doing 1:32.866, but Berger 1:31.549. Nigel Roebuck writing for *Autosport* sensed a 'simmering rage' within Winkelhock and not just about being a second slower than Berger, about everything. Nor did matters improve . . .

While Berger covered 12 laps in the Sunday morning untimed session (best 1:32.662, slow but safe; Prost for instance 1:31.698), Winkelhock's gearbox grumbled again. He limped a single lap of 2:51. A Touring Car would have been quicker than that.

On the parade lap before the race Winkelhock discovered — and it can have come as no surprise — that he had only fourth and fifth gears. He parked the car at the rear of the grid, clambered out and walked away leaving the mechanics to push the car to the pits. Winkelhock changed and went home. 'He was so disillusioned,' Stappert says, 'that he got out of the car and left it at the back of the grid and left the circuit, which was an unprofessional thing to do. He was so upset he lost his temper. While it was wrong it was understandable from a human point of view. All the weekend Gerhard had trouble with the gearbox and Schmid blamed him. "You cannot shift gear in a Formula 1 car like you do in a Formula 3 car, you have to be a little bit more careful." Gerhard said, "All my life I have always shifted gear the same and when the gearbox is right it stands up to it, when it's wrong it breaks anyway.'"

The world saw Winkelhock's departure briefly but watched the front row, Piquet and Prost, watched the second row, de Angelis and Lauda. The television cameras had to pan a long way back to Berger on the tenth.

Lauda, in pain from a slipped disc, drove a calculated and controlled race. Prost went on lap 3, engine, and when the leader Tambay went on lap 44 a clean run home spread itself before Lauda. Around half-way through Berger lost fourth gear but kept on, and as cars dropped out he moved up, modestly, almost quietly. 'You could hear that he'd lost fourth,' Stappert says, 'which is important at Monza, and Schmid left in frustration (to be scrupulously fair to Schmid, his version follows) and everyone was convinced Gerhard would have to stop in a couple of laps. Again, he adapted his driving style to the problem.' Across laps 18 to 30 he ran last — but ran.

At the end, while Monza paid homage to Lauda, who'd lapped Berger twice, the ATS moved into sixth place: last but sixth. 'It was the only race where three Austrians finished in the top six,' Stappert says — Lauda first, Gartner fifth. 'After the race Gerhard was excited, everybody was excited. Half the people were in tears . . . laughing with joy. For me it was a very satisfying situation. If someone asked me the most important thing about Gerhard I'd say, whenever you gave him a chance he took it, used it, put himself in a position to get a chance to take the next step. Every first chance he got he took and delivered.'

While Lauda now had 63 points against Prost's 52½, Berger's sixth didn't count in strictly bureaucratic terms. ATS declared at the start of the season they'd only field one car, so although they could enter two at their discretion the second driver would have to content himself with self-satisfaction. In the big, immortal tableau of points gained officially, Berger's first is missing and will always be missing. He got it but couldn't keep it.

Some reports — and Stappert — suggest Schmid left enraged by Winkelhock's leaving. He insists he had a ticket for an early plane anyway, not as bizarre a notion as it sounds. If you have business to do elsewhere it is not necessary for you to watch every lap of every Grand Prix, particularly since the team should be able to handle it. 'I couldn't stay to the end. I reached the airport and some people came over and said, "Oh congratulations, you finished in the top six," and this was a big surprise for me . . .'

A week after Monza Berger went to Nogaro in European Formula 3, the race where Nielsen returned and dominated absolutely. Dumfries recalls, 'There was a swimming pool near the circuit, and we went up there for a swim, Berger and I. We sat around relaxing and hanging out and chatting. I remember feeling quite uneasy about it.

He was a rival and I thought, do I really want to be getting too friendly with this bloke?

'Anyway, we talked and we arrived at a bit of an agreement because overtaking at Nogaro was particularly difficult and we were both behind Nielsen and Capelli. (In qualifying Nielsen did 1:12.54, Capelli 1:12.87, Berger 1:13.00, Dumfries 1:13.09.) So we made a pact: we wouldn't fight each other too hard, we'd concentrate on getting past Capelli and gain maximum points over him. It didn't matter whether Nielsen won because he'd missed so much of the season after his crash at Monaco and didn't figure in the Championship.' Both Dumfries and Berger could still win it depending on what happened here and in the last round at Jarama on 21 October. 'That was the agreement: if and when we got past Capelli then we'd start scrapping among ourselves. I reasoned I would get past Berger anyway.'

At the green light Nielsen led, Capelli behind, then Berger, then Dumfries. On that first lap Dumfries decided the agreement might not be such a good idea after all and 'I took a run a Berger, I made a mistake and hit his rear wheel with my front wing. I bent it up and that completely screwed the front of my car for the rest of the race. I couldn't do a thing about it. If I'd kept to the plan I'd have been all right (and possibly European as well as British champion). Berger probably didn't even feel it because it was only a slight impact, a real little touch. If I'd hit him hard I'd have given him a puncture or taken him out of the race. It just goes to show what can happen to the best laid plans of men.'

Nielsen, still in some pain from Monaco, led all the way, finishing in 36:58.16, Capelli 37:01.42, Berger 37:11.34, Dumfries 37:27.15. In scrutineering Capelli survived a protest from VW that his engine was illegal and Berger survived a protest that his Ralt was underweight. That could have been important with the points at Capelli 56, Berger 49, Dumfries 45, and only Jarama left.

It was Berger's last race for Trivellato and Pino says, 'We worked, tested, ate, cried together for a year and it was very nice, very good! Every day he made jokes with and against the mechanics. In one way he saw things clearly, very quiet — he could be asleep 10 minutes before the race started. Yes, I remember the water he put in my bed and the fights we had with shaving foam from canisters.' (Note: The picture in the photo section — and you can't miss it — of the young lady unadorned was probably taken at Mugello, although Pino Trivellato can't remember exactly. He does remember saying to Berger, 'Look, there is a girl waiting for an autograph' and when Berger saw her he dropped his shorts and kept them dropped. Trivellato coins another lovely phrase — 'with the bottom naked.')

Jarama clashed with the Portuguese Grand Prix, but the European Grand Prix, penultimate round of the season, lay between, on 7 October at the new Nurburgring. In mid-week after Nogaro virtually all the Formula 1 teams tested at the 'Ring. By then BMW had told Schmid they would not be supplying him in 1985 and Winkelhock had been reported as saying the further he was away from the team the better. A dark curtain was falling over ATS. Winkelhock went to the 'Ring, but wouldn't, or didn't, drive.

Because the circuit hadn't been used by Formula 1 cars before, the testing assumed particular importance, not least because of the return of Lauda. The world would watch that. Berger went well, although ATS only attended on the Thursday. Schmid says, 'Young drivers will be nervous but he was strong. During the testing he came into the pits and wanted some adjustments to the car. Five minutes later I asked where he was. The mechanics said, "Oh, he's going to the doctor, he's not well." I only discovered the truth afterwards. One pit was empty and he was in there with a girl!'

Two days later Berger went to Zolder for the penultimate round of the Touring Cars and he and Ravaglia qualified eighth. 'Gerhard was famous for being ultra quick,' Stuck says. 'In the team we had guys like Ravaglia, who was quick, and Dieter Quester, who wasn't so quick but was very funny. Against Gerhard I had to pull my socks up. For me he was the guy to beat and for him I was the guy to beat.

'This ended in a fantastic crash at Zolder, where we could make Quester Champion. I tried to put the car on pole, and going into the Kanaal corner (a sharp horseshoe right) to beat Gerhard's time I turned the car in so hard it flipped. I put it on its roof, and the guy behind couldn't believe it.'

Lamm says, 'We had a difficult season, overshadowed by the Jaguars and Rovers. Eventually we changed from Dunlop tyres to Pirelli and the car immediately went a lot quicker. Gerhard came back and you could see how much he had matured in his style of racing. He was a different driver to the one who had been with us earlier in the season. Gerhard and Ravaglia drove a very, very strong race in the wet.'

During the race lightning announced a storm and when it came Berger (and others) skated off. 'We were very close to making a pit stop,' Ravaglia says. 'Gerhard was in the car and I waited in the pits. It started raining and Gerhard stayed out on slicks, the rain became heavier and Gerhard did come back — because he'd had an accident. It was a mistake because of lack of experience.' Walkinshaw, third, took the Championship for Jaguar.

Meanwhile Schmid fired Winkelhock for alleged 'uncomplimentary remarks' about the team and evidently Schmid announced it to the press before Winkelhock had been informed — he was driving in the Mount Fuji, Japan, 1,000 km. Critics, studying what they saw as the death throes of ATS, pointed out Schmid's timing: going into a race in Germany, even though it was called the European Grand Prix, without the only German driver. Nor had Manfred Winkelhock finished. He wouldn't simply be elbowed out of the way. When he returned from Japan he rang his solicitor to ask some pertinent questions and received extremely pertinent replies. He'd be at the Nurburgring but not to drive the car, no. He'd *impound* it and impound Berger's car, too.

Meanwhile, too, Berger made an understandable decision to miss the European Formula 3 climax at Jarama and go to the Portuguese Grand Prix instead, but first he faced the 'Ring.

To quantify the build-up to this race remains difficult because it generated so much external emotion. If the media fed briefly on ATS in a macabre way, what to make of the return of Lauda? I remember, to select one example, South African newspapers demanding quotes from Lauda in the week up to the race, as many quotes as you could send, and I assume many, many other journalists came under similar demands from a host of equally distant places. What did Lauda think? How did he feel? How would he react? Would he, just this once, show unconcealed, uncalculated emotion?

Some chance of that.

Long before and in his own logical way he had detached himself from the events of 1 August 1976. He'd even consented to journalists taking him back to the place where the Ferrari snapped out of control and became an inferno. He just stood there wondering what the journalists expected from him. He'd watched the slightly out of focus film of the crash, too, and as he watched he felt it must have been happening to somebody else. This was not a man to return again now, especially to this new, neutered, bland strip of tarmac and go to pieces. He'd come and drive and go away, as he did at all the other circuits. It removed virtually all attention from Berger. He could theoretically make his progress quietly. If only it had been as simple as that.

In the Friday untimed session Berger went off into the armco heavily and bruised his knees. He did have a spare car, Winkelhock's, and used that to qualify eighteenth. Enter Winkelhock with an injunction, his lawyer and what a contemporary account describes as a 'very large policeman'. In essence the injunction empowered Winkelhock to seize the ATS cars in lieu of outstanding payments to him. ATS convinced both Winkelhock and his lawyer that 152,000 Deutschmarks had already been deposited at the High Court at Mannheim. Exit Winkelhock. Berger went out to celebrate that he still had a car and promptly spun a couple of times. He didn't hit anything.

Lauda had a wretched qualifying with car problems on the

Friday, and in the wet on the Saturday he couldn't improve on fifteenth place. Across 67 laps and 189.074 miles (304.314 km) Lauda could still be dangerous. Piquet had pole, Prost alongside.

Stefan Johansson (Toleman) caught a quite different mood when he pointed out that on a circuit it didn't matter what sort of racing you were in, single-seaters, sports cars, saloons even, the right-hander at the end of the starting straight always produced a crash. Johansson's race strategy became simple: keep out of trouble. He was proved right. Senna might have been squeezed by Eddie Cheever (Benetton) or he might have braked late, but he rode up and over Rosberg (Williams). Berger lost control of the ATS and, sideways, it struck and rose from Marc Surer's Arrows. Teo Fabi (Brabham) and Piercarlo Ghinzani (Osella) collided. Three separate crashes before you could draw breath.

Prost won, Lauda fourth after a most untypical spin and that took the Championship to Estoril, Lauda versus Prost head to head. On the same day, 21 October 1984, the European Formula 3 Championship went to Jarama, Capelli versus Dumfries head to head — well, almost.

The Formula 1 world gathered at Estoril, a new track to virtually all of the drivers. Some had been there in Formula Two but not many. The track was as you see it today, the long, long flat out straight, the nip and tuck loopers all the way round the back, and like every track it needed learning. A special session was held on the Thursday. Late that day news came through that Fabi's father had died and he returned to Milan immediately. Brabham tried to contact Stefan Bellof, a very, very promising young German driver, as Fabi's replacement, and when they couldn't they rang Winkelhock. He'd travel on the Friday, maybe his whole career back in play.

That Friday heavy rain fell at Estoril, delaying the untimed session until midday and pushing the first qualifying session back. The rain abated when qualifying did begin and Johansson took a swift run at it, during which as he skimmed across puddles he saw wisps of droplets on his visor. More rain coming in. Berger, also out quickly, spun and clouted the armco, bending it and the car. That delayed the session and when it resumed, the conditions drier, Prost went quickest from de Angelis (Lotus) and Lauda, with Berger last.

Fog shrouded Stuttgart airport, holding Winkelhock impotent.

At Jarama the track was opened for practice (not qualifying) on a strictly voluntary basis. It rained here, too, drowning the session.

On the Saturday Winkelhock arrived, clambered into the Brabham and after six laps in the final qualifying session said wistfully, 'You can't believe how much nicer this car is than the ATS.' He qualified nineteenth, Berger twenty-third. In the session the world watched Lauda struggle with his McLaren and, the pressure mounting, 'incredibly stupid defects' on the car led him to make mistakes. He complained that the car made a 'rattling noise' and at one stage missed his braking point and flowed down the escape road, flat-spotting a precious set of qualifying tyres. (If you hit the brakes of a Formula 1 car hard they bite enough to lock the wheels, scalping each tyre in mid-rotation at the instant of the locking; hence flat spots where the scalping took place.)

So: Lauda eleventh quickest, sixth row of the grid and Johansson, Warwick (Renault), Alboreto, Tambay (Renault), Mansell, de Angelis, Rosberg and Senna between himself and the front row of Piquet (pole) and Prost. Assuming Prost won, Lauda needed to finish second to steal the Championship by half a point.

At Jarama there would be two qualifying sessions this Saturday. In the first Nielsen gambled and used all his special tyres. That gave him provisional pole, 1:23.24 against Dumfries at 1:23.26. In the second session Dumfries adjusted the settings of his car and took pole, 1:23.13, Nielsen achieved no quicker than 1:23.70 — but his first session time was good enough for the front row of the grid. *Autosport* reported that Capelli 'was confused to find himself in eighth place. The Martini driver was magnificent through the twisty sections of the track but handicapped by lack of dry testing.' Capelli had another problem, the lingering possibility of losing all his championship points in the aftermath of the Affair of the Air Box. He faced the race eight points clear of Dumfries.

Dumfries remembers that 'basically Capelli and I never used to talk to each other but, having said that, he was always reasonably friendly, reasonably approachable. However, there was a lot of tension after Monza and that seemed to make him withdraw into himself.'

At Estoril 70 laps, 189.210 miles (304.439 km); at Jarama 30 laps, 61.74 miles (99.34 km).

Lauda went quickest in the Sunday morning warm-up, Winkelhock twelfth, Berger twenty-second. What would Lauda do? How would he apply his logic to the problem of reaching second place? A peak audience of seven million in Britain alone would watch. Deep into the race Lauda came upon a gaggle of backmarkers and would remember, 'Berger is the only one who moves over; all the others make themselves important, put on a show of being involved in the race for the title.'

At Jarama, Dumfries stormed it, Nielsen churning wheelspin at the green light. Nielsen laid whatever pressure he could on Dumfries but Dumfries kept control. 'Jarama,' Dumfries says, 'was a great race and I was right on top of the job from the word go. Nielsen was really close to me the whole way. On any lap the most I led was by two seconds and a lot of the time just over one second, a stand-off situation because our cars were performing almost exactly the same on all parts of the circuit. Capelli was history, he couldn't get on terms with either of us. Nielsen got the gap down to 0.9 and I made a mistake then, right near the end, just put it up on a kerb. Then I pulled the gap out again and won it by nearly two seconds.' Capelli finished third, champion barring the aftermath. 'If I'd finished in front of him at Nogaro — the race before — I'd have won it,' Dumfries says. 'Did I have to prove I could beat him when his car became legal? I don't know. How much does it prove? The Championship proves the most, doesn't it?' Capelli 60 points, Dumfries 54, Berger 49.

At Estoril, while Lauda moved towards second place — he'd get it when Mansell retired, brakes — Berger engaged in an animated scrap with Gartner which lasted from lap 53 to lap 65 before Gartner pulled clear. Towards the end Gartner ran out of fuel and Berger finished thirteenth but two laps down on the winner, Prost. Lauda, crossing the line 13.425 seconds after Prost, had stolen it.

An end and a beginning. Lauda would never win the Championship again and retired forever at the end of the next season. ATS would never race again. 'There was a lot of confusion,' Schmid says, 'and BMW said they would not give us the engine any more, maybe because of pressure from other people. In 1984 we were very good in practice but in the races the exhaust system broke all the time, and the system was supplied by BMW to us. It was not our choice to have it. We weren't allowed to touch the engines, we couldn't change them, even adjust them. BMW had one engineer and two mechanics for that. We had no engine and we said OK we'll stop. We informed Gerhard and he said, "That's a shame." Then he went round trying to find a drive for 1985.'

Trivellato asked him to compete in the Macau Formula 3 race on 18 November and they'd do some prior testing at Mugello. A week after Estoril, driving the short journey from home to his office to collect his overalls — a journey so short he didn't bother to put on his seat belt — his BMW was struck from behind by another car, rolled several times and thrust through the railing of a bridge, Berger pitched out of the rear window. The BMW came to rest in a brook. He did not lose consciousness but felt searing pain from his neck.

By immense good fortune two doctors from Munich happened to be passing. They examined him and saw immediately how dangerous it would be to move him. Two vertebrae in his neck were broken. Someone estimated the survival rate for such injuries as two per cent. The doctors kept him still until an ambulance came to take him to hospital in Innsbruck where his condition was pronounced 'serious but not critical'.

In hospital he was offered a choice, six months with his neck in plaster while it healed naturally, or an operation bearing risks. 'I was lucky,' Berger says, 'because the hospital was one of the best in Europe for this kind of problem.' That did not dilute the choice. Six months in plaster would take him to April, by which time every team would long have made their driver arrangements and two Grands Prix would already have passed, Brazil and (ironically) Estoril, now moved to the front of the calendar.

Three days after being admitted to hospital he had the operation. Surgeons assured him it had been successful and he began a ferocious struggle to get himself back into condition to drive. 'The accident,' he would say cryptically, 'came at the right moment, one week after the end of the 1984 season, and it gave me enough time to be fit for the start of the 1985 season. I worked very hard in hospital and Niki called me up, gave me Willi Dungl's number, and told me to talk to him about my neck. (Dungl was the fitness guru who'd helped Lauda recover from the Nurburgring accident in 1976.) The papers are always writing about Dungl looking after sportsmen so everyone thinks he earns a lot of money. I can tell you I never paid him anything. I always asked him but he said no.'

So, Berger lay in hospital. Saward recounts what he now considers a 'silly story but somehow it illustrates the way we were. I heard he'd had the accident so I rang up his house. Nobody spoke a word of English and my German consisted entirely of *Ja* and *Nein*. I said, "Gerhard OK?" loudly and a voice said "*Ja*," and I said, "Gerhard p-a-r-a-l-y-z-e-d?" and a voice said, "*Nein*." I put the phone down and I started laughing and I couldn't stop. An absurd conversation! He was into Formula 1 and he'd driven off a bloody cliff. Somehow you expected him to do something completely ridiculous like that. When he was all right, typically he took it as a joke. He'd got a scar from ear to ear, he was held together by wire, but at least he was all right.'

His visitors included Mansell. Berger says, 'I'd taken him to hospital in Innsbruck once after he'd had a skiing accident. When I came out of the hospital he picked me up. We had a good relationship.'

Berger was 24, lucky to be alive, his future extremely uncertain after the briefest flirtation with Grand Prix racing. Mansell was 30, he'd driven in 59 races and not won one of them. Lotus had recently fired him to take Senna, and Williams had hired him as a good 'journeyman who will score points'. As Mansell drove Berger away from the hospital towards Worgl, could either have imagined that within five years they'd be sitting side by side again — in Ferraris, Formula 1 Ferraris?

6

Slings and Arrows

What should have been easy, smooth and natural — marrying BMW, Berger and the Arrows team for 1985 — proved to be an authentic Formula 1 saga played out among a variety of vested interests, some so vested that it almost didn't happen.

'At the end of 1984,' Stappert says, 'it started to get serious because I knew Arrows were unhappy with Marc Surer and Jackie Oliver was quite happy with the way Gerhard had gone on. Jackie phoned me in November and said, "We watched Gerhard over the last couple of races and were impressed. We could try to take him but it's going to be difficult because of the money."

'Surer had a strong connection with the Arrows sponsor, Barclay. BMW also had to be careful not to push too much, so I found myself in a very delicate situation. I was convinced Gerhard would be good for Arrows, fresh blood in the team, and Arrows good for Gerhard because if they weren't a top team he would start his first full Formula 1 season on a sensible basis. Arrows knew what they were doing. And it wouldn't be too much pressure because people wouldn't expect a lot from Gerhard.' Arrows (now Footwork) had been founded in 1978 by Oliver and Alan Rees.

The unfolding saga . . .

Berger: 'After I got out of hospital a big Austrian sponsor came and told me they wanted to go into Formula 1. I organized for Jackie Oliver to meet them and after about a week it was all arranged. I signed a contract. Three weeks later the company phoned me and said that they had changed their minds. I was back where I began.'

Stappert: 'We started to have discussions with Barclay and the whole Barclay operation turned out to be extremely complicated.

Gerhard had to find some money. Oliver wanted to take him, Gerhard wanted to go there. BMW — at least myself — wanted Gerhard to be there, but obviously BMW weren't going to pay for it and Oliver wouldn't get a discount on engines when he took Gerhard. No way, no way. Gerhard had found a good co-sponsor, an Austrian company which made little glass animals. You see them all over the world. We had a big meeting and everything was all right. In the end it collapsed because one side of the co-sponsor wanted to back a football team and suddenly Gerhard had no money. And another complication — suddenly Gartner was fighting for the seat.'

Berger: 'Jackie phoned me to say that Jo Gartner had told him he had a million dollars for the drive. I didn't have any money, but Jackie said he would wait and try and find a sponsor for me.'

Stappert: 'Gartner pretended he had money but I knew he had none. I told Jackie that Gartner had no money and Jackie was upset with me because he thought I was lying to try and get Gerhard in! The whole thing went to the top of BMW and became a nightmare, a real disaster. I found myself in a strange situation and at one point a BMW executive told me, "If I find you are playing any tricks to put Berger into Formula 1 you leave the company today." Gartner had two sources he pretended to get the money from. When we found out the truth I immediately sent a telex to Jackie and he didn't believe me. Quite the opposite. He was angry because he thought I was trying to get him to turn real money away.'

Stappert understood Oliver's point of view. 'After all, Jackie is a businessman, you know, and if you have one guy with millions of money and a good guy with zero money, maybe you wouldn't like it but in the end you'd have to decide to take the millions.'

Rees, ruminating on how compact Arrows were, says, 'Those days teams were a lot smaller than these days. People were still running teams with 40 personnel. You could just about do that. I suppose teams like Williams and McLaren had 90 or 100 so it all moves up: now we have 130 and they've about 200. Jackie looked after all the sponsorship and I ran the team, looked after the finances to a certain extent. I didn't really know Gerhard. OK he'd done the four meetings with ATS and he'd done European Formula 3, but of course when you're in Formula 1 you just don't have the time to watch races like that.'

Oliver: 'What happened with Gerhard was that Dieter Stappert had been constantly on to me telling me how good Gerhard was. The trouble is that when a German-speaking friend impresses on you how good a German-speaking driver is you always wonder whether they have some ulterior motive and clearly they do. But with Gerhard, Dieter was right, no doubt about that.

'We listened to Dieter a certain amount but the only way the

Arrows team then could ever bring a driver into Formula 1 was to augment his budget. We were always on tight budgets. Throughout the history of the team we'd been responsible for looking at promising drivers who would have some national backing — people in their own countries who saw a future in them and would help them on their way. That enabled us to pay for the programme and give the driver the opportunity he deserved.

'No, I hadn't met him before. Dieter arranged a meeting and I said to Gerhard, "What we've got to do to give you the chance is raise some money." We'd done the same with Thierry Boutsen the year before and Riccardo Patrese two years before that. Jo Gartner was pushing hard as well, yes he was. Gartner had some money, but Gerhard's personality was clearly the best. He had that charisma which is associated with successful drivers, laid back, easy but the kind who does the business. I preferred Gerhard, too, because he wasn't like Gartner in the sense that Gartner had always paid for his rides whereas Gerhard had earned many of his in the lower formulas, although he had had a little bit of support.

'The driver has to start somewhere and it's unlikely — although it does happen on occasions — that he's going to go straight into a top team and be paid to do the job when he'd totally unproven. Even if a top team judges the driver has the talent they're not going to do it immediately. The risk is great then because he's going to make mistakes during his first and second years. The odd exceptions to this, I believe, prove the rule.

'Drivers at the stage of their career that Gerhard was raise money not to pay for their programme but to contribute towards it. You can't assume the money they bring in pays for the whole thing, all they're doing is contributing. You've got to find the rest from other sources. We toured around Austria and Germany trying to add to the budget he already had. He'd got one sponsor in his pocket.

'We had a fondue party in Gerhard's small apartment in Worgl with his mother and father. We were sitting around and his father didn't speak any English at all and I spoke hardly any German so Gerhard acted as translator. His father asked me through him, "My son wants to be a driver. I don't know if that's a good idea or not. I don't know whether he can make any money. I think I'd prefer him to stay in the family haulage business, but if he wants to do what he wants to do I suppose that's fine — but tell me, Mr Oliver, he must bring some money along to secure this drive. Has he got to do this every year? If he has, he's never going to make any money, you're the one who's going to make the money!"

'I said, "Well, I suppose you could look at it that way but if he does well enough with us after bringing money for a year or more then a team will notice him, they'll sign him up and he will be a successful driver in terms of results and earnings." Gerhard's father said, "Well, who might hire him?" and I said, just thinking of a name, "Ferrari, for example . . .""

Berger: 'I agreed with Jackie to give him all my personal sponsorship money if he would pay for my flights and hotel bills, so I would be driving in Formula 1 for nothing. We still needed more money but then Jackie telephoned me and said he was going to Italy to talk with a sponsor, it was all going to be OK again and I could sign a contract. When he got back he told me the sponsor wanted to be in Formula 1 but Gartner had contacted them and tried to get the drive for himself! I was angry about that, and a few moments later a journalist phoned me and I said Gartner was an idiot. I shouldn't have said it but I was annoyed and it all came out in the press.'

Like Winkelhock, Gartner is not alive to defend himself. The Viennese was killed at Le Mans in 1986. He made Formula 1 in 1984 with Osella and finished in that fifth place at Monza. He competed in Formula 1 only in 1984. He moved to sports cars and died in a crash on the Mulsanne Straight. The evening before he'd told Ian Phillips of *Autosport* that sports cars were just a job, just a way of earning wages while he tried everything he knew to regain Formula 1. As late as February 1985 Oliver said wryly, 'Jo Gartner looks like number one choice this week.' Oliver admitted Berg and Berger were also candidates but 'the situation ebbs and flows and there is no real indication who it will be right now'. Oliver did find a sponsor although evidently it didn't cover the whole cost.

Stappert: 'Later Jackie realized the money Gartner said he had maybe wasn't there. I took Gerhard and other BMW drivers for our annual winter training and I got a telex from Oliver saying maybe another company would pay for Gerhard — but in the end they didn't either. Gerhard phoned Jackie and Jackie explained the situation. Gerhard needed about $200,000. We sat looking at each other and he said, "What are we going to do now?" I replied that it was easy for me to say because I didn't have to provide the money, but there's only one thing to do: send a telex to Jackie and guarantee him the money. Stop your fitness training, go home tomorrow and start to find it. We phoned Jackie and he was a bit reluctant because he didn't think Gerhard would find it.

'I sent Jackie a telex from BMW and took the copy from the machine so that nobody would see what I had done. In the telex I said the money would come, but if it didn't then somehow it would come out of the family business. Gerhard also made a deal that Jackie could buy two trucks for the team and this is how it worked in the end.'

End of saga.

Berger phoned Charley Lamm and said, 'I have an Arrows contract now but I haven't driven a racing car since my accident. I'm looking ahead to the season and I don't know how good I still am. I need to do a test.' Lamm said they could take a car to Mugello. It was a secret test because Berger didn't want anybody to know, because as he said, 'I just want to see what I can do.' They took the BMW 635 and asked Ravaglia to be there to provide a comparison. Berger drove for two or three days, seeing how long he could stay in the car. On the third day he asked Ravaglia to drive a series of laps. Then Berger got in and was within a tenth of a second. He said, 'It means at least in Touring Cars I'm still where I was before'.

Rees says, 'I knew very little about him until he appeared in the ATS.' Rees had had a great deal of experience, driving against Clark, Graham Hill, Brabham and Rindt in the 1960s. 'We were doing the deal with BMW for engines and I know Gerhard was close to them but the two factors just coincided. It was when the turbos were coming in, you absolutely had to have them and the BMW was a pretty good one. Although he had just started in Formula 1 most people thought he was a good driver anyway, so it wasn't just the engine connection; and he was good. BMW were obviously interested in him, we wanted the engine, he wanted to be in Formula 1. It all fitted. He'd just had his road accident and when he first came to the factory he still wore a neck brace. He could take it off if he needed to, apparently, but he left it on all the time.'

How did Berger strike Rees? 'Well, you see, the trouble is you meet a new driver and let's face it you think OK he's probably good but let's see what he's really like. Nothing more than that. It's during the year that you get to know him better.' Rees's initial impression was that Berger was 'quick, and that was quite clear from the start but he didn't have the experience. Thierry Boutsen, our other driver, did. (This would be Boutsen's third full season.) They performed the same in terms of speed but Thierry was more polished. Gerhard got better, got quicker, but really it takes two or three seasons to gain the experience.

'The first time he drives your car you have to say, "Look, get to know it, get to know things, take your time. You've a lot of time in front of you. You don't even have to try and do it all in your first year. Think about it, take it easy to start with because the more confidence you have the quicker you will go".'

Is that difficult because by definition they are racers? 'You can't damp them down too much. Of course they want to go flat out. All of them do. Gerhard had a lot of natural ability and if you get into the occasional difficult situation you can get out of it. The drivers who do it by sheer perseverance and effort don't. I know he had a spin or two but he did get out of them.'

What is natural ability? 'That is a question. Balance plays a part, personality can play a part. When I say balance I mean physical and mental, and racing drivers must have a well-developed sense of that. If they have they can do extraordinary things. Obviously you also need co-ordination between your hands and feet, a quick-thinking brain.

'A driver with it all has a tremendous initial advantage. Compare Jimmy Clark with Graham Hill. Jimmy had more natural ability although in the end, you know, there wasn't a lot of difference between them. They both gained experience, they both knew what they were doing and got themselves into the right cars, but even then natural ability is always going to tend to be that little bit better. There is no question Gerhard had that natural ability and you could see him getting experience during the year.'

Berger tested the Arrows at Imola in late March. He says, 'For the first half a dozen laps I thought there is no way you can drive a car at this speed! I soon got used to it and I felt really good but the engine blew. My neck was not really a problem. The only time I was aware of it was under braking.' He did a respectable 1:35.10, Boutsen quickest of all with 1:28.75.

Boutsen says, 'I didn't know Gerhard before. I'd never met him and I don't think I'd even driven against him in the Touring Cars, but truly I found him a fantastic team-mate, a great team-mate, and we had good fun together. For sure he was learning but so in a way was I. Anyway I was able to help him. We began to work very hard and closely and it resulted in a very, very good contact. That year was probably one of the best human years of my career.

'Socially Gerhard is a crazy man, the man is totally mad. He always made jokes and there was no limit for him, absolutely no limit, absolutely everything happened, every day another story. The worst I remember? We were spending a night in a hotel and a man from Mercedes was there who'd just been to Boss and bought new clothes, suitcases full of them, very expensive. Gerhard found a way to get into his bedroom, opened the suitcases, turned on the hot water tap in the bath and put everything into the bath . . . including the shaver, even the hair dryer.

'He opened the tap full blast and left the room! The water was almost boiling hot and it started to come over the top of the bath, *and* when the episode was over and the clothes dried they dried a size too small. They'd shrunk! With me he'd play terrible jokes in rental cars and in hotel rooms. He'd take the fire extinguisher and blow it under your bedroom door.

'We had different driving styles and he made a few mistakes like we all do, spins and things, but it was normal. At the beginning he had a few problems because he was just coming out of the big road accident and his neck was really sore, but he learnt quickly.'

At Rio, Berger qualified on the fourth last row and rose to eighth on lap 28, but dropped out, rear suspension. Portugal was wet, he came within a fraction of Boutsen in qualifying (1:24.842 against

1:24.747), but on lap 13 the BMW engine responded so quickly under acceleration that it pitched him into a guardrail. He qualified eleventh at Imola but the engine let go after four laps. He qualified mid-grid at Monaco.

Oliver says, 'The driving part he has to decide himself, although you can give him a lot of help. Gerhard was pretty confident so he didn't need any moral support. What you've to try and do is warn him about certain things — about tyres, about the start of a race, to watch for this and watch for that — remind him at the appropriate moment so that he doesn't forget. That's normally just prior to a race or just prior to his going out on a qualifying lap. Then you chat about the mistakes afterwards. It's called the learning curve.

'At Monaco I said, "Right, you've qualified at the back of the field. That is very dangerous because when you reach Ste Devote or the Loews hairpin you'll come to a standstill — it's impossible to get all those cars through and in fact you may have to put your clutch down. You have to keep your eyes open for all that, otherwise you'll knock the nose cone off the car. Then just go for a finish.'

(Knowledge is passed down. In *Colin Chapman, The Man and his Cars*, Jabby Crombac quotes Oliver on what happened when Lotus hired him in 1968. 'I remember the first thing Chapman said to me at the start in Monte Carlo. "Now, lad, if you finish here in the whole history of Monte Carlo you finish sixth. Let's stay out of trouble and don't have an accident on the first lap." Those words were still ringing in my ears when, as I came out of the tunnel on the first lap, I collected Ludovico Scarfiotti and Bruce McLaren who had just had an accident before I arrived! That made the old man furious and he fired me on the spot.')

Now, in 1985, 'Berger misjudged it and of course he knocked the nose off at the first corner. You can tell someone but they have to learn by their own mistakes.' Berger made a good start and moved into the centre of the track. Tambay and Johansson (Ferrari) crashed. Tambay thought he hit Berger, Berger took to the escape road at Ste Devote and so did Tambay who arrived with no brakes and bumped the Arrows.

At Brno Berger partnered Ravaglia in the first round of the Touring Cars. Lamm says, 'The old Brno was a road circuit 11 km (6.8 miles) long and Gerhard said, "OK, I want to do this race because I have heard such a lot about the circuit." I knew how dangerous it was but Gerhard said, "This is the kind of circuit I like." He really squeezed in qualifying. There was a start-finish straight of about 2 km, then a series of left-right corners through a village taken in fifth gear — top in the 635. Gerhard became convinced he could go through the village flat. First run he tried, not possible.'

Or as Berger says, 'I thought I was finished for sure. I spun for a full 300 m from one end of the village to the other and only hit the armco at the end of it. The damage wasn't so bad, the problem was that the track was so narrow I couldn't turn round. I reversed out of the village until it was wide enough to turn.'

Lamm says on the second run Berger said, 'I can do it, I can do it,' and he did; 'but then he came across Armin Hahne (Rover), our biggest competitor. Arguing and fighting. Gerhard ran into the back of him! He damaged the cooler, came into the pits. We changed the cooler, by this stage not thinking about the grid, so nobody thought of checking the car. It was purely to give Gerhard the pleasure of driving round the circuit. Out he goes, third run. He takes the village flat. He climbs because Brno had a steep hill, then down to a hairpin, after that the long straight to the finish. At the top of the hill he finds he's got a puncture but he keeps on, very dangerous but very brave, very assertive. If he'd gone off . . .'

Berger and Ravaglia ran strongly in the race, third.

At the Canadian Grand Prix he finished thirteenth three laps behind the winner, Alboreto, and was eleventh in Detroit. At the Salzburgring in the Touring Cars, Ravaglia said something very naughty. 'We will make a lot of stops today. We stop for tyres, then for coffee, then maybe some tortellini.' They finished eighth. Berger accelerated at the French Grand Prix, qualifying eighth and getting as high as ninth before colliding with Martini. At Silverstone he qualified mid-grid and finished eighth.

He found he needed to abandon the smooth style he'd used in Formula 3. 'I started in the Arrows like that, smooth. People came and said when they looked at me in the corners I was quick but when they looked at my times I was not. I found it impossible to drive the car smoothly and go fast so I had to change.' At the old Woodcote chicane during qualifying for Silverstone, he approached sideways, controlled that and got through to a great cheer. 'It was very difficult for me, always driving sideways with wheelspin.'

He partnered Ravaglia and Surer in the Spa 24-hours. Thus far 1985 hadn't been happy for the Schnitzer team but, as Lamm says, 'At Spa everything changed and we had a very, very good week. We stayed in a *pension* at Malmedy and Gerhard called it The Hell Hole. The team had one floor, the weather was very hot and there was no air-conditioning, of course. Gerhard said, "Let's take all the doors off, better for breathing and easier for us to communicate with each other." The owners weren't exactly happy. I mean, we'd made the place into a youth hostel.

'We decided to spend as little time as possible in this place — nobody wanted to be in the sticky rooms — so every evening after midnight we'd go to a little place which sold Belgian beer, small glasses of it but cheap, and we'd spend the hours enjoying ourselves, all the team, Gerhard and Ravaglia. A lovely atmosphere.

'Ford were running their Ladies' Cup race and one of the women was Austrian. She asked Gerhard if he could give her some tips about the circuit. He took her round in her Ford Fiesta and said, "This is Eau Rouge, you should be able to take it flat," and she said, "Not possible", and he said, "Let's try it." He did take it through flat then when she went into the Ford Cup practice she tried, missed the line up to La Radillon and had a big shunt . . .'

Berger expressed the opinion that if the BMW lasted they'd surely win, something drivers rarely venture. He, Ravaglia and Surer qualified fourth behind the Rover Vitesse of Walkinshaw/Percy/Heyer, the Rover Vitesse of Joosen/Walkinshaw/Brundle, and the Volvo of Lindstrom/Brancatelli/Sigi Muller. At the start Ravaglia (first stint again!) settled into sixth. When Berger took over, Saward reported in *Autosport* that he 'began what was to be a fabulous stint at the wheel, clocking a lap of 2 minutes 44 seconds, during the course of it going two tenths quicker than the fastest lap of the early stints, set by Ravaglia. "Gerhard always wants to go quicker than we let him," muttered Charley Lamm in the Schnitzer pit. The car, though, seemed quite able to take it and it was no great surprise when the car moved into the lead. Brundle, however, fought back and led once more by the four hour mark.'

At six hours Berger and Ravaglia were in front again although they and Brundle had covered the same number of laps, 127, the rest a lap and more behind. In the night Berger pushed the BMW three laps clear as 12 hours approached, four laps up at 18 hours. With 90 minutes to go and rain threatening, Ravaglia pitted for repairs to a broken propshaft. The repairs took 3 minutes 45 seconds, and Surer got in. A few minutes after that Spa drowned in a rainstorm. Surer spun, caught it and won.

'They could run at such a strong pace,' Lamm says, 'and it was Gerhard's first major Touring Car win. I felt the race changed him because he could say to himself, "I don't just drive in the Touring Cars for the money, I've proved something." A milestone in his career.'

At the Nurburgring for the German Grand Prix Berger qualified down the grid complaining of understeer but finished seventh. Between the Nurburgring and the Osterreichring Winkelhock was killed at Mosport in the Canadian round of the World Sports Car Championship. He 'lost' his Porsche in an adverse camber downhill left, normally taken at near 150 mph (240 km/h) and struck a concrete wall. He died in hospital a day later.

Memory holds him as a chunk of a man with a ready smile, approachable, frequently affable and one of those curious drivers who felt initially no burning fires to conquer the world in this medium. Friends, evidently, persuaded him to have a go and when he reached Formula 1 he liked it. You could ring him on his Stuttgart number — he had a garage where he repaired old three-wheelers — and he'd chat happily about this and that. Like Berger he did not permit Formula 1 to seduce him into becoming what he was not.

Lauda announced his retirement at the Osterreichring and it dominated qualifying, Berger and Boutsen within a fraction of each other but low down the grid. Berger stopped on lap 34, turbo, and Lauda six laps later, turbo. Berger took the car to the end at Zandvoort, ninth.

A week later Stefan Bellof was killed when his Porsche crashed trying to overtake Jacky Ickx at Eau Rouge in the World Sports Car Championship. It came 22 days after Winkelhock. Memory holds Bellof as another good man, still perhaps in the impetuosity of a career, a racer not a pacer, and arguably the greatest unfulfilled talent of the last 15 years in Formula 1.

Quentin Spurring, who covered this sports car season, says, 'We had Monza when in a hurricane trees came down and people were killed in the park. Jonathan Palmer rounded a corner to be confronted by a tree. Then we had Hockenheim, nine fires in the race, Winkelhock killed at Mosport, Spa where Palmer had a bad accident in practice and Bellof was killed, a typhoon at Shah Alam, Malaysia, the whole track flooded with 2 ft of water, we had the Mount Fuji 1,000 km and an earthquake . . .'

Oliver said he expected to keep Berger for 1986 and Boutsen had already re-signed, but reports suggested the Benetton team had secured BMW engines. Peter Collins ran Benetton then. 'I had spoken to Gerhard a few times before and I knew a little about him. He was a mate of Nigel Mansell's. (Collins and Mansell were also mates from Lotus days.) When Gerhard drove in the Austrian Grand Prix in 1984 Nigel gave him a few clues about how to handle turbo power.'

Berger qualified well in the Italian Grand Prix but the gearbox went after 13 laps, qualified well in the Belgian Grand Prix and finished seventh. At Zolder in the Touring Cars, he and Ravaglia finished fourth. Amazingly it seems to have been an uneventful race for them although Walkinshaw crashed heavily at the start. Berger ran to the end of the European Grand Prix at Brands Hatch, tenth, he and Ravaglia ran to the end of the Touring Cars at Estoril, third.

The rumours of a Benetton-BMW engine deal, and that BMW would like to see Berger using it, gathered pace during the South African Grand Prix where in a reduced field — some teams unhappy about going because of apartheid — Berger survived a wild moment when Ghinzani's Toleman (the team Benetton bought and would soon call after themselves) blew up, laying a smokescreen across the track. Berger, blind, somehow got by and despite holding up Prost late in the race finished fifth.

At Adelaide, last race of the season, BMW confirmed they'd supply Benetton. Berger said he'd be happy to stay at Arrows but added that a place with Benetton would be 'nice'. He qualified on the fourth row and moved up to fourth before he pitted for tyres. Towards the end, with no fifth gear and faulty brakes, he held off Johansson for a couple of laps before Johansson dived inside him. Berger, bounding into the corner, went straight on but kept the engine running, reversed and finished sixth.

'Gerhard was a quick driver,' Oliver says, 'and towards the end of the year he began to finish in the points, quite unusual in a mid-field-running team as we were, but he did.'

Boutsen says, 'Gerhard was able to beat me a couple of times in the year which I was upset about, but generally I out-qualified him, 13 times out of 16. Mind you, I'm never happy when someone beats me.'

What should have been easy, smooth and natural — marrying BMW, Berger and Benetton for 1986 — proved to be an authentic Formula 1 saga played out among a variety of vested interests, so vested that it almost didn't happen.

The unfolding saga . . .

Collins: 'I had been watching Gerhard for a fair while and I'd spoken quite a few times. We met in Monza and we met in Australia. I thought he was bloody quick, very brave, good car control, and when I started to get to know him I liked him immediately. We got on because he was very direct. "This is what I want to do." He was very fair. "This is where I want to go." We had a meeting at Adelaide and I said, "As far as we are concerned, we are very happy to have you but obviously we must see what is going to happen." He had support from BMW and they were keen for him to drive for Benetton BMW, but they weren't in a position to specify a driver. They were, however, pushing very hard.

'BMW could have made it a condition of supplying us with their engines but they didn't. I said to Gerhard, "OK, we can't make a commitment at this moment, we have to talk to Benetton and so forth." I discussed it with Rory (Byrne, the designer) and basically we said, yes, we were keen to do a deal but we had to get Benetton's approval.'

Byrne: 'Peter and myself really thought Gerhard was the chap to have. Between us it was 50-50, in other words we both agreed. What attracted me was the fact that he'd done very little Formula 1 and once he'd got over the effects of his road accident in 1984 he was quick straight away. That's always a good sign. The people who really make it in Formula 1, all of them have been quick straight away, Prost, Senna, Schumacher. I didn't know him personally, I'd never spoken to him.'

Collins: 'Then it became rather a political thing because a lot of pressure came from Italy for Eddie Cheever (an American who'd long lived in Rome) or Andrea de Cesaris. We felt neither of those guys was the right person for the team at that stage. We already had Teo Fabi, Italian of course, so we hung out for Gerhard. It got pretty frantic at one stage and Benetton's representatives felt — against me in particular — we were just doing what BMW wanted, which wasn't the fact. We wanted Berger, he was the best prospect on the way up, he'd shown a lot of *bottle*, a lot of bravery, a lot of power and control and he was quick. In 1985 with Arrows he had put in some very good races.

'It reached the point where I received a letter from Benetton saying I didn't have the best interests of the team at heart and I was jeopardizing my position with the team. We had a meeting between Benetton and BMW. A lot of it was really principle, saving face and in the end we won. It was an interesting test for my relationship with Benetton because I'd only been with them for six or seven months and maybe they really did feel I didn't have their interests at heart but looking back it was a useful test of the relationship because after that it flourished with them and BMW and also with Berger. Benetton wanted Gerhard to bring some money — so many dollars, whatever it was — and he'd be able to have some space on the side of the car (to advertise to get the money back). Again it was Benetton not wanting to lose face' — by being seen to pay him fully.

Complex negotiations went on over Christmas and into mid-February.

David Paolini, chairman of Benetton: 'Berger was the first choice, then Warwick, then Cheever, then de Cesaris. In fact the man we really wanted was Thierry Boutsen but he was already committed to Arrows. We decided on Berger a long time ago — there was no disagreement over the choice of driver with BMW, although there were some personality problems between our two companies. BMW had no power to impose a driver of their choice on us.'

End of saga.

Oliver reflects on a driver lost. 'We had a three-year contract with Gerhard, but he had the opportunity to go to Benetton and it was going to be difficult for him to raise further money for us. We had someone else in mind so rather than cause problems we let him go. We'd have liked to have kept him but at that time our programme was driven by funds more than anything. BMW were pushing hard, Benetton were well financed by Flavio Briatore, Benetton were getting BMW engines so we weren't going to fight it.'

Alan Rees reflects on a driver lost. 'A lot of people were looking at him at the end of the year. He gained so much during it. Our year wasn't successful enough, but we had a good atmosphere. Gerhard and Thierry got on well and they both drove well. There was no way we could hold Gerhard because Benetton had done better than we had, BMW were obviously interested in him and Benetton had the BMW engines. We wanted to keep him, no question about that, but from his point of view it was a better proposition and you can't blame him, sure. None the less, we did try pretty hard.'

* * *

Conversational interlude

Hilton: 'It is a most frustrating thing, like a Third Division football manager who's got a terrific player . . .'

Rees: 'I know . . .'

Hilton: ' . . . who wants to go to a bigger club and you say, "Well, you must go there."'

Rees: 'That was always the trouble. Unless you can become one of the top two or three teams you will always have this problem. You find a young driver, he will become a winner and all the top teams wait. The only way you can keep him when they come for him is to be a winning team yourself. Top teams want the best drivers and drivers have to go to the best car, the best engine, the best of everything.'

Hilton: 'Did it ever get depressing that you had Berger and he could have done a lot for the team?'

Rees: 'Yes, in one way, a bit of a wrench but not too much pain because there's always someone else coming along. OK, maybe you lose drivers regularly but you're well aware that if you can make the car really good, get the best situation you could keep those guys.'

Hilton: 'Stretching that, what is the difference because, say, Marlboro McLaren are like Manchester United. For a start they have more money than you.'

Rees: 'It's not money. You need all the other things before you get the money. McLaren are very well organized, they haven't any big names in terms of chief designer and so on, but they have a good team, they do all their research, they do their projects and turn up with a first-rate car. Once you have that you're on your way to the money and at that stage there's no doubt the money helps to buy all the right things, get there a bit quicker than other people. You can't live without money but the other things do come first and of course they hire top drivers like Senna and Gerhard.'

Hilton: 'One thing that strikes me is that drivers often leave teams in acrimonious circumstances.'

Rees: 'Well, people don't leave here in those circumstances and I believe most people don't leave any team in those circumstances, either.'

Hilton: 'Look at Prost at McLaren with Senna.'

Rees: 'Yes, but you are talking about two of the top drivers of all time. Maybe there's a clue in that they are so determined, so competitive, those two guys and if it is not absolutely right for them they are going to fall out with the team.'

Hilton: 'Let me put to you a nasty question. If Gerhard had had that overwhelming desire to do well to the point where he started excluding all the things in his life which might interfere with it — like smiling, joking, shaking hands, chatting, being normal — do you think he might be World Champion by now?'

Rees: 'I think it could only have been an advantage, although maybe a small one.'

Hilton: 'But we are talking about small advantages in this business.'

Rees: 'Yes, and that is what some of them have done. Senna will debrief way into the night if he thinks he can get something out of it.'

Hilton: 'And Prost as well.'

Rees: 'Yes, Prost as well. I think it would be an advantage for Gerhard. He and Senna and Prost are the ones who win virtually all the races but Senna and Prost have won the World Championships so I think in a way your question answers itself.'

Hilton: 'You didn't laugh when I bracketed Berger with Senna and Prost.'

Rees: 'No, because he has that ability, he has determination and you can see that in his whole driving. Many times he's raced Senna, raced with Prost and Mansell. Maybe the problem in effect is his preparation, what I call his slightly laid back attitude. I don't want to make a big point of this. He has a dry personality, a great sense of humour, he enjoys things, enjoys life, enjoys racing, but slightly laid back and I just think that takes the edge off him. There was always laughter, you know, with Gerhard around, leg-pulling but not practical jokes in his year with us. Perhaps he kept that in check because it was his first full year in Formula 1.

'You take a really super driver like Jimmy Clark, everybody who drove with Jimmy disappeared off the scene (except Hill) because you couldn't touch his performances. Gerhard is one of the very few drivers over the years who doesn't seem to be affected in that way. He was team-mate to Senna, Senna was on top all the time but I think Gerhard eliminates that from his thoughts, goes off and does his own thing and does not worry about it. Very few people can do that.'

Hilton: 'You look at Senna's other team-mates, it always ended in tears.'

Rees: 'This is where Gerhard's personality, the fact that he is slightly laid back, might have helped him. The thing about our year with Gerhard that I remember most is that he and Thierry did a good job, they both improved and we had a happy atmosphere. Obviously we had a bit of a problem with Gerhard's feedback because he was so new. Gerhard, I am sure, can do that now no problem but you're talking six or seven seasons on.'

End of conversational interlude

*   *   *

Berger would judge that 'Boutsen was good, one of the quickest drivers in Formula 1. He always drove hard — always the same, free practice, testing, the race, always on the limit. I worked hard to beat him, to be quicker. I drove very hard.' Boutsen would judge that Oliver was 'running his business to survive, but not yet running it to win races. It proved a big problem.'

The year before, Boutsen partnered Surer. 'Marc had a lot of experience and was a good fast racer when it mattered. He was very good at setting up a car as well,' Boutsen says. 'I wouldn't say I learnt a lot from him but we could work perfectly together. That was one of the weak points of Gerhard. With Marc, he could do some development with the car and I could go into something else.

'In the end we put our results together and we had a well settled car. We also had similar driving styles, which made it easier to switch to the other's car. We really could work in the same direction. With Gerhard it was different because he had so little experience. A lot of what he learnt he learnt from me. I think Gerhard put a lot of pressure on me and that's what makes it more interesting although I could resist the pressure pretty well.'

Benetton were born, as I've said, Toleman. Collins initially judged Berger a bit 'ragged' after such a short time in Formula 1, although quickly found him 'a very nice young bloke and he's never really grown out of being that. It's one of his lovable assets: he does love life, that's the great thing.'

Collins's judgement about the raggedness is a forgivable one. We've already heard Berger explain why. Now in the Benetton he worked on the mechanisms of turning back to the smooth European Formula 3 style. 'If you change the car you are driving, sometimes you have to change your style.' He tested the Benetton in Rio in February, Senna quickest, Fabi tenth, Berger slowest: he covered only six laps before changing into first instead of fifth, which blew the engine. 'I wasn't used to the gear change, which does not have a spring on the gate.' Moreover Berger's height made it uncomfortable for him to fit into Fabi's car (Benetton took only one).

'He fitted into the team really well,' Byrne says (no pun intended on the paragraph above!). 'He's a very nice, personable bloke and yes he fitted in super well straight away, really no problem.' Soon enough, you see, he'd be given the initiation and then they'd see what sort of a chap they'd hired.

This initiation, more properly The Dreaded Lung Test was, as Byrne explains, conducted 'with a device invented by one of our fabricators and consisted of a tube but internally split into two tubes. You didn't know these two tubes were in there. The top tube turned the propeller on a canister, a bit like a kid's toy: you blew and the air spun the propeller. On the face of it, you tested your lung capacity by taking as big a breath as possible because the longer you could spin the propeller the greater your lung capacity. The bottom tube went into the canister and the canister was filled with carbon black which is carbon dust, a pigment.

'When you demonstrate the device to the unsuspecting you put your tongue over the bottom tube to cover it so that you're only blowing into the top half and that spins the propeller. Then you give it to someone. They take a big breath and blow down both tubes — which means they are also blowing into the canister and into the carbon dust. The dust is blown into the propeller and the propeller flicks the whole lot back into your face.

'Normally people closed their eyes and gave this thing a hell of a blast, and of course when they opened their eyes they were absolutely covered — pitch black, faces black, the front of the shirts black, everything. We used this to some effect. We caught Flavio Briatore with it, we caught Gerhard, and Gerhard actually caught the BMW engine engineer who wore glasses and took a full go at this. You wouldn't believe how black his glasses went. When he took them off he had two little white rings where his eyes were. We even caught the inventor of the device by reversing the tubes . . .'

It's this sort of thing which establishes an atmosphere within a team and the laughter is precious if only because the rest is so serious.

Berger qualified sixteenth for the Brazilian Grand Prix, the engine down on power, and slogged out a sixth place in the race. 'My happiest memory of the year,' Collins says, 'is Gerhard's point at Rio. The indications were there that he could do things like that but, because we didn't have the entire power of approval from Benetton for having chosen him, the sixth place vindicated us and very quickly.'

Donington in April offered rain, snow and sleet for the second round of the European Touring Car Championship, the first Berger contested this season. He and Ravaglia qualified sixth. Into the race Berger and Jeff Allam (Rover Vitesse) tangled and, *Autosport* reported, 'The BMW gave Allam a hefty bump amidships and the two cars, locked in a metal-bending embrace, cut a near semi-circular path towards the concrete wall by the top of the pit lane. After a short disentangling Allam made for the pits while Berger, always one for a bit of drama, drove off with bits of the BMW falling here, there and everywhere and his front left tyre being shredded by the mangled bodywork. The Austrian pitted next time round for the mechanics to rip the remains of the front spoiler off. For the rest of the afternoon the car looked, but did not behave, like a chinless wonder.' Berger and Ravaglia finished second to the Rover Vitesse of Walkinshaw/Percy but more than a minute behind.

That was not the whole story of Donington. During qualifying Quester completed a lap wearing a monkey mask, causing much laughter when he returned to the pits. The stewards were not amused. Lamm says, 'Quester hoped the stewards would understand the nature of the joke. They brought him up to their office on the first floor and five stewards sat at a long table, Quester in front of them. Quester was questioned. There was a glass door to another office behind the stewards and Gerhard went up there, positioned himself behind it. As Quester explained what he'd done Gerhard made faces at him, arms waving. Quester already faced a heavy fine. Each time the stewards turned, suspecting something was happening behind them, Gerhard ducked away out of sight. The stewards didn't understand why Quester found the matter so funny, which he did and which they didn't.'

In Jerez for the Spanish Grand Prix, Berger was second only to Prost in the Friday untimed session and qualified seventh. In the race he ran to sixth place or as Collins puts it, 'Then, you know, we went to Spain and that was points in successive races.'

Berger reached a Formula 1 podium for the first time at Imola, a curious race even as curious races go, and with much happening in the background as well as the foreground. The rules had cut fuel from 220 litres to 195 and Imola is traditionally thirsty. Others ran dry but Berger, despite driving the last 30 laps without a clutch, had enough left to mount a late charge. As Prost struggled towards the line, draining the last of his fuel, Berger poised himself to go by and unlap himself, realized that if he did he'd have to complete another lap and backed off.

'Ferrari,' Collins says, 'were impressed with the way Gerhard had driven and with the way he backed off. Gerhard was very, very mature for his age and he adapted quickly. He had driven a good race. One of the sticking points with Benetton had been that I wanted Gerhard on a one-year contract with a two-year option, but Benetton said, "No, we only want a one-year contract, we are not happy with your choice." By Imola Benetton started saying, "Ah, now we can discuss it" and the subject of Gerhard bringing some money was forgotten. They wanted to talk about retaining him but by then it was too late, the horse had bolted — Ferrari were interested.'

As Misano in the Touring Cars Berger and Ravaglia qualified third, which prompted Ravaglia to say, 'The team is catastrophic, the car is bad and my co-driver is terrible. I want to change everything!' He and Berger won by four seconds from the Volvo of Cecotto and Anders Olofsson . . .

At Monaco Berger qualified fifth, visibly fearless in Casino Square. He ran sixth, slipped to seventh and retired because a wheel nut broke during his pit stop. At Anderstorp in the Touring Cars the brakes locked on the parade lap, the mechanics cured that but on lap 45 the differential went. At this meeting, as Saward remembers, 'I was following Gerhard and Ravaglia in their hired car and Gerhard threw the ignition key out of the window and everything locked. Astonishing! The car went up an embankment. Not only that but Roberto then had to get out and walk back and try and find the key. (Ravaglia's version of this is given later.)

'Anderstorp was in the middle of nowhere, nothing there. The town had one hotel and all the Swedes went to bed at nine o'clock at night. I was sitting in the restaurant and a green bean landed on my ear thrown by Gerhard who sat in a corner by himself. I went over and said, "What the hell are you doing here?" He said, "I've tried the receptionist three times and she doesn't do it!" In the end he went off to watch Benny Hill in Swedish on television because he was so bored.

'Everybody remembers those days in Touring Cars as if it was a big family travelling round Europe like a bunch of crazy gypsies, a bit like European Formula 3 where Tommy Byrne and Gerhard had been madmen. Mind you, Gerhard and Ravaglia got up to plenty in the Touring Cars. Once they got Dieter Quester's road car on to its side using planks and Dieter went wild. To get even Dieter told the police that the house where Gerhard and Ravaglia were staying had terrorists in it, so when Gerhard opened the door he was surrounded by armed men.

'Dieter got into trouble, too. Once at Donington he did his qualifying lap wearing a monkey mask (see above) and was fined by the stewards. If the telephone in the pits rang he or Gerhard would answer it with a tirade of abuse. But you'd see the other side of Gerhard in, say, qualifying at Spa, amazing to behold the BMW in Eau Rouge. Worrying. He didn't have any fear, you see. I think the first time he felt real fear was after the crash and fire at Imola when he was with Ferrari. I think that did change him.'

By the Belgian Grand Prix at Spa on 25 May Berger had established himself. In context this had happened swiftly: Imola and the podium only his twenty-third race, which is swift enough in Formula 1. Now in Friday qualifying:

1	G. Berger	1: 54.468
2	N. Piquet	1: 54.637
3	A. Prost	1: 55.039
4	N. Mansell	1: 55.345

A misfire prevented him from improving on the Saturday, but the 1:54.468 proved good enough for the front row, the first time he'd been there. Piquet had pole, Prost and Senna on the second row. A savage start: Berger slow away and wheelspinning, he, Prost and Senna surged at the La Source hairpin together, Senna turned in, Berger had to turn in harder and turned into Prost who struck the Benetton. Berger and Prost came round and pitted, Berger emerging two laps adrift and minus the clutch. He flogged on to the end, tenth. Flogged? Yes, because lacking the clutch he daren't risk a stop for tyres in case he stalled.

'I think,' Byrne says, 'that even more impressive than getting a point in Brazil was his third place at Imola. For me, that proved to be one of his best early results. We thought he was pretty good and by the time we reached Spa and he took provisional pole the first day, only slipping to second the next day, we knew it for sure.'

'We went to Spa,' Collins says, 'he took provisional pole and by then he was being hounded by Ron (Dennis of Marlboro McLaren). Ron had been on to him, he'd been across to Ron. You know, once that starts to happen it's difficult to stabilize the driver, little frictions build up and you're never quite the same until it is out of the way. We went through a difficult period, really, from Spa to I'd say around the British and German Grands Prix.'

Before that, at Brno, Ravaglia came upon the spinning Mercedes of Denny Vjotech, a Czech. Ravaglia could do nothing but clout it and he and Berger finished sixth. And the mid-season in the Grands Prix was difficult: a turbo failure in Canada, electrics at Detroit, gearbox in France, but not before an incident. 'At Ricard,' Collins says, 'you noticed first of all the interest being shown in Gerhard, the press going very strong. I did feel at the time the pressure was starting to tell. He was impatient for results, he wanted to run at the front with Prost and Piquet and Mansell and the rest of them, he was frustrated by Christian Danner (Arrows).' Berger and Danner crashed while Berger tried to lap him. 'It was because he so desperately wanted to prove himself, to build his career. He was making some pretty rash decisions.'

He came to Brands Hatch for the British Grand Prix ninth in the table with six points.

Dumfries muses, 'How did I get on with Berger in Formula 1?' — Dumfries with Lotus and in his first season. 'Not bad, but people get much less friendly in Formula 1, Formula 1 is a very unfriendly environment. Certainly you find some hostility in qualifying, things get heated, you have rivalries that go on all the time between certain drivers. If you screw somebody's lap they're going to get you, screw you on one of your quick laps. You know what it's like: everybody's out there on a slow line, heating their tyres, deciding not to go for it on their first lap, they're creeping down the right-hand side of the track. Some people make a big effort to get out of the way and some really don't give a damn.

'Berger did me up once, he did me up like a kipper at Brands Hatch because I'd blocked him some time before. I was going on to the straight at Hawthorns, two or three cars in front of me and I went for the gap. He pulled over into the space intentionally and I really had to take evasive action. At the drivers' briefing the next day he came up to me and said, "I screwed your qualifying lap yesterday, didn't I?" I said, "Yes, you did." He said, "Well, you know why I did it, don't you?" I said, "Yes, I do, it's no problem." So we sorted it out and that was the end of it. Berger is like that.

'I had a thing with Johansson, it got silly, it got out of control, we were really screwing each other up in qualifying and it was probably exacerbated by the fact that I had an accident with him in Canada, but that's part of Formula 1, that's part of the edge Formula 1 has over other formulas, that vindictive side to it. It's an aspect of what makes Formula 1 what it is. It hones everyone, gets everyone hyped up, and they end up becoming much more competitive, wiser. When I reached Formula 1 Berger said to me, "It takes a year to learn this," and it proved good advice. He was right.'

At Brands, Berger qualified fourth, Dumfries tenth. The start was aborted after Laffite (Ligier) crashed but at the restart Berger surged past Mansell (in Piquet's spare car) at Pilgrims Drop and set off after Piquet in the lead. On lap 3 Mansell retook him and — with Piquet and Mansell locked into a gathering assault on the whole circuit and on each other — Berger couldn't stay with them. He held third until lap 23 when the engine failed.

At Hockenheim in the German Grand Prix Berger flew, qualifying fourth, pressing Senna for the lead on lap 1 but lost turbo boost, pitted and finished tenth. This did not prevent him setting fastest lap on 35, 1:46.604 and only two others, Piquet and Mansell, dipped into the 1 minute 47s. 'There was a reason for that fastest lap,' Collins says. 'We'd told BMW the turbo pipe was gong to blow off and they said, "No, no, it won't." It blew off. Gerhard lost two or three laps while it was refitted so it meant he had two or three laps' more fuel than he would have done, and of course we'd fitted fresh tyres. So he went for it and good luck. He was quick . . .'

At Spa he and Ravaglia finished third and the day after he visited the Ferrari factory to have a little talk. In the Hungarian Grand Prix he lay fourteenth after the opening lap, but had worked his way up to fourth when the transmission failed. At the Osterreichring the statistics tell it:

First qualifying:

1	K. Rosberg	1: 23.956
2	A. Prost	1: 24.346
3	N. Piquet	1: 25.090
4	N. Mansell	1: 25.515

5	G. Berger	1: 25.638
6	M. Alboreto	1: 26.152
7	T. Fabi	1: 26.421

Second qualifying:

1	T. Fabi	1: 23.549
2	G. Berger	1: 23.743
3	K. Rosberg	1: 23.903
4	R. Patrese	1: 24.044
5	N. Mansell	1: 24.635

That second session Berger had provisional pole but Fabi took it two minutes later. Berger made a final lunge but a misfire slowed him. 'The car engine combination at that stage in the season was very quick on all high-speed circuits,' Collins says.

The pressure of expectation can be hard to contain, particular if you're on the front row of your own Grand Prix and you've yet to win a race; and this pressure increased because with Gartner dead and Lauda retired, Berger became the lone Austrian in it, moving towards the succession from Rindt. Moreover, the small crowd were mostly Austrian. In years gone by, the Italians flooded over the border to savour their Ferrari (and cause extensive traffic jams to Udine, Venice, Bolzano and all points south after the race), the Czechs and more numerously the Hungarians came from the east in their *put-put-putting* Trabants and Wartburgs and Skodas and, if they were careful (which they were), did the whole trip without spending hard currency except to get in — namely, bring your own beer and sandwiches. This year of 1986 the Ferraris weren't competitive and of course the Eastern Bloc had its own Grand Prix at the Hungaroring.

No particular international hum, more the stolid Austrians camped out up there at the top of the track by the white church, across here on the grassy banks by the start-finish straight going pink in the sun but never dehydrating. Five or six litres of frothy beer prevented that. Not that you need a vast crowd to give the Osterreichring atmosphere because Mother Nature does that, offering smooth hillocks to loop round, loops which descend almost in tiers so that you witness a gallery of action. The loops are fearfully fast, too. Fabi's pole lap represented an average speed of 159.722 mph (256.993 km/h), Berger's front row lap represented 158.722 mph (255.384 km/h). In the era, only Silverstone was quicker, Rosberg lapping it at 160 mph (257 km/h) the year before; and if you think Spa is ultra quick, consider that earlier this season Piquet had taken pole with 135.808 mph (218.515 km/h).

Perhaps in a nationalistic sense it was better to have a crowd that was mostly Austrian. They'd savour fully each moment after the red light blinked to green. Berger, clean, outgunned Fabi up to Hella Licht, the first corner, and the Benettons began to construct a gap from Prost, third. (Collins describes Berger's start as 'fairly blinding'.)

	Berger	Fabi	Prost
Lap 1	1: 37.458	1: 38.152	1: 40.804
Lap 2	1: 32.640	1: 32.312	1: 33.530
Lap 3	1: 32.213	1: 32.595	1: 32.836
Lap 4	1: 32.039	1: 32.654	1: 32.755
Lap 5	1: 32.321	1: 35.288	1: 32.955

Berger and Fabi, then, had driven all five laps decisively quicker than Prost except Fabi's fifth — Fabi had a set-up which meant his car bottomed, and somewhere out there on the sweeps and loops it bottomed so hard once that it flung third gear into neutral. The rev counter went wild and Fabi knew he couldn't go the distance. The question for him became *when* it would happen, not if, but he did what a racer does and raced in the interim.

By lap 12 he'd sliced Berger's four-second lead to two, Prost circulating prudently 10 seconds further back. By lap 17 and in a broad gesture of defiance Fabi hustled all round the back of Berger and approaching the Boschkurve flicked by. It didn't last long. In the Boschkurve Fabi thrust an arm up to indicate *I'm slowing* and Berger pounced, fled through. Fabi's engine had let go.

	Berger	Prost
Lap 18	1: 34.211	1: 34.201
Lap 19	1: 34.511	1: 33.567
Lap 20	1: 34.190	1: 33.550
Lap 21	1: 34.201	1: 38.658
Lap 22	1: 33.553	2: 01.564

That lap 22 came at Prost's pit stop when he'd been stationary for 13.3 seconds, a long time even in the era. Berger did not pit until lap 25 and only then to report a misfire: dead battery. (Collins: 'We'd never had any problems with it previously, never had a failure.') The repairs cost three laps but racers race and although he finished seventh, three laps behind Prost, in a furious final salvo he set fastest lap, 1:29.444. Prost had been nearest on lap 32 with 1:30.751.

A happier postscript to the weekend from Byrne. 'Gerhard knows quite a few of the World Cup skiers and he invited them, Franz Klammer among them. We all had a couple of beers one night and that was good fun, that was a good laugh.'

Rumours, rumours, rumours. Benetton wanted to keep Berger but did Ferrari want him too? Enzo Ferrari declined to comment, which cynics took as a yes. Enzo said he'd reveal all after the Portuguese Grand Prix on 21 September.

At Monza, as Collins remembers vividly, 'Gerhard was on his pole lap and three-quarters of the way round when the engine exploded in the biggest possible way. He had just set the fastest ever speed-trap time on a Formula 1 circuit (214.391 mph/344.955 km/h). He got back to the pits and said, "Sure it would have been but a very quick lap — but an unbelievable sound when the engine went," and he accompanied that with a big smile. Gerhard had an infectious smile, and infectious grin.'

He lined up on the second row and ran third for a tract of the race before engine troubles pressed him back to fifth a lap behind the winner, Piquet. At Nogaro in the Touring Cars he arrived late, unkempt and unshaven, the pressure of Formula 1 consuming his time, ribbed Ravaglia about the way he'd set up the car. ('If you can do better, go ahead,' Ravaglia said. Berger did.) After the normal cut and thrust Ravaglia stroked the BMW home in front of Cecotto's Volvo after Berger had duelled mightily with Walkinshaw's Rover Vitesse.

Portugal and the announcement? Berger qualified on the second row and ran third but went out after a duel with Johansson and a dispute over who owned the first corner, Berger finding Johansson on the outside but holding on down the inside, partly on the grass, and clouting Johansson's *Ferrari*. Johansson, enraged, used his full command of Anglo-Saxon (which is extensive) after the race.

Collins says, 'I'd a notion he'd go to Ferrari by the middle of the season. He played it down a lot, he handled himself well overall and anyway he wasn't necessarily going to Ferrari. I had an idea by Hungary, a pretty good idea by Monza and I knew for sure at Portugal. Gerhard told me. I felt it was a bit early for him, I felt that he didn't really appreciate what he would be walking into. I was a bit worried for him because he was pretty wild, he used to press on. If it went wrong he'd find himself in a difficult environment. We obviously tried to keep him but on the day you have to be realistic about it. Maybe not today but certainly then any driver wanted to drive for Ferrari at some stage and of course John Barnard was going there, all the rest of it. I can't say if he'd have benefited by another year with us but he did suffer initially with Ferrari, I don't think he settled, Barnard wasn't doing particularly well, the car had problems.'

Rory Byrne feels, 'It's very difficult for a driver to turn down a drive at Ferrari, any driver, and that's for sure. Gerhard went for it like he normally does. It was discussed but it's very difficult to discuss something like that when you have a vested interest. I portrayed our side of things and what we were planning to do and let him make up his own mind. I don't believe in trying to twist someone's arm or browbeat them. And what if we'd had a bad second year and he was looking at us as if to say I could have been a Ferrari driver. Difficult.'

The week after Portugal, Enzo Ferrari confirmed at Maranello that Barnard would be joining and Berger, too. Enzo said, 'We regret that we cannot continue our relationship with Stefan Johansson, who is a popular figure with the Italian press, and who is rated to have done a good job for Ferrari this season. It is our opinion that he has not been fast enough in qualifying. He has driven well in the races themselves, but you cannot gain a good result if you start so far back on the grid. Otherwise we have a high regard for him.'

'When you are in Formula 1,' Berger said at the time, 'you have to be lucky and be in the right team. I have been lucky. Benetton gave me the chance to show how quick I could be.' Collins, gazing back, says, 'Our relationship is just the same today, fondly irreverent. He refers to me as an Australian **** and I refer to him as an Austrian ****.'

The week after the Maranello announcement Berger and Ravaglia contested the Touring Cars at Zolder.

* * *

Conversational interlude
Hilton: 'Did it all go to Berger's head?'

Ravaglia: 'For me what I like about Gerhard is that he didn't change as a man, which I think is very important. He got more and more experience, he was famous in Formula 1 but that made no difference. From the beginning we'd had a joke every hour and also some risk jokes.'

Hilton: 'What do you mean by risk jokes?'

Ravaglia: 'Well, we were in Touring Cars in 1986, we had a hire car and I was driving it. We were in a corner and he leant over in the middle of it and took the ignition key out of the car, opened the window and threw it away. The steering wheel locked and we stopped, I swear, 5 cm from a tree.' (Saward, of course, was following.)

Hilton: 'What about some of the other jokes?'

Ravaglia: 'Well, there were so many because together with Stuck and Dieter Quester they were really terrible. I remember one morning I tried to open the bedroom door of my hotel to come out and I couldn't. They had roped the outside handle of my door to the outside handle of the door opposite and I couldn't move it. This is one of the reasons why people like him, because he still does the same things.'

End of conversational interlude

* * *

At Zolder Ravaglia said, 'Do you know a terrorist?' Someone asked why. 'Because I want this place blown up.' Zolder can get you like that, bland nowhere land. Berger had influenza and the Schnitzer team couldn't make the car handle. They qualified twelfth. Lamm says, 'Gerhard was under so much Formula 1 pressure with Benetton but told us, "I'll do this further race because I know Roberto can win the Championship." He told me, "Look Charley, it's most likely this will be the last Touring Car race I'll do for some time, I'll drive the best I can".'

Berger took the spare car and scythed through the field, Ravaglia spun late in the race but they finished second to Cecotto and Lindstrom. Saward remembers the team put up a 'little banner with the legend *Thank you Gerhard* just behind the Villeneuve memorial, because they had the top pit. They were like a family, it was all like a family." Lamm remembers, 'Straight after the race Gerhard had to leave to get back to Formula 1. He took his clothes and went because an aeroplane waited for him.' His destination: Mexico.

Yes, his last Touring Car race. 'At Zolder,' Lamm says, 'it was already clear he had a Ferrari contract, and Ferrari wouldn't allow him to do this any more. However, at one stage Gerhard did say to me, "I'd like to drive for you in the future," and I said, "Gerhard, don't you think you've got other things on your mind?" He said, "Well, you could give me a different helmet and balaclava and I could do a stint at Spa. Nobody would know! It's always good to go to the Belgian Grand Prix if you've done some laps before, which you can't do in Formula 1 (Spa is partly public roads which precludes any Formula 1 testing). I could do a stint for you and it will refresh my memory for the racing lines when the Grand Prix comes along later in the month." Impossible to translate such an idea into reality, but that was the way his mind worked.'

The Formula 1 season moved towards a climax in Mexico. Mansell could become the first Briton since James Hunt to win the World Championship. Whatever people tell you, the main weight and thrust of Formula 1 is British and a concentration of many pressures gathered around Mansell.

No Grand Prix had been run in Mexico City for 16 years and when you got there you saw why — or rather sensed why. I flew in on KLM via Houston and all those who had a choice got off at Houston, leaving about 20 of us for the five-hour slog to Mexico City and when the plan descended to, I suppose, 10,000 ft a pretty hostess drifted by, paused and wondered, 'Can you smell it?' 'Smell what?' 'Mexico City.'

I mention this because the whole weekend was frankly strange, slightly unreal, a dimension away from reality: an earthquake had devastated the city a year before but searching for it you couldn't tell. The whole teeming city seemed locked into decay; and at traffic lights — before the red tuned to green — you could have your car washed by urchins, shop from haggard-looking women who proffered vegetables and light domestic goods or be entertained by fire-eaters who moved between the static columns of cars dressed like the Prince of Darkness.

The time you got to the circuit on the outskirts and heard the cars going round you grasped at the noise as normality. So: we watched Mansell come third in first qualifying — Berger quickest — and third again in second qualifying. The grid: Senna, Piquet, Mansell,Berger.

All unseen at Benetton something significant happened. 'Basically,' Byrne says, 'we were running a different compound of tyre on each corner of the car. We'd gone for a rather unusual solution but Teo Fabi opted for a different one. There was some discussion as to whether we should go for the more conventional solution which would have been a harder compound on the left, a softer compound on the right, but then we decided we'd stick with the combination we had.

'It was different tyres left to right and different front to rear — which means completely different tyres at each corner of the car. I must admit we've only ever ended up being able to balance the car and set the car up on that sort of idea once and that was in Mexico. It has not worked at other circuits at other times — it's difficult to get the tyre pressures correct, all that sort of thing. We took the risk and Gerhard just had to play it by ear, see how it went. Obviously we felt confident tyre-wear wise, we knew we didn't have a problem but we were worried about the consistency.'

At the green light Mansell fluffed the start, couldn't find first gear and they crossed the line to complete lap 1 Piquet, Senna, Berger, Mansell eighteenth. Forgive me for race-reading it from eighteenth. It was why I went, why I was sent, and I didn't think about the fate of Berger at all. So: Berger ran third until lap 7, when Prost went by, just moves in a race, sub-plots because *he* had already thrust himself up to eleventh, angry as a bull and bullish with it, nothing to lose and all to gain. Berger ran fourth from laps 7 to 29 and stayed with Prost. Only once did either gain a whole second on a lap, Prost (1.377) on 20 which, I assume, was traffic. They were lapping cars by then.

On lap 30, when Prost sought fresh tyres, the gap stood at 0.278. As Prost peeled away Berger assumed third place and three laps after that assumed second when Piquet sought fresh tyres. Senna would do the same four laps later. The Benetton — day-glo colouring all over it in fluid flecks, nearly psychedelic, flower-power blended to real power — led Senna, Piquet and Prost. 'Gerhard stayed out,' Byrne says, 'and of course all the Goodyear runners pitted but what's interesting is that they weren't any quicker on their new ones than Gerhard still going round on the old. It proved a remarkably consistent set-up.'

Where was *he*? Eighth, no man's land. The Championship would go to Australia. Nimbly, rationally, carefully Prost took Piquet and when Senna pitted for a second set of tyres ran second. That was lap 46, the gap Berger to Prost 34.267.

'I had a temperature before the race,' Berger says, 'and I took some oxygen just before the start to make me feel better. Once I got into the car I forgot about feeling sick and concentrated on the race, but I had already made up my mind I wasn't going to stop for tyres and break my concentration'

	Berger	Prost	Gap (+ = Berger)
Lap 47	1: 21.392	1: 21.252	-0.140
Lap 48	1: 21.441	1: 21.033	-0.408
Lap 49	1: 21.037	1: 23.210	+2.173
Lap 50	1: 21.315	1: 21.029	-0.286
Lap 51	1: 21.371	1: 22.502	+1.131

Fractions only, but cumulative and at the end of lap 51 — the race over 68 — Berger held a lead of 36.737 seconds. Prost needed to gain around two seconds a lap during the run-in and only three times did he approach that. 'The car suited the circuit very well,' Collins says, 'and on that day went very well. Gerhard drove coolly, did all the right things. He didn't realize that the onboard radio was cutting and shorting which gave us a strange sound in the pits because you'd only hear part of the laps. At one stage he was obviously speaking to himself and it sounded like *dee-dee-dee-dee* which we thought meant he was saying *easy-easy-easy-easy*, but the way it sounded we didn't think he was telling himself to take it easy, he was saying this *is* easy, this *is* a piece of cake. I lost track of where he was on the last lap, I became convinced that he'd stopped, that he was long overdue — so convinced that I just about missed him when he came past. That was my mind working. I panicked — *well overdue* — because you know one way and another we'd had so much crap over the season.'

Gerhard Berger won the Mexican Grand Prix, 12 October 1986, by 25.438 seconds, and it would have been more if he hadn't slowed over the last couple of laps, no danger now, which just goes to show how when you're intoxicated by anxiety and fulfilment so close to hand, like Collins, time (as Einstein proved) is relative to where you happen to be.

They arranged themselves on the podium, Prost with a subdued semi-grin, Berger no smile at all, Senna partially masked by Jean-Marie Balestre of FISA. 'Your first win is always your best, isn't it?' Byrne muses. 'Oh yes, it was tremendous. How did Gerhard take it? He's fairly level-headed, old Gerhard, but it was all . . . fantastic.'

Berger thought it would be a good idea to offer the victory as his leaving present to Benetton, suggesting that they'd have many more, which is the sort of thing he'd say and mean. The following day he phoned from his hotel in Mexico to the Schnitzer team hotel in Jarama to see how Ravaglia had done in the second last round of the Touring Cars (Ravaglia won). The Schnitzer people were deeply touched. He hadn't rung to talk about his own victory, not at all, he was interested in *them*.

Collins says, 'I repeat: my happiest memory is his first point in Rio. I suppose Gerhard would say his happiest memory was Mexico, because, perhaps, he thought he wasn't ready for that. There is a last thing I want to say: we became like brothers, well, not quite that close but our relationship was based on mutual affection, respect and trust. We'd both put our balls on the line pretty well for one another and it worked out.' Question: did you ever pull practical jokes on him? 'No, I don't think I did, but he certainly did on me. I can't remember what they were . . .'

Adelaide, the consummation of other drivers' dreams, went not to Mansell — the immortal tyre burst — but Prost, Berger a bit-player only. He qualified sixth, ran sixth and fell away, clutch; and that was farewell. He felt genuine sadness at leaving, considering Benetton a tight-knit, homely team.

He journeyed to the Great Barrier Reef for a holiday after Adelaide and in time would listen to the words of Niki Lauda who said Alboreto, the resident driver at Ferrari and now Berger's team-mate, will be a hard nut to crack. There would be a lot of hard nuts to crack at Ferrari — hence the anxiety of Collins — but if you're a racer and Enzo Ferrari wants you what else would you do?

Enzo Ferrari knew that. Enzo Ferrari had always known that. It was why the drivers had kept coming and coming, generation after generation of them. The latest did not intend to be overawed. Surely Enzo Ferrari knew that, too.

7

Memories of Monza

To cover *the announcement* at the Maranello Press Conference the week after Portugal more fully, listen to the sonorous voice of Enzo Ferrari saying he had reached an agreement with Berger as early as 4 August. 'Today we are able to confirm our arrangement with Berger because we have found a happy solution to the problem of his commitment to BMW, thanks to the co-operation of the competitions director, Peter Flohr.'

Ferrari also confirmed the team thought they had an agreement with Mansell ('His subsequent behaviour has amazed us and our lawyer will treat the matter in the appropriate manner.') and had spoken to Senna ('He came to Maranello after the Belgian Grand Prix but we did not come to an agreement.')

The arrival of designer John Barnard after his triumphs at Marlboro McLaren was widely heralded as a new dawn after the lean years: a couple of Ferrari wins in 1985 but none this year of 1986 when Ferrari finished fourth in the Constructors' Championship behind Williams, McLaren and Lotus, their lowest since 1981. Moreover they scored only eight more points than Ligier.

Berger confirmed, 'The decisive meeting took place in August, right after the Spa 24-hours. We reached an agreement and from that day everything was set for Ferrari, but I had to get a release from BMW. This happened by Estoril.' Berger consulted many friends before he signed, among them Pino Trivellato — Italian of course — asking him for his 'impressions' of the team.

In November Enzo Ferrari presented Berger and Barnard to the press and said, 'Berger's first tests for us have confirmed what I thought originally. He is fast, determined and very quick to learn. I have great faith in him.' A couple of days before, and in only his second drive of a Ferrari, Berger had lapped the test track at Fiorano in 1 minute 6.62 seconds, fastest time of the year. (Without belittling the achievement, new Ferrari drivers traditionally either did that or broke the Fiorano record. Why? Something to do with the cars getting faster every year, something to do with vindicating Enzo, and something to do with trying to frighten the opposition.)

Berger commented, 'It's difficult to say much at this stage. The engine feels to have about the same power as the BMW, but with six cylinders it has a wider power band. The chassis has a bit of understeer but the most noticeable change after the Benetton is the cockpit, which seems huge and is very comfortable.' He added that he'd continue to live in Austria and estimated that he'd cover the 250 miles (400 km) between there and Maranello in three and a half hours. Hmm.

Autosport caught the mood when it reported that 'all Maranello continues to rave about their new signing, Gerhard Berger, whose initial spell at Fiorano produced the fastest lap of the year'. Mind you, a handful of days later and in damp conditions Berger crashed testing a new 90° V6 turbo, although the damage proved so light he continued later in the day after repairs (to the car).

Alboreto, his new partner, says something familiar. 'I didn't know Gerhard before he came. I'd met him of course, because he drove for Benetton, but I didn't have a close relationship with him before. It was a new time for Ferrari with a new designer, in a sense a completely fresh team and in the beginning a little bit difficult. The car was very bad and then after a few months' work we began to find the solutions. I got on very well with Gerhard, a very funny guy.' (Berger says that Alboreto can be difficult, but we'll come to that.)

John Barnard says, 'I didn't know Gerhard and I was even a little bit doubtful because, you know, you watch these young drivers and draw conclusions. I'd seen him at Benetton and I thought, well, a little bit wild, a bit up and down. He was much more of the gung-ho lad then, hang it on the edge no problem, but the ability to dissect a car and extract its problems in detail just wasn't there. And going into Ferrari is a situation where you have to have your head on straight if you're to last, so I was a little bit nervous about Gerhard; and of course he was in with Alboreto, who had years of experience and was a political animal. He used and manipulated the Ferrari system to a large extent, which was an added problem.

'There is no question of it: mutual dislike between Alboreto and myself. I want to be a bit careful about what I say but someone did approach me specifically to help a person, but, you know, this was the way Ferrari was then. Anyway, Gerhard is coming into this lot.

'I really do try and split myself between the two drivers, as I did at Ferrari in 1987. I am in charge, I cannot be seen to favour one driver or the other but the business of working with a driver from a technical point of view requires a close liaison. Effectively you need to know how his mind works before you can really extract all the information and understand what he is telling you. You need to get to the point where you have established a mental link, a mental relationship. There can be a language barrier (Barnard British, Berger Austrian, Alboreto Italian) and one driver may express a problem in a different way to another while in fact it is the same problem. You need to know what they mean when they express these problems.

'It is a fact that you find a natural affinity with some people and other people you don't. In that situation when you get a guy who is prepared to sit and talk hour after hour about what he thinks of the car — what he thinks if you did this, if you did that — you naturally gravitate to that person because you feel you are getting more back. This is what really happened at the first year at Ferrari with Gerhard and of course once you have built the relationship it carries on.

'A designer knows how long it takes to produce a new car but no driver has time! All they have is the next race and it is very difficult. One thing I have learnt is that it takes a number of years to make a top line Grand Prix driver unless you are Ayrton Senna, and even then if you go back to the early stages of his Formula 1 career, boy, didn't he make some goolies! There is almost no case where you can say a driver came straight in and was super from the word go. Prost made mistakes. Prost is The Professor now, but then (the early 1980s) you'd think, that was a stupid move he made although he was unbelievably quick.

'The ability is this: one half of the mind is thinking about what the car is doing while the other half drives and races it. The real key to the top guys is that they can split their attention, whereas the ones that are not the top guys, and will never be the top guys, are using 80 per cent of their minds just driving it quickly.'

In March, Ferrari unveiled their challenger for 1987, the F187, and tested it at Imola where 5,000 *tifosi* (outright Ferrari fans) came to watch and cheered every time they glimpsed Berger. 'It's just more pressure,' he said. 'I don't really care about the pressure, but if I don't deliver they will all think I am slow. Things change quickly in Italy. I am more recognized in Italy now than I am in Austria. It's a lot but that's part of the Ferrari magic.' Later he crashed heavily at 130 mph (210 km/h) at Ravazza when the rear brakes gave problems, but didn't hurt himself.

In testing at Rio two weeks before the start of the season he went tenth quickest but felt unwell and (paradoxically in view of what he'd said before) couldn't get comfortable in the cockpit. At the Brazilian Grand Prix itself he qualified seventh, had a fuel injection misfire in the Sunday morning warm-up and moved to the spare car, but fourth gear kept jumping out. He slogged to fourth place 1 minute 39.235 seconds behind the winner, Prost, so exhausted he could barely lever himself from the car. When he did he tottered away in a daze.

At Imola he qualified fifth and ran fifth until the turbo went after 16 laps, but something delightful happened at the Autodrome Enzo e Dino Ferrari. According to Dieter Stappert, Hans Berger espied Jackie Oliver walking along about 50 m away and 'shouted at him "Ferrari! Ferrari!"' You remember how at the fondue party two years before when the subject of money came up Oliver explained that if Gerhard did well a big team might pick him up, and plucked the name Ferrari from the air to illustrate that. 'In fact,' Oliver says, 'for a long time after Gerhard did join them, whenever his father came to a race he'd say to me "Ferrari! Ferrari!" as if I'd known all along.'

Already rumours circulated about how unhappy Alboreto was and that he might well leave the team at the end of the season for Williams, although reflecting he says, 'Gerhard was always very happy, very easy to find in a good mood. That was helpful for the team, especially in the beginning when our results were not very good.'

Spa might have been the breakthrough. First qualifying:

G. Berger	2: 6.216 (122.998 mph/197.946 km/h)
N. Mansell	2: 6.965 (122.273 mph/196.779 km/h)
M. Alboreto	2: 7.459 (121.799 mph/196.016 km/h)
N. Piquet	2: 8.143 (121.149 mph/194.970 km/h)

Berger dropped to fourth on the Saturday and spun coming out of the bus stop (the entirely artificial left-wham-right contortion before the start-finish line) on lap 2 of the race. Boutsen couldn't avoid him. The race was stopped — Palmer couldn't avoid Philippe Streiff who'd crashed — and two laps into the restart Berger's engine blew.

'When he was with us at Benetton,' Collins says, 'always before every race I'd sit on the grid and talk to him. Keep off the kerbs, keep away from the maniacs and all this sort of thing. Drive cleanly. Sometimes during qualifying or even an untimed session and he was coming up to making his run I'd say don't drive over the top, you're pushing too hard. After eight or 10 races it became something of a joke. "I know, I know, don't use the kerbs, keep away from the maniacs," he'd say. We'd have a laugh, but I still tried to get the message across.

'Up to Spa he'd had a terrible time at Ferrari, a lot of problems. I saw him in the paddock and he said, "Last year you told me slow down, slow down, be careful. I used to think — well, I used to laugh at you. Now all they say to me is you must go faster." That's the sort of mental pressure you get at Ferrari and it was difficult for a young man to handle.'

At Monaco he crashed by the swimming pool in first qualifying, was eighth in the second and again slogged the race out to finish fourth a lap behind the winner, Senna. At Detroit, Ferrari announced they'd re-signed Alboreto for 1988 and taken up their option on Berger for 1988. Alboreto said, 'Mr Ferrari asked me to stay in the team so I decided to. I have a good relationship with Frank Williams but at this moment the conditions are not right to change.' In the race Berger finished fourth yet again, but this time he wasn't lapped.

During the French Grand Prix at Paul Ricard, and from the third row of the grid, he virtually stalled at the green, waving his arms to warn the cars coming up. Alboreto, immediately behind, flicked to the right, Warwick flicked to the right, Patrese to the left, Cheever to the right, but by then Berger was moving. As the front runners jostled towards turn one, the sharp right, Berger jostled amidst those at the back. When the field sorted itself out only three cars lay behind him.

Cheekily, at the approach to the right-hander, he went wide on the outside taking one car, and completed the opening lap nineteenth. On lap 2 he took Danner (Zakspeed), Capelli (March) and Ghinzani (Ligier) and, with Johansson in the pits for repairs, he'd risen to fifteenth — fourteenth when the engine of de Cesaris (Brabham) caught fire. He took Satoru Nakajima (Lotus) and that was thirteenth, took Brundle a lap later and that was twelfth.

He ran smoothly to lap 12 when he took Alessandro Nannini (Minardi). Eleventh. Patrese pitted four laps later. Tenth. Immediately he took Warwick (Arrows). Ninth. He chased, caught and took Arnoux (Ligier). Eighth. Nine laps later Alboreto pitted. Seventh. The electrics on Boutsen's Benetton failed and Berger — in the space of only 32 laps — had carved a path to the points. Fabi (Benetton) pitted a couple of laps later. Fifth. Berger pitted himself, was stationary for 7.42 seconds, then came back out sixth, Alboreto up ahead. He took him three laps after the pit stop. Fifth.

Berger moved politely aside so that the leaders, Mansell and Piquet, could lap him and the two Williams pulled instantly away, demonstrating the power that the Ferrari didn't have. Berger pitted again to change the spark box and three laps later he spun off, suspension.

I've set out this race because within it you have the gathering maturity of Berger in no more than his third full season. This is a comparatively short span in a Formula 1 career, particular since he'd been constantly adjusting to the demands and nuances of different cars, ATS, Arrows, Benetton, Ferrari. The charge from nineteenth was handled securely, no histrionics, exactly as mature drivers do handle these things. Perhaps this race established him. Enzo Ferrari always liked racers and part of that is the charging.

Berger spun out at Silverstone, crashed heavily in qualifying at Hockenheim and dragged himself up to sixth in the race before the turbo went. Just when the season seemed to be drifting he produced a storming lap of the Hungaroring, quickest of all in the second session and only Mansell's time from the day before prevented him taking pole. Moreover he had an upset stomach. 'I feel much better than I did earlier in the week,' he said. 'My main problem is that I'm weak. I get tired quickly. The car feels good here, really good. What we don't understand is that everyone else said the track was slower than yesterday but it seemed to me there was a lot more grip.'

Before the race he sat on the grass, his back resting against the armco, holding a parasol in his left hand while a pretty Marlboro employee (a nurse?!) checked him (his pulse?!). He did look weary, slack, almost listless.

Mansell made an enormous start, a great gush of raw power leaving swathes of burnt rubber to mark it. Piquet, in line on the grid behind Mansell, gripped the inside and reached turn one before Berger, but Berger took a slingshot around the outside. Second. In the twist and snap under the bridge after turn one, a sharp little dip towards turn two, Berger settled behind Mansell and stayed there. At moments out around the twisting back of the circuit he crowded Mansell who needed a full 10 laps to pull away from him. Berger was proving something: if the car could deliver, he'd deliver. At lap 13 the gap stood at no more than 3.9 seconds and Mansell had the Williams, the car of the year. It ended that lap, Berger pulling the Ferrari off beside the pit lane wall, the differential gone.

In Austria he qualified third but it was a chaotic start, cars crashing everywhere. Berger had made a slow getaway, Fabi ducking inside him. At the restart Mansell limped forward and, as Berger drew abreast, Fabi tried to duck between them, couldn't, braked hard and then . . . cars crashed everywhere. At the re-restart Mansell crawled forward again and Berger went by, Boutsen surging between them. Threading out into the loops and sweeps Berger held third but Mansell, recovering strongly, prepared to attack. Boutsen squeezed the leader, Piquet. On the rise at the end of the pit lane straight, going into lap 4, Mansell powered by. A couple of laps later Berger's turbo failed and he parked on the grass, got out, shook his head in a gesture of great resignation, and walked away.

'I must admit,' Berger says, 'that in mid-season, if I'm honest, there were times when things were not good at all. The politics is something strange, sometimes too much, but anyway I enjoy a bit of politics. Drivers are different, some just turn up and drive, some like to know what is going on around them. I always keep my eyes and ears open for the politics.'

At the start at Monza Piquet got away comparatively slowly, Mansell moving hard, Berger trying to nose between them. Piquet pulled ahead, Mansell slotting in behind for the first chicane, Berger slotting in behind Mansell. Crossing the line to complete lap 1 Piquet had eased away from Mansell who had eased away from Berger. Almost magically Berger drew full up to Mansell while simultaneously Boutsen crowded Berger. At the second chicane Berger made a heavy thrust on the outside but was never alongside and Mansell fended him off. The impetus proved so strong that Mansell slewed into the chicane, ran over the inner kerbing and — moving out of the chicane — Berger punted Mansell's left rear wheel with his right front. The Ferrari made a little hop, was pitched on to the outer kerbing, and that let Boutsen through into second place.

Berger immediately took Mansell. At the Parabolica Mansell tried a move on the inside but Berger baulked that. Out of the Parabolica Mansell maximized the power from the Williams and as they drew level with the pits had drawn up behind him. Mansell jinked left, kept the power on and jinked back on to the racing line for the chicane.

Mansell moved past Boutsen and Berger moved on Boutsen, and a race within a race developed after the tyre stops, Berger emerging from the pit lane first, Boutsen hounding him, and side by side they rushed the first chicane. Boutsen reached it in the 'lead' but thumped the inner kerbing and it pressed him wide on the exit, leaving a gap which Berger turned into. Boutsen covered that by coming back across. At the second chicane on lap 34 Berger nipped through and pulled away. He ran there — fourth — to the end, 59.979 seconds behind the winner, Piquet.

Clues, suggestions, hints, moments, moments, moments, all suggesting that Ferrari had a gathering impetus, and a question became more and more insistent. When will it come right? Today? More clues at Estoril, although you had to search for them among the statistics. Berger ended first qualifying no higher than fifth, but at the timing point recording maximum speeds was quickest, 204.973 mph (329.802 km/h) against Mansell's 204.349 mph (328.798 km/h). The timing point at the finishing line made Berger quickest, too: 197.261 mph (317.393 km/h) against Mansell's 197.029 mph (317.020 km/h).

A red hot lap is getting speed constantly so that maximums at check-out points are impressive but not conclusive. A driver with a taut, snappy, meaty car through the corners can make it all up and more, and if he's also fast in the check-outs . . .

A single lap at the edge is an art form, a communion of a dozen

random factors, some human, most mechanical, tyres, temperature, surface, the state of your car, what you've learnt it can do
from previous laps, what you judge you can make it do, where
other cars are on their laps, who is driving those cars, what they
might do to you. Pole can be decided by thousandths of a second,
an Einstein (well, Einsteinian) concept of time and as hard to com-
prehend as his Theory of Relativity. (This is why I've included, and
will include, so many comments Berger made about his qualifying
laps, to show when and how he got the thousandths and how and
when he lost them.)

And while you're finding more and more speed the others may
well be, either from the machinery or themselves. Thus on the Saturday these timing points recorded Berger as third quickest
behind, in both cases, Senna and Alboreto. Rain had fallen after 25
minutes so it depended when you'd gone out. Before this, Berger
did his flying lap, his eighth, incidentally, and on his second run.

'One corner was getting wet,' he said. 'Actually my fastest lap
should have been the one before when it was completely dry, but I
made a mistake, got sideways and lost time. The first lap on new
tyres is always the best for grip so they weren't so good after that.
Also fourth gear was jumping out and I had to drive the first corner
with one hand holding the lever. It wasn't too much of a problem
but it wasn't perfect either, you know.' One minute 17.620 seconds,
and the only lap to beat Mansell's Friday time of 1:17.951. It gave
Berger the first pole of his career in his forty-eighth Grand Prix,
and Ferrari their first since Alboreto in Brazil in 1985, 43 races
before.

What should have been easy, smooth and natural — marrying
Ferrari, Berger and the circuit of Estoril — proved to be an authentic Formula 1 saga, played out among a variety of vested interests,
so vested that it did happen but in the wrong way.

Mansell thundered the start, Berger churning wheelspin. Cars
behind darted like nervous fish but at turn one Mansell led, Berger
second. Piquet and Alboreto jostled, Warwick spun and several
cars met in a mêlée of a crash. Frighteningly the race was not
stopped until the leaders had come all the way round and threaded
through. Before they reached it Berger took Mansell, clean and
swift.

At the restart Mansell thundered again, Berger pitching the Ferrari to mid-track muscling Piquet half on to the grass, and they
moved into turn one Mansell, Berger, Senna, Piquet. Mansell held
Berger until just after the line starting lap 2 when Berger swept by,
a genuinely imperious sight. Berger stretched a gap corner after
corner, the Ferrari taut, snappy, meaty, and by lap 5 that gap had
become 2.8 seconds. The race settled. Mansell set fastest lap on 12,
clawing back some of the gap, now 4 seconds. Deceptive. Mansell

dropped out, electrics, and by lap 21 Berger led Piquet by 9.5 seconds.

Berger struck fastest lap himself and Alboreto took Piquet, Ferrari one and two. Berger's pit stop lasted 8.3 seconds, giving the lead temporarily to Alboreto, who lost it when he pitted. In fact Alboreto lost four places and Prost took Fabi and ran second. At lap 39 the gap Berger to Prost stood at 16.358 seconds, 31 laps to go. Prost began the hunt and set fastest lap on 53, cranked his speed up and up and the gap tumbled.

Lap 53	8.126
Lap 54	6.376
Lap 55	5.171
Lap 56	5.731
Lap 57	5.270
Lap 58	5.471
Lap 59	4.341
Lap 60	3.937

On lap 64 Prost set fastest lap again, the gap down to 2.776. Berger responded with his fasted lap, 1:19.668 against Prost's 1:19.591, but crossing the line to complete lap 67 the gap stood at 2.402. Berger spun, the Ferrari *facing* Prost as the Frenchman went by. Berger rotated the Ferrari and set off again, the race lost.

Berger: 'I had a sixth gear which was too short, a mistake. As the fuel load lightened I picked up speed on the straights and hit the rev limiter more and more. Towards the end I was on the limit for maybe three-quarters of the straight, *pah-pah-pah*.

'About 30 laps from the end I thought, perfect, Prost cannot catch me, but I came up to lap Johansson and he made his car very big. On the straight I couldn't get by because I was on the limiter and in the corners he wouldn't let me pass. I lost some important seconds and then Alain was getting closer and closer and I had to drive on the limit. You may say why not wait until the last lap and make your car big? The problem was that if Alain got into my slipstream at the end he could hit the boost and pass me on the straight.

'I could hit the boost, too, but then I would only get the limiter so I said to myself, right, I have to start the last lap without him in my slipstream. This is what I did and I went too hard and I spun. I was tired and they showed me a board saying how many laps were left. And I knew I had to fight for my contract for next year — how could I get good money if I gave in? So I fought to the last lap like crazy. Stupid that money should figure in thinking like that but it does.'

Prost in his autobiography *Life in the Fast Lane*: 'The chase was on as of the thirty-first lap, and, believe me, it was quite a chase. Berger was some 15 seconds up on me but I was convinced he would be easy meat. I couldn't have been more wrong. I piled on everything I could, driving one fastest lap after another, sliding, opposite locking, and turning up to full boost. What did I have to lose?

'Quite frankly I don't think I have ever driven a Formula 1 race like it. Berger held on. My brakes were beginning to overheat and above all the McLaren's tyres were taking a terrible beating. I told myself the same things must be happening to Berger's Ferrari. I had just corrected the start of a slide when I looked up to see that I was only 3 seconds behind him. At that moment there was a little puff of dust up ahead. Berger had spun off.'

End of saga.

Prost's victory took him past Jackie Stewart's total of 27 while a storm broke all over Italy about Berger's spin. That night Quentin Spurring of *Autosport* 'went back to my hotel where I'd arranged to meet somebody. I was having a beer. Gerhard walked in looking, I assumed, for people he was to meet. I said, "Hard luck, just one of those things." My people arrived and we went to a restaurant and Gerhard was in it with his people. After the meal I was walking back to the hotel and there was Gerhard leaning up against a lamp-post with a girl . . .'

Work hard, play hard, see life in its true perspective.

In Spain he qualified third, set fastest lap and ran fourth early on, ultimately halted when the engine let go. In Mexico he was quickest on the first day, just eclipsed by Mansell on the second, led the opening lap of the race, ran second to Boutsen to lap 15 when he regained the lead and the turbo failed.

'It could all have been quite bad,' Barnard says. 'What really saved it was that we had wins at the end of the season and we were able to go into the winter like that. We started being competitive, the result of doing all the work through the first half of the year. If we hadn't, the winter would have been even more difficult.'

It did come right at Suzuka, a weekend initially overshadowed by Mansell's crash in first qualifying which took him to hospital and the Championship to Piquet. Berger had pole with a lap which, he confessed, had been less than perfect. 'Fabi held me up a little, going very slowly. He kept out of the way but you never really know in these circumstances and I lifted a fraction. Then on a sixth gear corner later in the lap I put two wheels on the grass. It was a hard moment and I lifted and the car came back on to the track. A perfect lap, I think would have been 1 minute 39.8 seconds, but I'm quite happy.' He'd done 1:40.042 with Prost, Boutsen and Alboreto also in the 1 minutes 40s. 'It's kind of funny,' Berger added, 'that Honda should dominate this year with Williams (and Lotus) and then come to Japan and qualify fifth (Piquet 1:41.144).

Berger seized the lead at the green light and Prost briefly harried before he realized a rear tyre had a slow puncture. Berger put the hammer down and led Boutsen by six seconds after a couple of laps. After the pit stops Berger led from Johansson. 'I'd had a big lead before the stops and afterwards I went a little bit asleep. Suddenly I saw Stefan in my mirrors and the next thing he was nearly under my wing. Then I really had to push again.'

Lap 29	1:49.496
Lap 30	1:48.459
Lap 31	1:47.013
Lap 32	1:46.526
Lap 33	1:46.020
Lap 34	1:45.540

Johansson found himself hampered by using too much fuel and on the last lap Senna moved past him. Berger won it from Senna by 17.384 seconds. 'It's sometimes easier to win than to finish sixth. I had no real pressure — certainly less than in Portugal, although I'm particularly pleased I made up for the mistake there. Alain had his puncture right at the start and of course Nigel wasn't in the race at all. I was lucky, really.'

Lucky? Maybe, but he'd been growing in stature as the Ferrari had grown in potential. You need only glance at the lap times above to see how he could harness the car and make a decisive move to break Johansson. He also covered the final 10 laps by slacking off to 1 minute 48 seconds with a couple at 1:50 and a single lap at 1:51. That is not only controlling yourself and a racing car, it is also controlling a race.

He blitzed Adelaide, fastest in first qualifying which stayed pole. Nigel Roebuck caught that lap perceptively. 'No one could get close to the Ferrari. It was a typical Berger hot lap, all tiptoe stuff, using the kerbs, pitching into the corners. And he also said he was left-foot breaking. It wasn't flowing in the Prost style but mighty effective.'

Berger laid heavy rubber at the green but Piquet, to his left, drew level and Berger twitched towards him. Their rear tyres kissed — a fleeting kiss, not strong enough to disturb the balance of either car. Piquet reached the left-right at the end of the start-finish straight first, Berger behind, Prost eager behind him. Berger responded at the next corner, a 90° right-hander, pumping inside Piquet, running wide so that for an instant Piquet might have had a gap, but Berger was on the power very, very quickly, pitching the Ferrari to mid-track — the perfect placing for the corner after that, a hard left. That let Berger take command. Tiptoe? He danced the Ferrari round Adelaide.

Late on Senna attacked — 'I gave it everything,' he'd say, adding that his tyres were finished — and Berger made the Ferrari dance a little more deftly, a quickstep. He went into the final lap with a lead of 27.880 seconds. As he crossed the line he permitted himself a short, sharp wave of the right hand. No Ferrari driver had won back to back Grands Prix since Gilles Villeneuve in 1981. 'It was good to go on to Australia and prove that Japan was not a lucky win.'

Barnard says, 'The fact was, the wheels were changing for 1988. There was the business of will we run turbo engines, will we run normally aspirated engines? (The following year turbos would be banned.) Ferrari did some work on the turbo so we could run it for 1988 and in typical Ferrari style went off winter testing with effectively too much boost in the engine saying, "We will put up the boost because we know we are going to get *this* much from the engine when we do our new cylinder head *dee-dar-dee-dar*." You've heard it all before. So they go off and have a wonderful winter testing, quick everywhere, magic. Of course the expected step forward never comes. When the racing starts you step back to reality. That unfortunately was Ferrari in those days, but at least it had the advantage of carrying people through the winter feeling that they were doing OK. I think that helped Gerhard get through the winter, too.'

The dominant theme of 1988 would be revealed deep into the Brazilian Grand Prix, Rio, 3 April. Prost led in the Marlboro McLaren Honda, Berger second. On lap 42 Berger made a second stop for tyres and launched an assault, setting fastest lap of the race. 'It seemed as though Alain must have a problem so I began to push . . .'

	Prost	Berger
Lap 47	1: 37.029	1: 33.244
Lap 48	1: 36.917	1: 33.028
Lap 49	1: 35.758	1: 33.575
Lap 50	1: 35.893	1: 33.402
Lap 51	1: 35.064	1: 35.462

On lap 52 Berger dipped into 1:32.957, Prost 1:35.526, the gap sliced to 15.635, and soon enough to 10.538. Prost in trouble? Berger should have known better, as he admitted. 'Sure I got the gap down a lot but he opened it out again. I thought his tyres might be finished' — Prost made only one stop — 'but of course they weren't. He was just being careful with the fuel. Nothing I could do.'

	Prost	Berger
Lap 55	1: 33.720	1: 34.427
Lap 56	1: 33.865	1: 34.006
Lap 57	1: 33.540	1: 34.661

Prost was asked if he'd been worried about fuel. Yes, he said, and added that of course Berger would have to be worried about that, too, 'so I didn't worry too much. The car felt very comfortable and I was not even concerned when Gerhard started to attack. I knew I had something in hand to respond if necessary. You can see already that the season is going to be good for us.' *That* was the dominant theme of 1988, particularly since Senna had now departed Lotus for McLaren. Between them Prost and Senna gripped the season so hard they choked everyone else.

All you could do was keep on and hope, and in the matter of perseverance Berger earned profound admiration. At Imola he spun several times in qualifying searching for the right balance for the Ferrari, although 'you can change springs and bars but that won't give you 50 extra horsepower'. In the race he finished fifth, a lap down on Senna and Prost.

Monaco demonstrated perseverance, too. He out-dragged Prost at the start. Senna led and moved clear and by lap 23 had constructed a lead approaching 25 seconds, Prost still held behind Berger. Prost put whatever pressure on he could, which is what you do — and often all you can do — at Monaco. What you don't do is get desperate. Even the traffic didn't open up chances for Prost, Berger dealt with it crisply. Prost feinted a time or two at Ste Devote, feinted a time or two out of Casino Square, but Berger stayed on the racing line, plump, precise and persistent.

'I knew I could go much quicker than Berger if I could get by,' Prost said, 'but he was driving really well, not making mistakes or leaving gaps.' Rounding the Rascasse corner Prost came close, was closer *earlier* on the pit lane straight and reached Ste Devote first. Senna lost concentration just before the tunnel on lap 67 and thumped the armco, leaving Prost a clear run, Berger second at 20.453 seconds.

The theme of a season: a lonely third in Mexico and many fissures split Ferrari with reportedly factions emerging. Piero Lardi-Ferrari (Enzo's illegitimate son and for a long time the Prodigal Son) departed and insinuations insisted Alboreto would not be re-hired for 1989.

The theme of a season: Berger held third in Canada but 'it was hopeless. We ran as lean as possible with as little wing as we dared and still the consumption was too high. I backed off, saw the gauge still on the wrong side and backed off some more . . . then some more. It's not a way I like to go racing.' The ignition failed on lap 23.

The theme of a season: in Detroit he shared the front row with Senna and spoke about Ferrari politics. 'Of course it's not good for the team but it will change soon.' For the better? (Smile.) 'I don't know . . .'

He had a puncture on lap 7. At Paul Ricard he finished fourth a lap behind Prost and Senna. Immediately after Ricard, Mansell confirmed he'd be joining Ferrari in 1989 and added, 'I'm looking forward to working with Gerhard. We have always got on extremely well.'

Silverstone? A paradox, Alboreto taking provisional pole from Berger in the first session, Berger reversing that in the second with a thunderclap 1 minute 10.133 (152.402 mph, 245.215 km/h). The McLarens lurked on the second row, neither Senna nor Prost unduly concerned. They knew the Ferrari was too thirsty on fuel to challenge them across the 65 laps. A wet race might alter that and it rained hard. Berger took Copse comfortably in the lead but Senna swung past Alboreto and at Stowe, a rolling ball of mist and spray behind them, Senna tried to get inside. Berger blocked that and eased away.

'At the speed Gerhard was going,' Senna said, 'I knew that if I kept with him I couldn't make the finish on fuel. I was pretty sure he couldn't either.' On lap 14, approaching the *Daily Express* bridge, Senna pulled out and powered by. At that instant Senna nearly brushed against Prost, hobbled by handling problems.

'By half distance I was already the wrong side with fuel and as the race went on all I could do was reduce the boost, reduce the revs, forget about racing,' Berger said. 'When I was still second at half-way I didn't know what had happened to everyone else. The way I had to drive I could have taken my family along and gone on holiday. I still ran out of fuel at the last corner.'

Hockenheim? Berger did something completely amazing in qualifying which doesn't exactly fit into the theme of this or any other season. He spun at 200 mph (320 km/h) in the final session. 'I did a completely stupid thing. Eddie Cheever came up to me afterwards and said sorry. I told him to forget it — it wasn't his fault. Two laps earlier I'd got a good tow from Arnoux but he stayed in the middle of the road and Hockenheim is actually not that wide in the straights. I couldn't get by but I was running flat and I wanted to finish the lap so I decided, OK I'll overtake him on the grass. That at 12,000 revs in sixth. I put two wheels on the grass with the other two still on the track. The car twitched a little bit but came back so I thought, perfect. I wondered why I didn't do it more often. (!) Then I came into the same situation with Cheever and Ghinzani, two cars, the road completely closed, right? I thought, no problem I'll overtake them on the grass. I did the same again, but the difference was four wheels on the grass this time. There was a small bump in the grass and the car jumped and . . . well, it was stupid!'

At the post-qualifying press conference he was asked about the race. An ordinary question and one you'd expect to draw a vague, quasi-optimistic response. He eyes refracted hard as he explained that he had no chance and no point in anybody deluding themselves. It created a hush in the normally bustling press room, and not just because it represented the truth but because he had insisted on speaking it. He ran third to the end, 52.095 seconds behind Senna and almost 40 behind Prost. And that was the truth.

Hungary? Fuel again: fourth, watching the gauge the whole way.

A week later Enzo Ferrari died.

'I was very close to the Ferrari family,' Alboreto says. 'From March, Mr Ferrari started to be a little bit worse than normal. (He was 90 and suffering from a kidney disease.) I kept in contact with the family all the time. I was in Italy and the family phoned me. I expected the news because I had seen Mr Ferrari one week before and he was really, really bad.'

The Fiat company had long held a controlling interest, contractually dormant until Ferrari died. The first race after his death was Spa, Berger qualifying third and Alboreto fourth, Berger struggling for 11 laps before the engine failed.

Monza, two weeks after Spa, would have to be genuinely historical, all the players intimately connected with it pressing their emotions down, holding on to normality.

'It was one of the very few tracks where our car was good because of the power of the engine' Alboreto says. 'Equally it was my last race with Ferrari at Monza, a very special moment for the team, but in one way a very sad moment: we could offer a tribute to the memory of Mr Ferrari, especially there at the track he liked most. We knew also that our cars had the best chance of the year so we'd try and do the best we could.

'I had a good relationship with Mr Ferrari and his family. You can imagine how I felt when he died. Moreover the situation within the team was . . . well, me leaving and the team moving towards Gerhard, although that had started a bit before. He had a very close relationship with John Barnard and really I wasn't comfortable. With Gerhard no problem, nothing special with him, but the situation became bad for me over the season.'

Alboreto had just been turned down by Williams, late in the day to find another drive for 1989. 'I feel let down,' he confessed at Monza, 'but I wouldn't have wanted another situation like Ferrari where the chief engineer (Barnard) is not happy about me. It's better to forget it, right? I'd like to drive for a team that believes in me, where there is a good atmosphere, not like the disaster it's been here. I know the feeling I have now at Ferrari and I don't ever want that again.'

Part of driving is to isolate emotion and place it in the background. The foreground is dangerous enough at 195 mph (314 km/h), the speed Alboreto would achieve crossing the line in second qualifying. Berger might have grasped pole but spun. 'I'm not sure what it was but the car felt unsettled and the left rear corner had a funny feel to it.'

A perfect autumnal Sunday morning, warm but not humid, and in the untimed session Berger and Alboreto did enough in race trim to excite a vast crowd.

A. Senna	1: 29.820
A. Prost	1: 29.828
M. Alboreto	1: 30.784
G. Berger	1: 30.867

The meltdown to the Italian Grand Prix is high voltage and that's not just because of the weight of so much history bearing down on the present, never mind offering tributes to the memory of Enzo Ferrari. You cannot avoid knowing that this is an important place graced by virtually every great driver. The high voltage is the howl of the *tifosi* which grunts to a grumble to a yearn to a wild, wild shriek before the cars get a chance to shriek themselves; it's a mighty backdrop of banners and flags and home-made slogans full round the teeming circuit. The grid, arranged on such a broad, imperial sweep of a straight, seems more than usually important as if spread on a great canvas. The arrival of the cars on the dummy grid long, long minutes before the parade lap, becomes an event, the earthy thousands in the grandstands hissing some, applauding others and detonating when the Ferraris appear. It is at this moment, if he hasn't done it before, that the Ferrari driver must isolate the emotion or perish to it.

Berger had his plugs changed on the grid. An official in a yellow short-sleeved shirt held up the *five minutes* board just beside Senna's car. The official held up the *three minutes* board. Alboreto chatted on the intercom to a mechanic, Berger sat almost motionless in the cockpit, arms folded over his lap. The blankets were peeled from his rear tyres and a mechanic's hand smoothed the surface of a tyre with the palm of his hand, sensuous as a caress, to brush any particles from it.

The official held the *one minute* board as high as his arms would allow and walked stately up and down the chequered finishing line, let the board fall as if suddenly heavy. He exchanged the board for another, *thirty seconds*, and twirled that aloft, trotted away to the grass verge. A green flag fluttered and the cars set off on the parade lap, Berger's Ferrari seeming to hesitate for an instant.

They came round and settled, somehow breathless and breathing hard.

At the green light Prost took the lead, Senna behind but reaching to the first chicane Senna dived inside Prost and Berger dived inside Alboreto to be third. Senna drove a fine first lap pulling far from Prost, who had Berger close behind. As Prost accelerated from the starting line and shifted into third gear he'd had a misfire. Only Prost knew this.

Moving into lap 2 Senna led by 3.3 seconds, Berger holding station behind Prost. Alboreto advancing on Berger — 'the engine felt very good in the warm-up session,' Alboreto says, 'but when we started the race, there was nothing we could do with the McLarens.' Lap 2:

Prost at 3.377
Berger at 4.102
Alboreto at 5.227

The tale has been told before and a précis of it will suffice here. Prost, the misfire worsening, reasoned that he would not finish the race. How then could he help his Championship chances against Senna? Prost reached a rational conclusion. Senna couldn't know about the misfire and if Prost pressured him Senna would accelerate to hold him back and use more fuel than prudent. Interesting, come the end of the race. Prost started to move, Berger clinging. A gap flicked up.

Prost at 2.654
Berger at 3.546
Alboreto at 5.746

'My car kept jumping out of fourth gear,' Alboreto says, 'so I thought maybe if I took it easy the oil would cool and then it would be all right.' Alboreto slipped back, held station himself. Next lap the gap had become 2.4 seconds. Nannini, who'd started from the pit lane, lay between Prost and Senna, Nannini now going well. Prost stalked him while Berger set fastest lap, but in the rush to the Parabolica Prost slotted the McLaren inside Nannini.

Crossing the line Berger feinted right of Nannini, went right and followed Prost through. Prost had a clear road to Senna who responded by setting fastest lap himself. Senna held the gap at around 3.3 seconds, but couldn't slacken his pace — Prost set a new fastest lap on 11. The McLarens were beautifully matched and they circulated with a certain poise trading milliseconds.

	Senna	Prost
Lap 11	1:30.392	1:31.005
Lap 12	1:30.327	1:30.249
Lap 13	1:30.399	1:30.395
Lap 14	1:30.303	1:30.343

and this over 3.604 miles (5.800 km). I ought to add Berger:

Lap 11	1:30.987
Lap 12	1:31.188
Lap 13	1:30.912
Lap 14	1:30.343

Senna set another fastest lap, going hard as Prost had foreseen he would, and Prost waited placidly for the misfire to engulf the engine: then he'd go home. Berger began to fall away, the theme of a season again. 'I had to back off. In the first few laps I used too much fuel trying to stay with them.' The race (outwardly) unfolded as everyone anticipated, the strength of the McLarens against the frailty of the Ferraris. Lap 13, Senna of course leading:

Prost at 3.770
Berger at 6.269
Alboreto at 10.339

It would be (outwardly) a long pursuit, Senna and Prost ramming in laps of 1:30, 1:29, the poise maintained. On lap 27 Prost did 1:29.642, fastest, and two laps later Senna made the counter gesture with 1:29.569, fastest. Prost's misfire coughed and churned and a lap of 1:30 drifted to 1:36 on the next. Berger closed quickly, sliced by, and Prost melted from him, pitted. The mechanics lifted the bodywork off. Lap 35:

Berger at 25.631
Alboreto at 36.027

Prost sat a long time in the cockpit, eyes darting, and finally levered himself out, wandered into the crowd gathered at the mouth of the McLaren pit.

'Senna had gone away from us,' Alboreto says, 'and then Prost's engine blew and I started to catch Gerhard, and Gerhard was increasing his lap times to catch Senna. I pushed very hard. I did the quickest lap of the race.' A gap flicked up: 25.553 Senna to Berger. In the midst of this Berger permitted Nannini to unlap himself. Lap 40:

Berger at 23.412
Alboreto at 30.650

Senna lowered his pace and a hypnotic thing happened. Alboreto began to close on Berger — as he says, 'pushing as hard as I could' — and *that* gap came down to 4.006 seconds. On lap 43 Alboreto did thrust in fastest lap, Senna insisting, 'I was running on minimum power during the second half of the race, taking things easy to be on the safe side and allowing the Ferraris to close up. I was under no pressure.'

Berger was. He responded to Alboreto by dipping into the 1 minute 29s on lap 44. Alboreto responded with another fastest lap, 1:29.070, slicing the gap to 2.411. The other gap, Senna to Berger, sliced to 11 seconds with five laps to go, and then another Senna to Berger gap flicked, up, 8.944. They could all see each other on the main straight. Another gap: 6.132.

	Senna	*Berger*
Lap 46	1: 31.556	1: 29.209
Lap 47	1: 31.925	1: 29.113
Lap 48	1: 30.308	1: 29.225

Mansell, recovering from chickenpox, was not in the Italian Grand Prix. Brundle might have replaced him but didn't. On such threads hang motor races. Jean-Louis Schlesser, aged 35 and making his début (although he'd tested for Williams 14 months before) did replace Mansell. For most of the race Schlesser had been a lap down minding his own business.

Senna moved into lap 50, the Ferraris somewhere back there on the main straight but visibly closing. Senna moved to the first chicane. Schlesser tried to get out of the way and locked his brakes, leaving wisps of smoke. Senna bounded over the inner kerbing to give himself room. Schlesser wrestled the Williams.

Both went for the chicane exit. Senna turned into it but Schlesser had two wheels on the light brown dust beyond the kerb, his Williams out of control. He smacked Senna's rear wheel, punting the McLaren into the air. It pivoted on its front left wheel and slewed away, the Williams boring into its flank. The McLaren spun and travelled backwards half on to the run-off area beyond the chicane, beached on the arch of the kerbing. A great tide of Ferrari flags cleaved the air. Senna could do nothing, nothing at all, except watch Berger flow by, watch Alboreto flow by.

Schlesser insisted he'd tried to get out of Senna's way. Senna said he thought Schlesser was so far off line when he'd locked his brakes that he could get through.

Certain questions have never been answered, and likely never will. Had Prost's plan worked and, so deep into the race, Senna found himself short of fuel? Did that mean he'd lowered his pace and when the Ferraris came into view *had* to risk taking Schlesser at the chicane?

	Berger	*Alboreto*
Lap 50	1: 31.811	1: 32.042

On the last lap Alboreto made a final attempt to reach Berger, now behind the lapped Gugelmin. Into the Parabolica Gugelmin travelled fast enough to draw Berger with him, Alboreto unable to get closer. Berger slowed after the finishing line and waved and waved from the cockpit. Alboreto contented himself with more modest waving.

Berger: 1 hour 17 minutes 39.744 seconds.
Alboreto at 0.502 seconds.

When scrutineers checked Berger's fuel limit they found it to be

151.5 litres, clearly over the permitted 150 litres. Four times Ferrari tried before they got it down to 149.650. What might have happened if Berger had been excluded? A riot? Probably not. After all, Alboreto would have won . . .

Berger dedicated the victory to the whole team but particularly to the memory of Enzo Ferrari. A couple of months later he'd say, 'To drive for Enzo Ferrari was different from driving for Ferrari, a part of the Fiat company. Before, my boss was Enzo Ferrari. He decided how much money I got, how good I am for him, whether or not to keep me. He was a big personality, a great man, and I think most drivers would like to have driven for him. I've done it and I'm happy about that. But I would love to have been able to go to Maranello the day after Monza and to have seen his face.'

After that 1988 drifted, fastest lap in Portugal but the clutch went, a distant sixth in Spain, a distant fourth in Japan, an accident with Arnoux in Australia when he was leading. Berger took that philosophically, said that Arnoux had been scrapping with Modena and 'perhaps he didn't see me because of that'. Persistence had brought him 41 points and third in the Championship table behind Senna (94 but 90 counting) and Prost (105 but 87 counting).

Footnote to 1988. Berger evidently decided to thank his mechanics and race engineers and flew them all in his plane to Austria for a Christmas party. A fleet of limousines met them at Innsbruck and transported them into the mountains. Strange place to be going for a Christmas party, the mechanics thought. The limousines took them to a bordello. As Barnard says, 'We didn't see them for two or three days . . .'

In 1989 Mansell came. 'Basically I got on quite well with him,' Berger says. 'I'd taken him to hospital that time when he had a skiing accident and he picked me up there when I was coming out after my road accident in 1984. I liked him, no problem, but there was a problem when he came to Ferrari. I had a strong relationship with John Barnard and I think Nigel was warned by some people that this relationship would be an advantage for me. From the first day on he didn't trust anything.

'Today I understand it, but in those days I didn't because I didn't think about those things. I know exactly what was on his mind. However, I have to say that he was always nice to me, he tried to do it fairly and we maintained a good relationship to the end. Unfortunately at the end when I told Ferrari I was leaving some things went to his advantage, normal when you're leaving a team. I still like to see him. We never got very close because I think the nature of the job does not allow that.'

Barnard says, 'The problem with Nigel for Gerhard was that he was bloody quick and Nigel had a problem in that when he came he immediately said to me "Let's make friends." I hadn't worked with him before and Nigel, being an Englishman thought, "Ah, fine, this is my friend because we're both Englishmen." But being in my position I tried very hard to stay in the middle and work with both guys. Nigel didn't really want it that way. He wanted 80 per cent from the people working with me and 80 per cent of me, and Nigel wasn't going to spend that long discussing the car after practice: stop, finish and off and do something else.

'Again, you naturally gravitate to the guy who is going to sit there and chew it over with you longer and longer, and after a time Nigel felt I wasn't giving him all of my attention. It's difficult to explain but he just withdrew, yes withdrew, to try and work only with his race engineers. You know, "I want all the sweets and if I can't I won't have any" sort of attitude, and that I think is where the problem came.'

Barnard's Ferrari 640 with a semi-automatic gearbox would emerge as the only serious challenger to McLaren and even then only towards mid-season. The fact that Mansell won the first race, Brazil, was almost misleading. Berger crashed with Senna going into the first corner. 'The only way out of the problem would have been to go straight up in the air,' Senna said. 'Patrese and Berger trapped me and I lost the nose section. That's all there is to it.' Berger said, 'Senna chopped across me to try to make me back off, but he shouldn't try that with me. Never in my life will I back off in that situation.'

A month later on that gentle early afternoon the Angels of Imola took up their position behind the armco some 50 m from the corner called Tamburello . . .

A couple of happy anecdotes woven around the aftermath (leaving aside the happiest of all that Berger emerged comparatively unscathed).

Alboreto: 'We lived for a long time in the same building in Monte Carlo and in fact Gerhard took my apartment when I moved to a bigger one. He was on the ninth floor and I was two floors up. We'd go out and have meals together. After his accident at Imola he didn't drive in the next Grand Prix, Monaco, and my new Tyrrell had been finished so late it didn't arrive in time for first qualifying. Gerhard and I watched that first qualifying from his balcony. We were in the sun, looking down at our friends and we thought, "It's nice to be here, not down there driving like crazy and sweating like crazy."'

Berger did go to Mexico and ran third early on before the gearbox went. Les Thacker of BP says, 'I happened to meet him at the airport waiting to fly back. I shook his hand and he winced in pain. What is so delightful about Gerhard is that he then said something very funny. I just can't remember what it was, but I wish I could.'

Berger ran second in Detroit but the alternator went, second in Canada but the alternator went again, second at Paul Ricard but an oil leak stopped him, and at Silverstone he had a misfire before the gearbox failed. Prost, meanwhile, had announced he was leaving McLaren — his partnership with Senna now resembled a débàcle — and on the Thursday before Silverstone the team announced that Berger would replace him. Berger said, 'Obviously I'm sad to be leaving Ferrari but McLaren is the top team, the team everyone wants to drive for.' That encapsulated it perfectly.

Dieter Stappert advised Berger. 'At the beginning, when Gerhard was going to McLaren I said, "Let's do it because you have shown in the Ferrari you are the quickest man. Now if you want to be World Champion you have to beat Senna and to do that it's best you go to Mclaren, have the same equipment." We know, of course, how organized Senna was, but . . .'

At Hockenheim Berger lined up on the grid behind, inevitably, Senna and Prost. At the green light and instantaneously he flung the Ferrari full across the track to the left, hugged the rim, urged and urged, and took turn one in the lead. Honda power came in then and Senna went through at the first chicane, Prost on the outside at the second chicane. Berger hustled as best he could, riding the kerbing at the chicanes almost violently until, approaching the stadium complex on lap 14, his right rear tyre deflated. He braked and the suspension ground a molten flurry of sparks from the surface of the track. He locked his wheels, slate grey smoke billowing from under the side of the car.

He fought the car as it twitched and twitched again, hauled it into the first corner of the complex but it vaulted the kerbing, all four wheels off the ground, tilted as the nose cone was plucked away, this nose cone which peeled back over the car; it landed on grass, gouging that and, wrecked, flowed back on to the track. Berger crossed the track before Mansell got there and still the Ferrari twitched as it flowed off the other side, gouged brown dust now, the nose cone gone. It nearly struck his head. The car came to rest on the grass. He scouted round it when he'd clambered out, felt the front tyres, examined the gap where the nose cone had been and moved off, removing his helmet. The way it goes, some races.

In Hungary he ran third but the gearbox went, in Belgium third but scudded off in the wet. He came to Monza without a single point. He ran second behind Senna until Prost took him but not until lap 41, second again when Senna's engine went. He finished 7.326 seconds behind Prost.

He put the Ferrari on the front row in Portugal and stormed the race, but 'I pushed too hard and it was a mistake. I destroyed the tyres, particularly the fronts. It gave me big understeer at the last corner which meant I lost speed on to the straight.' Mansell came at him and ducked out on the straight and kept two back markers between himself and Berger and took the lead. During the tyre stops Mansell overshot his pit and had to reverse, something illegal. Mansell was black flagged although he vehemently claimed he couldn't see it with the afternoon sun full in his face. To compound it all, Senna and Mansell collided. Berger beat Prost by 32.637 seconds.

In Spain he put the Ferrari on the front row and finished 27.051 seconds behind Senna. In Japan he ran third until the gearbox went. In Australia he crashed with Alliott in the wet. It scarcely mattered that he'd finished the season seventh in the World Championship with 21 points. He'd elevated himself to one of the four leading drivers and, with Mansell, the only ones who could reasonably take the McLarens on — not beat them but at least take them on.

It begged questions. What would Berger do when he enjoyed McLaren's undisputed expertise and Honda's undisputed power? Beat Senna? Survive Senna?

'I suppose if I am honest,' Barnard says, 'going to McLaren was the only thing Gerhard could do. I couldn't fault him on doing that. I don't think it is a risk, I think it is something you have to face at some point in your career. How good are you? How do you find out? Go up against the best. I was leaving Ferrari, Prost was coming, a much harder decision for me because I am a Prost fan.

'Gerhard had the offer from McLaren. I knew McLaren, I knew how they worked, I knew they were very logical and it was a much more controlled environment than Ferrari. I thought I saw Ferrari going back to the way they'd been fairly soon. I think yes, I recommended him to go to Mclaren.'

8

Breaking point?

That March day in 1990 in Estoril Berger and Senna first tested McLaren's new MP4/5B and a psychological game was played out in the pits, the two drivers trading fastest laps. One would go out, do a time, return and sit in the cockpit *smiling* at the other, who'd go out . . .

Maybe that set the tone of the relationship. In time, Senna said he felt 'more comfortable in the McLaren environment now Berger has replaced Prost. The atmosphere is more relaxed, no pressure inside the team. Gerhard and I get on extremely well. On the personal side, he is very easy going and we've no problems at all. We've shared some moments of fun and made some jokes.'

Jo Ramirez, McLaren's team co-ordinator says, 'I'd first met Berger when he was driving with Benetton, but only to say hello and goodbye. I guess we at McLaren knew there had been early conversations about him joining, but I didn't know anything before that. While he was still at Ferrari we began to have a few words about measurements for his overalls and so on. My first impression was a good one, that here was a man who enjoyed life to the fullest, but what impressed me most was that he was not afraid in the least of joining a team with Ayrton Senna in it and everyone knew what Senna could do.

'Senna had driven with Prost when Prost was Number One. Prost was obviously the man to beat and Senna came up and beat him. So Gerhard signed and I thought, that's a good thing, he's really got what it takes, and I hope he is going to be good at it.'

At Phoenix, the first race of the season, Berger took provisional pole on the Friday after 'a good clean lap — not a super quick one. On this sort of circuit it's often the case that you go quicker if you drive more precisely.' Senna, with a slight misfire, could get no higher than fifth and these times stood before rain fell on the Saturday. Berger felt 'under no particular pressure' starting from pole. His priority, he insisted, remained 'getting to know the team and becoming accustomed to working with them'.

Jean Alesi (Tyrrell) made a superb start, outbraking Berger into turn one, and for eight laps that remained the order. On lap 9 Berger spun into the barrier. 'I was a little bit between the brake and the throttle pedal, already braking on the limit, and as I caught the throttle pedal I lost it. My fault.'

'Between Phoenix and the next race, Brazil,' Senna says, 'we spent some time together away from racing, enjoying the sun, the sea, playing on jet skis. With Elio de Angelis at the beginning at Lotus I did this but not with anyone else.' Maybe *that* set the tone of the relationship.

Senna took pole in Brazil, although in the second session, Berger says, 'I didn't really push too hard because I saw that the times were not improving — but I hadn't seen Ayrton's time!' Senna 1 minute 17.277, Berger 1 minute 18.504, the front row of the grid.

In the race Senna crashed with Nakajima and Berger finished 13.564 seconds behind Prost. 'Everything was OK at the start but I was still finding it a tight fit in the car and I had some difficulty changing gear. Soon after the start the car developed understeer so I decided to take it easy until the tyre stop. Then I pushed hard but I began to get severe pain in my foot from the braking effort so I had to take it easy again. Then I pushed once more but I heard a noise from the clutch and eased back.'

And he returned to Imola. Stan Piecha of *The Sun* sought him out and spoke to him. 'Berger said that yes, he had had recurring nightmares about it but that was all behind him now and he was quite prepared to race. After the first lap he did he said he'd come to that corner and momentarily the thought went through his mind but after that he was just back in the car, just back racing.' It's the process of isolating your emotions again.

Berger took provisional pole, 1 minute 24.027 against Senna's 1 minute 24.079, and immediately afterwards Berger said, 'I think it's going to be very close between myself and Ayrton throughout the season. At this rate I'll be feeling 10 years older by the last race!' In the second session Senna reversed the order, 1 minute 23.220 against 1 minute 23.781, the front row of the grid again.

Senna led from Boutsen (Williams) for three laps but felt 'something flexing at the right rear of the car'. He spun off and when Boutsen over-revved his engine — a gearbox problem — Berger led. Mansell powered past Patrese and set off after Berger. After 45 laps he'd caught him, tracked him, the Ferrari seeming prehensile, predatory. They moved through Tamburello and Mansell darted hard left to grasp the racing line for Tosa.

He did this very, very quickly, Berger already travelling left to grasp the racing line himself. That forced Mansell to put two wheels on to the grass and the impetus carried the Ferrari full on to the grass, rotating. That brought it back on to the track where it described another rotation, its tyres carving a wild pattern of burn marks. Mansell caught the Ferrari and set off.

'Gerhard moved over on me,' Mansell said. 'He's a friend of mine and my team-mate only last year. I can't believe what he did. There was nowhere for me to go.' Berger said, 'I took the normal line at that point and I looked in my mirrors and thought Nigel would try and overtake me at the end of the start-finish straight. After that I looked to the left and saw his nose out of the corner of my eye at the last minute just as he began spinning. I'm very sorry because I don't like things like that to happen. It was a very dangerous situation.'

They always will happen, the driver behind an opportunist making what he feels is a deft move, the driver in front not expecting it *here* and taking his usual lines. The sheer speed makes these moves virtually instantaneous and apportioning blame remains extremely difficult. It depends on, literally, your point of view.

Deep into the race Patrese took Berger for the lead, Berger baulked by a backmarker. He accepted he'd finish second and he did, making the points table interesting: Senna 13, Prost and Berger 12, Patrese 9. 'No,' Berger murmured, 'I'm not thinking about the Championship at this stage.'

Just as well: third in Monaco, fourth in Canada, but Canada wasn't as simple as that. Berger, sharing the front row with Senna, jumped the green. 'I did not gain any advantage from my over-eager start. I anticipated the light.' Senna led a very wet race, Berger tracking in second place. After the pit stops he out-braked Senna but had a one-minute penalty for the over-eagerness. He set fastest lap and dealt with the traffic ruthlessly, now in a race against time itself to regain as much of the minute as he could. It created a bizarre spectacle, Berger 'leading' on the road but actually working his way back into the top six. Einstein would have loved it. Moreover Berger had a 'slight brake problem. Sixteen laps from the end I had to ease back slightly due to the pedal movement becoming very long.'

He finished third in Mexico, fifth in France: Senna 35, Prost 32, Berger 25.

Senna would say that while Berger and he got on extremely well, as we have heard, 'We work very differently, particularly setting up the car. Some occasions his set-ups were better and on other occasions mine were. That makes it harder because information from him and myself doesn't really work in many situations and we can't split the work load. I found it strange when I first saw the set-up of his car.'

At Silverstone I needed a lap of the circuit and sought out Berger to get one. He sits and beams and people keep coming up to shake his hand or make little jokes. Before we come to the lap, I ask the inevitable question about life with Ayrton. 'No, it's not difficult. If you take a comparison, I've been twice on pole and he's been four times on pole and in Canada we were 66 *thousandths* of a second different in qualifying' — Senna 1 minute 20.399, Berger 1 minute 20.465 — 'so we are more or less the same. I don't compare myself to Ayrton, I race to win races.' You can't doubt the sincerity or accuracy of these words reflecting the overall situation in mid-July 1990.

Now the lap, and remembering it's round the *old* Silverstone without the 'complex' under the *Daily Express* bridge or the gelding of Stowe corner to slow it. Fasten your seat belts.

'I like Silverstone. You have just four corners and the chicane but the four corners are all difficult so it gives me more pleasure to drive than, for example, the last circuit we were at, Paul Ricard, where you have more corners but they are not as hard, except Signes.

'You cross the start-finish line in sixth gear and reach the right-hander (Copse) changing down to fourth and doing 135 mph (217 km/h). The camber falls away so the car begins to understeer. You use the kerb on the exit, go up to sixth but down again for the next right-hander (Becketts), your speed about 110 mph (177 km/h).

'You go back up to sixth on the long straight where you reach 198 mph (319 km/h), down to fifth for the very quick right-hander (Stowe) doing 150, 155 mph (240, 250 km/h). You use the kerb, flick into sixth and at the next right-hand corner (Club) go down to fifth, but it's very difficult because again the camber is adverse and the car begins to understeer in the middle of it.

'At the quick left-hander (Abbey) you're flat, up towards 198 mph (319 km/h). Towards the bridge you brake and go down to second for the chicane, go through it in second but it's very slippery and usually you have a little bit of wheelspin. Under the bridge and through the chicane you're doing about 50 mph (80 km/h) then straight back to sixth and you cross the start-finish line to do another lap.'

Mansell took pole from Senna and Berger with 1 minute 7.428 (158 mph/255 km/h) and across 2.970 miles (4.778 km) that's quick, that is. In the race, 'Right from the start the car was very difficult to drive although the engine was good,' Berger said. 'I thought I would lose control in the faster corners.'

As we've seen, a driver who knows his craft can drive around these problems so that you're unaware of how close to losing control he is. Senna led, Mansell second, Berger third, but Senna complained of handling, too, and on lap 12 he could resist Mansell no longer. Senna spun. At lap 15:

Mansell	18:33.255
Berger	at 2.773
Boutsen	at 5.521

and five laps later the gap Mansell to Berger had become 3.127, but the semi-automatic gearbox on Mansell's Ferrari kept jumping out of gear. Berger closed and went through towards Stowe. He led for six laps until Mansell's gearbox behaved again. Under the bridge Mansell out-braked him on the inside, took the lead, Prost swarming over Berger. Soon enough Prost went through under the bridge as well and when Mansell dropped out, gearbox, Berger lay second to Prost, but something in the throttle control mechanism failed.

During first qualifying for the German Grand Prix at Hockenheim, 'On my first run I tried to make room for Martin Donnelly (Lotus) coming into the stadium but I think he was a bit nervous and went off on the outside. Later on my second run, he blocked me into the Sachskurve. I think he was paying me back!'

'Went off on the outside?' Donnelly says. 'I went off on my backside! I wasn't nervous, we had qualifying tyres in those days, of course, and I was on my first flying lap — quite a good lap, Gerhard up ahead warming his tyres. As we went towards the stadium I knew he was looking in his mirrors because I could see his helmet moving from side to side. I assumed he'd seen me and would move over. At the right-hander going into the stadium he moved over and left me about the width of half a car! I went off. I honestly think he misjudged it and I don't remember blocking him later.

'That weekend we had onboard cameras, I watched a replay and you could clearly see his helmet moving from side to side. The press tried to build it up to a big thing, telling me Gerhard had said this and that and if I'd said anything it would have gone to and fro so I kept my mouth shut. Funnily enough after I had my accident (at Spain in September 1990) and Willy Dungl was treating me, we had a party and Gerhard came. We shook hands, had a chat and that was that. It had been a racing accident, no more.'

Berger finished third in the race and locked horns with Mansell in Hungary. 'In the early part of the race I could not pass Boutsen because he was quicker through the last corner on to the start-finish straight. I thought a change of tyres might help my overtaking. After I returned to the race I reached fourth. Mansell kept moving over on me, pushing me over towards the wall. In the end I tried to get him at the chicane but he moved over on me.'

Crash . . .

The season drifted, third in Belgium; the car kept sliding so he 'nursed the brakes' to third at Monza; tracked Senna in Portugal, Senna leading — 'I could have pushed Ayrton but he was fighting for the Championship so I backed off.'

After second qualifying in Spain Berger spoke with his accustomed candour (and please remember two factors: this was the aftermath of Donnelly's horrific crash *and* Berger is a man who habitually admits his own mistakes). 'What is there to be said about de Cesaris? It was unbelievable. My first run was a problem because I had trouble with the gearbox. De Cesaris spoiled my second run, and on my third naturally the tyres had gone off.' (One time when I interviewed de Cesaris he vehemently denied he is a blocker. I mentioned that James Hunt was repeatedly harsh about him during his BBC race commentaries and de Cesaris offered this riposte. 'Does Hunt really watch the races?' That said, de Cesaris did have a reputation, deserved or not, for being in the wrong place on the tracks at the wrong time.) In the race Berger touched wheels with Boutsen and spun off.

Japan? The infamous collision at turn one between Senna and Prost which gave Senna the Championship and coincidentally gave Berger the lead in the race. But on lap 2 he spun at . . . turn one. His first reaction was to distil this into a sound rather than a word. *Oops!*

He went straight for his hotel. 'There was oil and dirt all over the road from the Senna-Prost thing. Heading down towards the corner I thought maybe I should back off a bit but then I decided no, the track will be clean because the whole field has been through it. There were no oil flags. I didn't go back to the pits because I was so angry with myself. It was the worst thing that could have happened to me. I needed a win desperately and I had this one on a plate.'

He'd have to wait a full calendar year for that win, here at Suzuka and gifted to him by Senna.

Berger finished fourth in Australia, 'a really bad pain in my foot under hard braking and I even had to come off the throttle on the straight to give myself some relief from it. At one point I accidentally switched off the ignition and went over a kerb.'

Senna (78 points) had the Championship from Prost (73 but 71 counting), Piquet 44 (but 43 counting), Berger 43. The pressure of Senna on Berger? Consider it. He'd taken 10 pole positions and won six races, Berger two pole positions and of course no wins.

After this season Berger rang Lamm. 'He said, "Charley, if I look back I am a more mature driver now, but at McLaren they teach you a little bit like you are in the army. If practice started at Ferrari at 9.00 you arrived at 9.30. If practice starts at McLaren at 9.00 you are at the exit of the pit lane, helmet on and completely ready, at five minutes to nine. You don't have lunch. If practice ends at 5.00 it ends at 5.00. You have a two-hour debrief and then you can take your flight. At Ferrari practice ended at 5.00, but if you had a flight at 6.30 you'd stop at 4.30 to catch it. The attitude of the McLaren team makes it successful."'

Lamm continues, 'Gerhard started to concentrate on fitness. He'd phone Senna and asked how far he ran — 5 km — and he'd run that. Then Senna would say, "Well, I'll do another 5 km," and Gerhard would do that. Press-ups the same. He said that in all these disciplines Senna is further ahead and Gerhard employed a fitness trainer who'd worked with Boris Becker. Gerhard understood that you cannot do it on talent alone, if you're not fit after 30 or 40 laps you start to lose tenths. What is the consequence of not being totally fit? He said, "Maybe you have to take deep breaths and you lose time doing that." You must be so fit you don't put yourself in the situation of having to do that.

'He also said, "I can do the speed but there are moments in a corner when you are conscious of what you are doing but you are concentrating so hard you are not fully aware of how you did what you did and what the car did in the corner. I'd do the same speed as Senna. In the debrief Senna says 'At the beginning of the corner I was doing this and at the exit to the corner I was doing this with so many revs, but yesterday I was doing this and I was doing this with so many revs'." Gerhard said he didn't know how many revs he'd been doing *because he didn't have time to look*. Gerhard felt he had to show the same approach. Run as far, do as many press-ups. He added that it was tough, not such a lot of fun because the organization of the whole package was so obsessed by success. He said he couldn't go out in the evening and eat what he wanted, drink what he wanted. "All the time I have to behave myself".'

Berger will be discussing the pressure later in this book, but when the season ended he also rang Dieter Stappert and said 'he'd go testing and then he'd be fit and ready and so on. What happened? They came to the first race at Phoenix and he was 2 seconds off the pace. And the year before he'd been on pole.'

Or, as Ramirez says, 'At the end of 1990 Gerhard felt he needed to improve a lot in his driving, his mentality, everything. Senna was World Champion, he went back home and had three months' holiday, didn't get into his race car until he came to Phoenix and in the meantime Gerhard did all the testing and at the same time he prepared himself mentally and physically to really get into the system to beat Senna. He got to Phoenix and . . .'

Friday 8 March	*Free practice*	*First qualifying*
Senna	1: 23.525	1: 23.530
Berger	1: 25.966	1: 25.914

Saturday 9 March	*Free practice*	*Second qualifying*
Senna	1: 24.214	1: 21.434
Berger	1: 24.158	1: 23.742

During that first qualifying Berger spun 'trying too hard'. Otherwise

196

he masked the pressure well enough, certainly in public. Davy Jones, who'd raced Berger and Senna in 1983 in Formula 3 at Macau, went to Phoenix to watch. 'I hadn't seen Gerhard in years, I hadn't seen Ayrton in years and I had a chance to talk to both of them. It seemed as if they weren't only team-mates but friends. That's the sort of person Gerhard is.

'I know if it's a year from now and I go up to Gerhard and say, "Hey, how are you doing?" he'll say, "Hey, Davy, I haven't seen you in a long time, what have you been up to?" It's what makes him a neat guy. There are other guys, and it's hard for me to name them, who when they reach that level don't have time for you. That's not true of Senna either, incidentally. He has time for people. If Senna is focused or busy he's very difficult to talk to, but if he has 30 seconds it's no problem.

'I thought that nobody could really work with Senna except a guy like Gerhard because he can relax on the sidelines, he'll be the one to give in a little bit, he won't try and stick to his guns and go on and on and on until he gets his own way. He'd say, "Whatever, I'm going to make the best of what I've got." Because of that the two of them could have a good working relationship. Rather than create a difficult situation Gerhard would rather create a pleasant situation. It's almost like "We have to live together so let's make the most of it and enjoy it."'

In the race Berger made 'a very good start but I couldn't get past Patrese, so Alesi managed to come inside me. I pushed quite hard until my water temperature began to rise, giving me a slight loss of power. It was too early to take any risks. Eventually the fuel warning light came on a few times and then the car stopped.'

Senna won . . .

'That was the most depressing meeting of Gerhard's life,' Ramirez says. 'He couldn't believe it and it took him three or four races to regain his confidence. He is very honest. If you talk to him now, he will still say being second to Senna is not a bad place to be. Senna didn't need support, a very strong personality, very strong character. When he makes mistakes — rarely — he punishes himself just as much as he punishes the team when the team makes a mistake. Gerhard is different. He seemed to be a guy who needed a little tap on the shoulder and reminding you are good but you're doing certain things you shouldn't be doing. Ron took a lot of time trying to help him concentrate, you know, one lap at a time at places like Monaco.

'When he drove for Ferrari he won four races, he was a hero, quicker than Mansell when Mansell was there, quicker than Alboreto when Alboreto was there. He left Ferrari and came to us and after two years hardly anybody asked for his autograph, it was Senna, Senna, Senna not him. We gave them both the same equipment and the same kind of support, moral and physical. Gerhard realized that and he thanked the team for it.'

'Gerhard rang me,' Stappert says, 'and I went to Brazil and from there I think I did nearly every Grand Prix. I watched him a lot in 1991 because he was in big trouble. He made a serious mistake, he tried to copy Senna. By trying to do that he lost what was his strongest asset, his natural speed. It took a while to get him back on his feet. Not only did I watch the Grands Prix but also every practice and we discussed everything.

'The problem, as I say, was that in his head he tried to copy Senna, which couldn't work because he isn't Senna. He doesn't think the way Senna thinks. I learnt how Senna thinks, how he works. I watched, for example, Imola' — the race after Brazil where Senna had taken pole from Prost, Berger second row more than a second slower than Senna, Senna winning, Berger third. 'First lap, free practice at Imola, five, six cars bunched, crazy Italians amongst them. Senna came round and I thought, he's thinking "This is the last lap of a Grand Prix and if I overtake them all I win." You know what he's doing? He's practising that.

'Senna wins his races from the start, the first three or four laps when he is demoralizing others like Gerhard. As soon as somebody has to be lapped Senna goes *wham*. He doesn't just overtake, he virtually drives into the back of these guys and it becomes an automatic reaction for them: if they see a McLaren with a yellow helmet they get out of the way. That's what I saw at Imola. He went up to these guys . . .

'There are so many ways you can see how methodically Senna works. In trying to copy Senna, Gerhard lost a lot of time in slow corners. He remained as fast as Senna on the quick parts of a circuit. He wasn't so consistent as Senna and he didn't react as quickly as Senna to changes in the car. Before, in slow corners Gerhard used to throw the car around. Now he tried to do it like Senna — go in, turn in, everything perfect. Sometimes it worked, sometimes it didn't; maybe it worked 10 times out of 10 then it didn't. He lost time. For example in Montreal, just going round the tight hairpin before you come back towards the start-finish straight, Gerhard was losing half a second. Can you image that? Half a second just in braking going round the hairpin.

'I still believe that in the right team Gerhard has the potential to be World Champion but if he approached it like Senna — as he did — it wouldn't happen. He tried. Then he started to lose speed in the quick corners. Yes, I told him that. He was at breaking point. It took him a while to realise that copying Senna is nothing, took him a while to remember that he is Gerhard Berger, he has to go his own way: work as hard as Senna, be as concentrated, as logical as Senna, but stay Gerhard Berger. In time he did that, and it worked.'

Breaking point? Peter Collins watched from comparatively afar because he was in the Lotus enclave. (He'd joined, or rather rejoined, Team Lotus in December 1990.) He noticed that 'the saddest thing during his McLaren years was that Gerhard sort of lost his way a bit. Whether he suppressed his own personality I don't know but he wasn't himself.'

Ramirez says that 'Gerhard and Ayrton are very different. Senna has nothing in his life, absolutely nothing, except this. Maybe he likes to go to the beach, play around, but at the end of the day all he is interested in, in his life and his career, is racing and winning. He is a man who doesn't enjoy competing but winning. For him, being second is coming the first of the losers. He is not built to be that. Gerhard enjoys life and is full of what he is doing, you know just life in general. Ayrton is different and you can't compare them.'

At Imola Senna won, Berger 1.675 seconds behind — brake problems. At Monaco Jaguar held a support race to the Grand Prix, showing off 16 of their XJR15 sports cars which cost £500,000 each and good drivers contested it, Warwick, Nielsen, Juan Fangio II, Davy Jones, Bob Wollek. On lap 2 Nielsen turned into a corner along the harbour 'too quickly' and his car struck the shoreside armco, crossed the track and struck the harbourside armco. To walk back is no arduous journey, the race had another 25 minutes to run and Nielsen would be in the pits any minute now. He didn't come.

The truth emerged only later. Jones, chatting to Nielsen, asked whatever happened to you? Nielsen replied, 'Nothing happened. I hit the wall right in front of Gerhard's boat and Gerhard was sitting on it watching. As I walked past Gerhard called out, "Come on to the boat" so I did and I was watching all you guys from it.' Like Berger and Alboreto on the balcony in 1989, motor racing can seem extremely civilized from such vantage points, all those guys driving like crazy and sweating like crazy, and pass the champagne, would you dear?

In the Grand Prix itself and from the third row of the grid (Senna pole), Berger 'had a coming together with Piquet on lap 1 which forced me to pit and after I restarted I got a lot of oil from Minardi all over my visor. I had a problem with the tear-offs and I couldn't see anything. I tried to wipe the oil off with my hand, lost concentration momentarily and my foot slipped off the brake pedal.' The car thumped the armco — 'a big accident'.

The pressure: a misfire in Canada where he completed only four laps, an engine explosion in Mexico where he completed only five laps.

Ron Dennis gave a situation review at Magny-Cours before the French Grand Prix. 'Gerhard? First of all you have got to look at the facts this season. When I say this, I'm leaving aside last season.

Gerhard worked very hard through the winter to improve his own performance (the testing, testing, testing he'd told Stappert he'd do). Now look at the first six races and take away the car failures, the reliability problems. His performances in the remaining races have been 50-50, broadly speaking.

'I think that probably Gerhard has the most difficult seat in motor racing, being in a two-car team with Ayrton in the other seat. As has been shown in the past, it is an extremely difficult position to occupy but I still have a lot of faith and confidence in his ability to perform. It might be hard to believe that statement. One result would solve 90 per cent of the problem.'

Dennis, who prides himself on his management skills, and with great justification, broadened the discussion and because it involved all of the Marlboro McLaren Honda team and thus Berger I include it.

'In all relationships there is this stupid expression called the white lie, it's like saying someone is a little bit pregnant. In reality it doesn't exist, does it? You are either telling the truth or you are not telling the truth. The ultimate test of telling the truth or not is in your marriage. That's where it all starts, you know.

'If you get into definitions of a family, you may not like your mother-in-law, you may not particularly like your cousin, but you tolerate them because they are part of your family. You cope. Now talk about a motor racing environment: you can't put 30 people together and say they've all got harmonious characters, but they have a common objective which brings them together in a form of a family — which most people call a team. You could equally argue that a family is a team because when something serious happens the family comes together to try and lend support.

'There is one fundamental in our working environment and that is trust. If you don't have trust you don't have anything, absolutely nothing. That's in the team, that's in life. I trust everybody until they give me a reason not to and they go into the opposite column. I'm an elephant in those areas. I never forget. I never ever, ever forget. Ever.'

Berger's speed in qualifying had reduced, sixth on the first day at Magny-Cours, fifth on the second. The engine 'went bang' after he'd completed six laps in the race. At Silverstone, second row and a bump and bore with Patrese, who pleaded not guilty. Berger said, 'Patrese gave me a hard time at the first corner when I was level with him but on the inside line. He cut straight across into me, bending my left front wheel and leaving me with a tyre vibration that not only forced me to make an early tyre stop but also gave me a large blister on my right hand.' When Senna stopped (fuel pressure) on the second last lap Berger inherited second place and stayed there, crossing the line 42.293 behind Mansell.

Mid-season brought good and bad, a fourth in Hungary, a second (to Senna) at Spa by 1.901 seconds despite being 'low on power all through', a fourth at Monza. In Portugal he took provisional pole, lost it in second qualifying and a misfire stopped him in the race. By now, and with Stappert's guidance and advice bearing fruit — be yourself, not Senna — he started to become again the man and driver he had been.

'It wasn't only myself advising,' Stappert says. 'Helmut Marko was doing it, too. It's very hard to pinpoint one race where Gerhard changed and I don't think it happened from one day to the next. He didn't get depressed except at that first race at Phoenix where he'd worked so hard over he winter and told himself, "I know the car better than Ayrton, I know everything about the car" and then got blown away in qualifying by the 2 seconds. I think he was on the edge of giving the whole thing up then.

'He'd lost his easy way of approaching things. He was trying to think like Senna, live like Senna, and I estimate it took him six or seven races to realize it wasn't working. As I say, it's hard to name a particular race but I'd judge it was around Budapest and the Hungarian Grand Prix that his — how can I put it? — ease came back.'

In Spain the speed came back, too, with provisional pole on the Friday, to which Senna said, 'Gerhard did a really good job today and deserves to be fastest. I feel I could have done slightly better because when I changed cars (he took the spare for his final run) I really wanted to use a mixed set of worn tyres but due to a slight misunderstanding they fitted my original set. Under the circumstances it was quite good but I really don't know whether I could have equalled Gerhard's time.'

Berger said, 'The car was fine. I fought for the time because I wanted to catch Nigel Mansell (initially quickest). Now that the track has some rubber on it there is more grip and it is more enjoyable to drive. My engine was strong but I over-revved it on my first run and after that it lost some power, whether because of the over-rev or the heat of the day I am not sure.'

Provisional pole became pole on the Saturday. On a cool, overcast afternoon nobody could get under 1 minute 19 seconds, so Berger's 1 minute 18.751 and Mansell's 1 minute 18.970 stood as the front row. Berger led before and after early pit stops, the track drying but 'then two or three cylinders stopped working. A pity, but *c'est la vie!*'

He took pole at Suzuka, but listen to him talking after the first session when he'd gone quicker than Senna. 'They told me the chicane has been revised this year and it doesn't really make a lot of difference to me. I couldn't drive the last one, I can't drive this one!' When he had pole he added, 'In the past I feel I've tried too hard and it doesn't work. You think if you take it easy it won't work either but it does!' Yes, we were back to exclamation marks, back to Berger saying things which demanded them. 'My first lap was good but I had a blister on my right front tyre after the hairpin and I knew from the first session that I could be in trouble so I eased off for two corners and then pushed again by the quick one leading to the chicane. I took the chicane easy but even so I could feel I was losing a lot of time there.'

Mansell needed victory or the Championship went to Senna. A plan was born and Senna says, 'Gerhard and I agreed that whoever led the first two or three laps, the other would try and help him. Gerhard made a very good start.'

The race became an unfolding saga.

Ramirez: 'The Japanese Grand Prix showed how the team worked and how equal everybody was. Terrific teamwork. From the European part of the season, when he'd been really struggling, we improved the car, Shell improved the fuel and Honda improved the engine. We were a clear second quicker than Williams and therefore in a position to programme how we wanted the race to be. Ron, Ayrton and Gerhard worked out the plan the night before. We were in this comfortable situation. At the beginning of the race the plan worked as envisaged. Gerhard took off to be the hare, Senna behind, Mansell behind him and Mansell could see Gerhard going away, going away: 3, 4, 5, 6 seconds.'

Berger pulled out three seconds on the opening lap building that to 4.2 seconds next lap.

Berger: 'The biggest problem I had was giving the tyres too hard a time in the beginning because I wanted to get as far away as possible. I worried that Riccardo might overtake Ayrton.' Mansell needed the win and needed Senna to finish third or lower. If Mansell and Patrese, his team-mate at Williams, did get past Senna that made Senna fourth. If Mansell then caught and took Berger the Championship went to Adelaide.

Mansell, following Senna but radioing to the pits, 'Don't panic, I'm biding my time.' Later he'd say 'The McLaren drivers used perfectly legitimate tactics. Gerhard shot off like a bullet while Ayrton kept me slow through the corners.'

Ramirez: 'Mansell started to get desperate. He had to get past Ayrton but he couldn't because Ayrton paced himself, always just a bit quicker in places where he needed to be. It was pretty clear sooner or later Mansell would make a mistake.'

Patrese suffered a gearbox problem on the parade lap: 'It stopped me being able to chase the McLarens.' Berger didn't know that, Senna didn't know that. During the ninth lap Mansell went on the radio again saying he'd move on Senna soon. He drew up and going into turn one on lap 10 skimmed away on to the run-off area never to return.

Mansell: 'In the morning warm-up I had a brake problem. We thought we'd fixed it. Unfortunately when I went into the corner the pedal went soft. I went deep into the corner because the car was very quick and very stable round there and when I put the brakes on I was caught by surprise. I wasn't slowing down, I tried to make the corner and ran out of road.'

Senna: 'When I saw Mansell go off I cannot say I was sorry because I knew he was having a hell of a time in the turbulence behind me. After he retired it was almost an instant reaction for me to think, right, we've got to go for it and we can have some fun.'

Berger's radio crackled: *Mansell out.* 'I slowed down to take care of the engine,' Senna accelerated and his radio crackled: *remember the Constructors' Championship*. Berger led by 10 seconds but, with him slowing and Senna accelerating, that came down in a cascade at 2 seconds a lap.

Berger: 'Ayrton was pushing and I thought maybe he wanted to make a nice race.'

Ayrton did. Ayrton came past Berger in a muscular move on lap 18 and Berger pitted for tyres almost immediately but suffered a poor stop stretching to 10 seconds and making him third; second again after Senna and Patrese had pitted themselves — second to Senna.

Patrese: 'I pushed hard after the pit stop but then I had some gearbox problems which stopped me pushing any harder. The gear change was not as good as I would have liked.'

On lap 33 the gap Senna to Berger stood at 2.919 seconds, Berger reaching 195 mph (314 km/h) at one point and that's quick, that is. Patrese drifted back to slightly over 20 seconds from Senna.

Berger: 'I was about 2 seconds behind Ayrton when I heard a big engine noise and I thought it was over but the engine kept running.' Berger set fastest lap and with 15 to go had the gap down to 2.689.

Senna: 'I was having to drive 99.9 per cent.' Senna set fastest lap and at lap 42 pulled the gap to 3.370. Berger shaved it to 3.309 a couple of laps later, Senna responded, ramming it back up to 5.564 with five to go.

Senna: 'We had agreed that whoever led for the opening stages would be allowed to win. I couldn't hear the messages clearly over the radio and I knew nobody would believe me if I didn't give way. Eventually I asked the question but I couldn't hear the reply. I had to keep asking if Ron wanted me to let Gerhard through. I backed right off to cut the noise from the engine and asked again. Ron said yes, he wanted us to change positions.'

Senna moved into the final lap and as he flowed through the sweepers after the start-finish straight Berger wasn't in sight. Senna waved a clenched fist once, twice in those sweepers. At the hairpin at mid-lap Berger began to draw up but approaching the chicane Berger still lay some 100 m distant, perhaps a little more.

At the chicane, the last lunge of the circuit before the start-finish straight, Berger drew full up. Senna slowed and moved left-left-left allowing Berger to pass. Berger won his first race for McLaren by 0.344 seconds.

Senna: 'It hurt to do it but the pain was nothing compared with the feeling of having my third Championship. Gerhard has helped me in the past and it was my turn to give him some help, a small gesture because he was as fast as me in the race.'

Berger: 'Ayrton, I am happy to say, was thinking about me as much as I was thinking about him!' (Later, and more privately, Berger would describe 'winning like that' as a 'bit of a joke'.)

Ramirez: 'It was very moving, although I didn't think Ayrton was going to do it despite the plan! At the end of the day they're sitting there in the cockpits, it's one more Grand Prix victory for the taking and he let it go. In fact it was really moving and better because Mansell stayed around for the finish.'

Dennis embraced Berger and would say, 'Good tactics well executed!' Yes, time for exclamation marks again.

Senna pulled into the pit lane, the McLaren engulfed by mechanics, media and anyone else who could get near. Senna raised a fist again, stepped from the cockpit and now embraced Berger — a masculine bearhug of a gesture, Berger smiling, Mansell in the background smiling, too. He had waited to pay his respects to the Champion. It was nicely done with a handshake, an affectionate slap on Senna's arm. Berger handled the podium nicely, beckoning Senna up to join him on the highest rung, then beckoning Patrese.

Senna's decision remains contentious because of the ostentatious way he made the 'small gesture'. If he'd slowed a bit over the ebbing laps of the race and let Berger take him that would have been one thing; to demonstrate so graphically 'Here is my gift to you' after the chicane and virtually within sight of the line was another.

No one who understands the ferocity with which Senna approaches every detail of his career can doubt that he endured very real mental turmoil in reaching the decision, particularly since this would have been his thirty-third victory. To a man constructing records which might never be beaten, including the most wins by any driver — although that lay a long way ahead, Prost already on 44 — passing up even one did represent a genuine sacrifice. In fact, as he let Berger through and Berger reached for the line, Senna accelerated again, and for a naughty, naughty moment I thought he'd changed his mind; but no, he moved up but not fully alongside and let it go at that 0.344 seconds.

Ramirez: 'You can say that perhaps Ayrton should have progressively slowed and allowed Gerhard to catch him but then again, if he was going to let the victory go, he wanted the whole world to see he was saying thank you to Gerhard for helping not just in the race but all through the year to win the Championship. And yes, we did want Gerhard to win a Grand Prix.'

End of saga.

Australia might have been anti-climactic (if any motor race can be that) but it rained and rained hard. Senna said he'd only start because he felt a 'strong obligation' to the team. He had pole, Berger alongside. At the green light every car slithered, Senna leading, Berger tucking in and prudently keeping his distance peering into the spray which Senna threw. Mansell tiptoed behind Berger, went through on the straight and set off after Senna. Lap 3:

Mansell	at 3.919 seconds
Berger	at 8.091 seconds
Schumacher	at 8.895 seconds

Nicola Larini's Lamborghini battered itself into the wall on the main straight and three laps later Martini's Minardi did the same at the same place but on the opposite side of the track. That made a narrow neck in the straight, compounded because rescue workers beavered over and around the stricken cars. Officials stopped the race a lap later, Berger coincidentally spinning off in a floating motion.

'I only started for the Constructors' points,' he said. 'I closed my eyes and said, 'OK, we go.' It was very difficult to stay on the road. Some parts of the race were a little bit better but then it started raining again, my tyre pressures were low and I had aquaplaning everywhere. It was not possible to control.

'The worst thing was — well, to have some spins is OK and even to crash into a wall could be OK, but crashed cars were on the straight, people working on them, and that was the most dangerous place. The big aquaplaning was there. You knew every time you reached that point you couldn't control the car and there were people on the road so it was just impossible. It's your own decision whether you start or not. If you don't start you're right, if you do start it's OK. If you crash it's a result of your own decision, but if there are people working on the circuit and you hit somebody that's not acceptable.'

Senna, visibly concerned, lowered his voice (which always means he's going to be extremely serious) and said, 'I think it's very hard for the officials to make such a decision because there is a lot of pressure, television all over the world. We understand, but in a way it's our own fault. We should have got out of the cars, stuck together and made a decision ourselves. Then the race wouldn't have started.

'It's always very difficult to get everyone together because we have a lot of responsibilities to the teams and the sponsors who give us so much and there are moments when we have to try to give them something back. It's very difficult to find the equilibrium, the balance of making the right decisions every single time but, as I said, it was a mistake by all of us — not only the officials but the drivers, the teams. We should have had courage as a *group*.'

A sad, drowned, niggling end of a season and mercifully nobody was hurt on 3 November 1991 at Adelaide, the normally placid city everyone likes so much. Final Championship points: Senna 96, Mansell 72, Patrese 53, Berger 43, Prost 34.

And a final irony. Ferrari fired Prost before Adelaide but if they hadn't it's as certain as day follows night that he *might* have done a lap in these conditions but almost certainly wouldn't. The year before Prost had refused to start in similar conditions and which man can say Prost was wrong? It's not just that you might hurt yourself, it's that you might hurt others and either way it's not an attractive notion for a sportsman. Fastest lap, you see, on 3 November 1991 was Berger, 83.602 mph (134.545 km/h) round *streets* in a downpour. The legal speed limit on British motorways is 70 mph (113 km/h) . . .

Prost's replacement, Gianni Morbidelli, qualified on the fourth row of the grid and finished sixth. Not bad; in fact good — but worth risking your life for?

Testing time

Just before Christmas 1991 Mark Blundell spent a couple of days testing the Marlboro McLaren Honda at Donington, specifically doing work on the gearbox. Blundell, as approachable a man as Berger, was taking over from Damon Hill — now official tester with Williams — and found himself in a unique position to watch Berger and Senna.

'When I went into Formula 1 with Brabham Yamaha during the 1991 season Gerhard and I would acknowledge each other very briefly in the normal way, an experienced driver recognizing a newcomer,' Blundell says, 'and I didn't really get to know him well until I joined McLaren, stayed in the same places as they did. I noticed clearly that when he needed to be serious he was extremely serious, but as soon as that was over he was funny, always a joker, a normal guy, nice, straight.'

The sharp irony to this remains that during 1992 Berger found himself involved in two of the most dangerous moments since his own crash at Imola in 1989, an irony compounded by the fact that Formula 1 had become so safe. No one could give an absolute guarantee that danger had been eliminated and no one ever would, but you didn't then go to the races expecting the worst any more.

Berger stood completely blameless in one of them, at the tail end of the British Grand Prix, and arguably his common sense, and how he kept his nerve, helped prevent what might have been the greatest disaster since Le Mans in 1955 when the engine of a Mercedes scythed into the crowd causing carnage. The other? We'll come to that, we'll come to that.

After Christmas, during the annual ski trip, Ron Dennis asked Berger a pointed question. *Are you going or staying in 1993?* The conversation between Dennis and Berger wasn't as blunt as that, of course, rather the first exploratory step to negotiations.

A quiet start to the year, though, with Blundell and Berger testing at Silverstone in January, working on the push-button semi-automatic gear shift. McLaren, incidentally, have a company policy of attacking a new season only when they're ready. They don't like being hustled by the calendar and went to the first race, Kyalami, with a modified version of the 1991 car. Kyalami proved to be a very, very distant sibling of the track where Formula 1 had last raced in 1985. *This* Kyalami might have been anywhere. Some, drawn by a mingling of curiosity and nostalgia, sought out overgrown sections of the old, searched for the places with resonant names, Crowthorne Corner at the end of the immense straight where Mike Hailwood had hauled Clay Regazzoni from a burning car so long ago, the Jukskei Sweep where Jim Clark had smoothed the Lotus 49 through with such ease to win the last Grand Prix of his life; Barbeque Bend which Mansell had taken with such ferocity to hold off Rosberg in 1985; and even 1985 — when you surveyed the new Kyalami, the corners named after sponsors — seemed so long ago.

Berger caught a mood. 'It's a nice track, but personally I don't find it very exciting. I would have preferred some more high-speed corners — the fast corners you can take flat out anyway. It's difficult to get a good lap.' At the *old* Kyalami Berger averaged 141.720 mph (228.027 km/h) in the Arrows on his hot qualifying lap for eleventh on the grid. Allowing for the increase in technology, the *new* would be some 10 mph (16 km/h) slower but I only mention this for reasons of general interest. The comparison is in no sense valid otherwise.

Mansell forged the matrix of the whole season during the first qualifying session when he lapped at 1 minute 15.576, Berger next at 1 minute 16.672, then Senna on 1 minute 16.815. Berger complained that the biggest problem was the 'number of young drivers out on the circuit who are, in my view, not really experienced enough for Formula 1. If you have slower drivers who are only a couple of seconds off the pace it is easy to back off before a quick lap in the knowledge that you won't catch them before the end of it. With people who are 5 seconds or more off the pace you are obviously catching them more frequently.'

Taking Berger's 1 minute 16.672 as the yardstick, you need only glance down the times to understand perfectly.

G. Morbidelli (Minardi)	1: 21.027
P. Martini (BMS Dallara)	1: 21.134
B. Gachot (Venturi)	1: 21.447
E. van de Poele (Brabham)	1: 21.648
S. Modena (Jordan)	1: 22.020

P. Belmondo (March)	1: 22.022
U. Katayama (Venturi)	1: 22.129
A. Chiesa (Fondmetal)	1: 22.170
G. Amati (Brabham)	1: 25.942

Morbidelli, Martini, Gachot or Modena had plenty of experience but the others didn't. On the old Kyalami with that imposing ascent to Leeukop Bend and then the truly immense straight it might not have mattered, but here on a tighter circuit it did. And in second qualifying, maintaining the theme, Berger said, 'The problems of getting a clear lap just don't get any better.' Senna — 'I had a clear run' — thrust in 1 minute 16.227, good enough for the front row but not pole. Mansell had that in a firm grip, shaving his 1 minute 15.576 to 1 minute 15.486.

At the green Patrese, with a new anti-wheelspin device on his Canon Williams Renault, thrust between Senna and Berger and, almost in his wake, Alesi nipped past Berger. By turn two, a left, Schumacher had gone through, too. Berger drifted back from Schumacher and came under attack from Capelli's Ferrari.

'From quite early on,' Berger said, 'I realized I was going to have a problem with fuel. When I pushed hard it became obvious that there was insufficient so I had to back off to get to the finish.' He watched Alesi and Schumacher play out their duel and when Capelli went on lap 28, engine, the pressure behind went with him. Alesi himself went on lap 41, engine again, all smoke and dust and the race finished Mansell, Patrese, Senna, Schumacher, Berger, Herbert (Lotus).

Akimasa Yasuoka of Honda commented that 'from our telemetry neither engine seemed to have any problems apart from the fact that Gerhard's car was consuming too much fuel. Because this is the first race to be run to the new fuel regulations we allowed a slightly greater than usual margin of error when calculating our fuel load and, fortunately, this is what got us to the finish.' Berger limped across the line and immediately parked the McLaren on a small segment of grass. He'd made it by less than 50 m.

In the background Berger and Dennis discussed 1993 again.

Allan McNish, a young Scot, tested the new McLaren (MP4/7) at Silverstone, a fly-by-wire car (an expression borrowed from aerospace, electronics replacing many human actions), although the team were reticent about when they'd race it. Senna tested it the week after South Africa, Blundell and Berger tested it, too

* * *

Conversational interlude
Hilton: 'How frustrating was it to you as a racer to set the car up, go round and round and round trying this and that without neces-

sarily going for a time, then Berger might come along and blitz your best time?

Blundell: 'Of course it is frustrating for any driver to actually pound around and develop stuff and know you're carrying the full weight of 100 litres of fuel and one of the race guys — Gerhard or Ayrton — turns up and the team might drain out the fuel and let him go for it. At the same time you acknowledge that you will be working in certain areas and you're not there to prove your speed. I have to say I had real support from Gerhard and Ayrton. I was, I felt, doing a good job and they were very happy with the response I gave them, the feedback. Now and again the team drained the fuel out for me so I could show what I could do and my times were always up there with theirs.'

Hilton: 'I remember you saying once that you did a time in the morning and Ayrton came in the afternoon, drove the same car, same spec, everything, and was no quicker.'

Blundell: 'It happened the other way around. We were testing at Silverstone and Ayrton used the car all morning and I used it in the afternoon. We changed the seat, changed the seatbelts, and I matched identically the time he'd done, so in that sense there was no problem for me. I think everyone in the team knew if we needed a fast lap I could do it as well, perhaps, as Gerhard and Ayrton could. Of course this was a testing environment. I wasn't up against them in races.'

Hilton: 'Did you think Gerhard and Ayrton sympathized that you were doing a lot of the hard work and they reaped the benefit?'

Blundell: 'I don't know. I think they did take on board that in some ways they were fortunate — I'm not, I sincerely hope, being big-headed — that they had a guy there who was giving the same information about the car that they were giving. They knew we were all going in the same direction. If they were away and I was testing, they didn't have doubts about me going in the wrong direction. At the same time they knew I wasn't pussy-footing around, I was pushing the car, which is nice background knowledge for them. They never turned round and said, "Oh, it must be hard for you" or whatever, because I am sure they understood that anyway. I was a driver as much as they, they knew what feelings I had about being around but not being able to get at it in a race.'

Hilton: 'Especially if the team said, "We're doing a full race distance, today, thank you?"'

Blundell: 'Yes, there was that.'

Hilton: 'Especially if you might do a long run in the morning and another in the afternoon?'

Blundell: 'We had an inhouse joke. I'd be there trying four or five different floor variations and they'd roll into the motorhome and say, "How are you getting on with the floors?" In fact it became a standing joke.'

Hilton: 'How would you contrast the two men? After all, Senna has been known to play a practical joke or two when he puts his mind to it.'

Blundell: 'Yes, I think that is precisely what it is — when he puts his mind to it. Nine times out of 10 the guy is very focused, very stable, he doesn't come out of what I might call the Formula 1 driver's shell, whereas Gerhard tends to switch off from that easily — from concentrated driver to concentrated funny man. Gerhard is also a lot more relaxed in his attitude. With Ayrton there always seemed to be a tension surrounding him, he had a certain presence. They are completely different characters.'

Hilton: 'If you look back, all Senna's team-mates have fallen out with him or been overwhelmed. Suddenly Berger's there and they go on holiday together and genuinely like each other.'

Blundell: 'Yes, they got on extremely well because they were so different. Maybe when you had Prost and Senna together they were two totally focused guys and neither could quite get to grips with that. I think Gerhard always acknowledged that if he was to do well he'd have to really buckle down and knuckle down. I also think at the end of the day he respected Senna had the sheer ability and speed and talent, so much of it you'd need a lot to knock him off.'

Hilton: 'Psychologically it's an interesting point. Senna is Senna, Berger is manifestly not like that. Berger wants to be alive, making people laugh as well as driving the car. Maybe to compete with Senna he would have had to change himself and he was not prepared to do that.'

Blundell: 'I'm not sure whether he did try, I'm not sure that he actually did try to change himself. Maybe at the beginning he did say to himself, "I will be like Ayrton, I will try and do that, focus on it 24 hours a day", but it is just not Gerhard. His attitude is to get back to his normal self as quickly as possible because that is the way he is.'

End of conversational interlude

* * *

Senna became the focal point of the first qualifying session in Mexico. In the esses, flowing across the bumpy surface, the McLaren twitched, rotated and struck the barrier. Berger felt his session was 'OK' — he was fourth — 'but that's about as fast as this car will go in these circumstances. Perhaps there are a few more fractions of a second to come. I like this circuit but it is very bumpy and Peralta remains as difficult as ever.' Prophetic. In the second session going into Peralta the car snapped out of control.

Berger applied opposite lock but not enough to contain the momentum. The McLaren spun full round and off. 'You can't take the risk of pressing hard over the bumps because you just don't know what the car is going to do. I crashed because the car got thrown slightly on a large bump and I slammed into the barrier sideways and very hard. A big accident.'

After a spate of jostling at the start of the race Berger was squeezed back to fifth, sixth when Brundle hustled through. 'Being stuck behind Brundle held me up at the beginning and the car was not very good on full tanks, but it got better and better as the race went on. I was flat out all the way but the car jumped out of fourth gear over the same bump every lap and so I had to change gear earlier than usual and this lost me some time. I couldn't go quicker.'

On lap 19 Berger mounted an attack. He got a tow down the straight but Brundle moved to centre track, Berger having a look at the right-hander at the end of the straight. Not close enough this time round. Nor next time. Out on the back of the circuit he tried again, turning the pressure up and up. It's tantalizing how a circuit 2.747 miles (4.420 km) long rations and rationalizes itself to just a couple of overtaking places. Both drivers know this and take their precautions so that laps dissolve into a kind of waltz, the same steps each time. There might be a flurry of movement at the overtaking places before the waltz resumes.

At the end of the straight on lap 41 Berger did get inside as Brundle turned in. Brundle estimated the distance between his right front wheel and Berger's left rear as the equivalent of 'three fag papers'. Brundle flicked away, ceding the corner to Berger. That took them through the right-hander on to a little surge to a left-hander and Brundle moved outside Berger — another three fag papers. Now Brundle sliced in front forcing Berger to brake heavily.

'I had a lot of electric moments with Gerhard all through the season,' Brundle says. 'He seemed to be good in qualifying but fighting the car in the race, I was fighting the car in qualifying and very good in the race, so very often we met in the middle, as it were. I actually out-qualified him in Mexico, I was running fourth and he was running fifth. He was quicker through the last corner leading to the straight and quicker down the straight, I was quicker through the twiddly bits. He started to crowd me and I kept blocking him without being too obvious about it. Finally he did squeeze up the inside.

'I'm sure it looked good on television (it did) but for me it was a normal thing. I knew what I was going to do before we even got to the corner: he'd try to come inside, he'd have to brake late because my car was very good under braking, I'd take the corner in second rather than third and squeeze him on to the dirty line on the inside where the track had a few per cent less grip — he'd slide wide and I'd zap him up the inside and shut the door.

'That's the difference between a Formula 1 driver and non-Formula 1 drivers, if you like. You have much more capacity left to work out what's happening around you. Driving the car is actually like going to the office, it's relatively easy for us, and the best drivers — and Senna most of all, probably — have more percentage available to examine what is happening around.

'Gerhard's hard to dice with and I'd get very frustrated. He tends to leave the door open and when you get there shut it very firmly, which usually means you meet in the middle . . .'

They waltzed again.

Berger gathered himself, waited, began to position himself, caught Brundle and at Peralta went inside, went clean through. Lap 43: Mansell, Patrese, Schumacher, Berger. As Berger chased Schumacher he set fastest lap but finished almost 12 seconds behind.

A week after Mexico, McLaren announced that they'd be taking six cars to Brazil in two weeks' time, three of the MP4/6Bs they'd been running so far, three of the new MP4/7As. Ron Dennis insisted, 'We'd always considered the option of running the MP4/7A in Brazil,' and that option now pressed hard: Mansell 20 points, Patrese 12, Schumacher 7, Berger 5, Senna 4.

The pressure mounted in the first Brazilian qualifying session, Berger fifth, Senna ninth, mounted again in the second session. I give you unadorned the official Marlboro McLaren Honda view of the Saturday.

'Ayrton Senna will start his home Grand Prix from third place on the grid, having earned this position at the wheel of the new MP4/7A. It was an achievement which rounded off a difficult day during which all six of the team's cars were used during the morning's free practice session. In the morning session Ayrton suffered an engine failure on the MP4/6. This afternoon Gerhard briefly tried Ayrton's spare MP4/7A but set his time in another MP4/6.'

'It's a shame I had traffic on my best lap with the old car,' Berger said. 'I couldn't drive the spare MP4/7A with Ayrton's pedal set-up and I was disappointed I had to keep jumping back and forth between the two types of car.'

After the parade lap and before the race Berger angled into the pits, engine overheating, and started from there, last. He dropped out after four laps, engine overheating.

The rain in Spain fell all over the second qualifying session, Senna third on the grid, Berger seventh, and although Berger went quickest of all in the Sunday morning warm-up, the rain in Spain fell all over the race.

The grid: Mansell — Schumacher — Senna — Patrese — Capelli — Brundle — Berger — Alesi. At the start, Berger says, 'I must say I

213

was surprised to see Alesi alongside me on the starting grid when the light was still red!' Alesi made the start of a 100 m runner, body taut and tight, poised to react. He turned the Ferrari's nose towards the channel between the twin columns of cars but only actually moved forward when the red light was still on but the green had come on, too: both colours up there on the starter board simultaneously for an eye-blink. And an eye-blink later Alesi's wheels churned smoke but neither Mansell nor Schumacher had yet moved, Alesi already between the twin columns.

Patrese, scarcely expecting to find a car there, clouted Alesi wheel to wheel into a gap on the far side of the grid in front of Senna. Berger, taking the outside of turn one, slotted into sixth while Senna swarmed him. Through the spray you could glimpse move and counter move as Senna took Berger. 'I just didn't have enough downforce early on in the race and my gearbox started playing up but then the fault seemed to disappear.' Brundle spun off.

Wonderful moments in the right-left loop, Schumacher slicing inside Alesi — they touched — and simultaneously Berger stealing inside Senna, drifting full across the front of Senna and so far that Senna stole back through. Senna took Alesi on the straight, a simple power play, and now Berger circled behind Alesi, predator. He tried on the inside — they touched — and Alesi spun away. At lap 14: Mansell, Patrese, Schumacher, Senna, Berger, Capelli.

On lap 30 Senna and Berger took a backmarker and Senna did slither wide. Berger drew alongside and into a right-sweeper held the racing line, forcing Senna to follow. In traffic they surged to a left-hander and Senna tried on the inside — a prod — but Berger resisted that and Senna had to catch his breath, settle before he resumed the assault. During that assault he angled inside Berger on a right-sweeper and edged away.

Berger pushed hard, narrowing the gap to Senna. By now the rain fell harder and Senna spun — 'I was lucky to go back on the circuit but the car was aquaplaning everywhere.' Lap 58: Mansell, Schumacher, Senna, Berger, Alesi, Capelli. Alesi pitted for fresh wet tyres, caught Berger at a savage rate and surged by, set off after Senna, but Senna spun again and this time 'I just couldn't hold it'.

The Spanish Grand Prix finished with Mansell 23.914 seconds clear of Schumacher, Alesi third, Berger a distant fourth.

The talk naturally centred on Mansell who bestrode the Championship with a maximum 40 points and why Patrese — 18 points — couldn't stay with him; the talk was of Schumacher and his golden horizons. Berger had only eight points. Easy, as the sodden crowd tramped home, to overlook his race. He'd started seventh on the grid and been engulfed at the start. He'd taken Senna in a fluid, opportunist's move and when Senna struck back he behaved in a pragmatic way. OK, you can go. When Alesi sprang out and grasped a right-hander, Berger had the finesse to hold the McLaren steady and safely away from the Ferrari. He understood perfectly well that Alesi could not be held on fresher tyres. OK, you can go. Across 65 laps Berger made no discernible mistake, and this when 10 cars spun off. It stands as a statement about the art of the possible and more poignant because so easily overlooked.

They tested at Imola a week after Spain, Mansell rapping out 1 minute 22.236, but Senna did 1 minute 22.727. Hope for McLaren? Maybe. Berger did 1:24.310 but had a major accident at the Variante Alta, the car travelling off sideways and beating against a wall, the suspension pushed into the side of the monocoque.

During the San Marino Grand Prix Senna moved out and took Alesi comfortably enough but, as Berger moved inside to follow, Alesi pincered him and they collided, Alesi's Ferrari briefly airborne. Alesi drifted to the rim of the track and jack-knifed back towards Berger clipping the passing McLaren. Debris flew and Berger halted. 'The incident with Alesi was just a racing accident, not my fault and not his. There was a gap. I had to go for it and he was obviously going to fight me for it. We touched wheels which was OK but he lost control and I hoped I would squeeze past. I was out of luck.'

In first qualifying at Monaco Berger crashed heavily and said shortly afterwards, 'To be honest I'm really surprised to have got away from that accident without hurting myself. I was pressing really hard and it was a big shunt. I went straight in at Massanet (the left-hander feeding into Casino Square) at about 155 mph (241 km/h), absolutely on the limit. It felt as though something broke on the left rear because the front right wheel locked up suddenly, as though the wheel wasn't touching the track.'

'At the race track,' Ramirez says, 'one of the differences between the two is that Senna could concentrate every second, every corner of every lap. He is on the pace all the time. He understands the electronic gadgets we have nowadays and he can keep doing it lap after lap. None of the other drivers we've had at McLaren including Prost — although when he was with us the cars didn't have that much electronics — could use all those gadgets to gain a bit here, a bit there which adds up to getting a few tenths.

'Gerhard and the others couldn't do it. They can't programme themselves. They are too busy driving the car. Ayrton can drive the car *as well as* optimizing absolutely everything and you see it on the telemetry: Ayrton will extract every ounce out of the engine and the gearbox and the brakes, *everything*, and a lot of the others will only extract 75 per cent, which isn't bad . . .

'At Monaco, second qualifying, Gerhard had this problem where he just couldn't concentrate a whole lap. Last lap of qualifying, look at the telemetry: up to the tunnel he and Ayrton were exactly the same. Gerhard was really good. His problem: he thought the last corner was fast, his brain didn't tell him it was slow. He threw it away. He missed it completely. He tried to slow the car too much with the gearbox, put it into first gear and first gear broke. He came round again, had to use second gear and lost a lot of time, lost a second.'

In the race Berger went only to lap 33. 'I had a big problem trying to change the mixture setting and nearly went off twice because of that. Just when everything settled down again and I started to push the gearbox stopped working. No hydraulic pressure.'

In Canada Senna took pole from Patrese, Mansell and Berger. At the green Senna moved fast. Mansell surged past Patrese, Berger fourth and it settled like that, Senna nursing and guarding the lead, Mansell tracking, searching. A queue formed behind him circling more or less equidistant. 'It was quite hard because in the opening stages it was impossible to overtake,' Berger says. 'It became a question of waiting a little bit. The first six cars were all together but there was too much risk involved in trying to overtake and I decided to stay behind Patrese.'

Mansell, eager for the World Championship, tried to take Senna at the chicane on lap 15 and failed, locked his brakes and spun. 'Ayrton was in front' Berger says, 'but he didn't have the quickest car and everyone behind waited for a mistake by someone in front of them. Everyone knows that if you want to try really hard to overtake someone you have to go off line and off line the track is dirty. You lose grip. This early in the race there was no reason for anyone to do it. I'd tried to overtake Patrese at the same place and if I'm honest there was no way, it was never going to work. Then I saw Nigel go for it and I thought the same thing, it's never going to work. After that I did get past Patrese.'

Berger moved off after Senna and 'I realized I was able to lap a little bit quicker'. For 20 laps he chased him but faced the same problem as Mansell: where to find a way through. The problem solved itself. 'Eventually,' Senna said, 'the engine just cut out.'

Berger led, Patrese hard on him, the Benettons of Schumacher and Brundle hard on Patrese. 'Just as Ayrton got problems I did too, with the gear change, which meant I had to spend seven or eight laps trying to adapt to a new driving style.' At 38 laps:

Berger	58:10.445
Patrese	at 0.445
Schumacher	at 1.281
Brundle	at 1.776

The new driving style? 'I couldn't shift any more using the button and I had to shift with my fingers. That's a completely different way and one I hadn't used since my days at Ferrari. I had to learn it again. Tyres were on the limit and once in the middle of the race I thought to change them but they didn't get worse.' (Technical note: the McLaren had a button which allowed a driver the freedom to change down from, say, fourth to second and so on; if the button failed the driver had two switches, one to go up and the other to come down through the gears, but only sequentially, first to second to third.)

Patrese remained within striking distance until Berger set fastest lap and had a straight run home. Patrese went out — gearbox, lap 43 — and the gap Berger to Schumacher stood at slightly more than 8 seconds on lap 46 of 69. Berger drove those last laps masterfully, nimble but incisive in traffic, set a new fastest lap and emerged from the car smiling broadly. He'd beaten Schumacher by 12.401 seconds.

Leaving aside Senna's 'gift' of the Japanese Grand Prix the season before, Berger had now driven 39 times for the Marlboro McLaren Honda team before he reached, if you can put it this way, his first legitimate victory for them. The team, and Honda, were visibly delighted for him. In the background the discussions with Dennis became, as Berger says, 'more concentrated' in Canada.

The two sides of Berger are well illustrated at the French Grand Prix at Magny-Cours. 'We stayed at a chateau half an hour away from the circuit, a fantastic place,' Blundell says. 'There was a big bust on the mantlepiece, very human-looking and probably the owner's pride and joy — certainly a valuable thing. Everyone else was at dinner. Gerhard spotted the bust, took it under his arm and upstairs we went. He likes to have someone with him so they can be in on the joke as well.

'Into Senna's room he goes, takes all the sheets off the bed, lays the bust down on the bed, arranges the pillows under it so they look like a body when the sheets are pulled back over it all. The lighting in the chateau wasn't terribly brilliant so Gerhard knows that when Senna walks through the bedroom door he's going to crap himself — *somebody's in my bed*. We went back downstairs and the evening wore on. Eventually Senna did go up, opened the door and we could hear an exclamation. Typical Gerhard. He though it hilarious.

'You'd go into the Marlboro Suite, big pictures on the walls of Nigel and other drivers. Gerhard would take out a felt-tipped pen and draw goggles over their eyes . . .'

The other side of Berger? In first qualifying, 'I pressed really hard throughout but an incident with Erik Comas (Ligier) was unbelievable. Belmondo always seems to be in the middle of the circuit.' Comas, hammering in his Ligier, came upon Berger trying to get past Belmondo and struck the rear of the McLaren. 'Comas was really lucky, I tell you. I saw the whole underside of his car as it passed over me.' (Comas subsequently said, 'Gerhard acknowledged that he had been in the wrong and came to apologize afterwards.')

In second qualifying Berger went 'absolutely as fast as I could go under the circumstances. I really don't think I could have gone any faster. Towards the end of the session I got a little too close to Alesi's Ferrari and locked a front wheel when I lost downforce but by then my tyres were finished anyway.' It gave Mansell, Patrese, Senna, Berger on the grid.

Patrese stormed away at the green light, Mansell behind. As they reached the end of the start-finish straight and moved into the long left-hander Berger, hustling Senna, 'braked late, on the limit and Ayrton and I came very close'. Berger, on the inside, overshot Senna and Senna's car jerked under breaking, veered away. They flowed round to the hairpin and whey they reached it Schumacher tried to slot past Senna, struck him amidships.

'I made a bad start,' Senna said. 'Gerhard and I ended up side by side at the first corner. It was close but OK. I followed him down the straight, he braked very late so I was being careful and then Schumacher just came up and hit me from behind. I think he totally misjudged his speed and his braking point.'

'After Ayrton was hit,' Berger said, 'I saw him coming towards me and I thought we were going to collide.' Berger ran third but with no real hope of catching Patrese or Mansell and on lap 11 his engine 'just stopped and as I pulled over a small fire started'. Fire marshals sprayed it while Berger clambered out and stooped over the cockpit looking for causes.

Silverstone will be remembered for something more than a race which Mansell dominated absolutely. Berger ran seventh early on but 'in the first half of the race the car was difficult to drive and after my pit stop (on lap 29) I felt that the engine was slightly down on power. There was a strange vibration in some corners. Despite this I pushed as hard as I could but three laps from the end the temperature warning light came on. I couldn't back off because Schumacher was right behind me. Then on the last lap it just went.'

This demands much closer examination. On that last lap intoxicated sections of the crowd began to invade the track while Mansell moved towards the finishing line. As he crossed it someone ran across the track, a spectre from a nightmare. At Copse the crowd flooded the track forcing Mansell to slow very urgently. Patrese crossed the line 39.094 seconds after Mansell and by then several hundred people ran along the grass verge at the side of the track towards the oncoming traffic. Berger, fifth, crossed the line with a plume of smoke beginning to billow into a cloud and he pulled up near the pit lane wall, parked it. He did this very calmly, taking care to keep the McLaren under tight control and taking care to keep the oil from his blown engine as far from the centre of the track as he could.

Eleven cars behind him still raced.

The concept of any of them contesting a place side by side and reaching Berger's oil with an uncounted number of unprotected spectators a few feet away did not, and does not, bear contemplation. Patrese, back in the Williams pit, remonstrated with expressive arm movements about the invasion. His face looked stunned and haunted. Brundle admitted candidly he'd been frightened. Alboreto became equally expressive. 'It was very dangerous. We (he, Comas and Capelli) arrived at Woodcote flat out and there were people everywhere. Crazy.'

No spectators had been killed since 1977, when Villeneuve's Ferrari plunged off in Japan killing two and, as far as I could see, the people who felt impelled to take themselves on to Silverstone on 12 July 1992 looked no older than their early 20s, many clearly younger. They'd have no memory of 1977 and the mood they were in it probably wouldn't have made any difference if they had.

Berger moved towards respectability in the points table, Mansell 76, Patrese 40, Schumacher 29, Berger 20, Senna 18. The Williams held superior in its totality and virtually every lap of every race thus far had proved it. Senna and Berger handled this professionally: they made the right public noises, never disguising or belabouring how far behind the Mclaren was. In Germany after second qualifying Berger said, 'We look as though we have everybody under control except Williams.' They'd play the season to the end, drive tactically, search out advantages and, moreover, after a wretched German Grand Prix — a misfire claimed him after 16 laps — Berger began a strong run.

In the background, he flew to Bologna with Niki Lauda, now Ferrari's technical adviser, to talk to Luca di Montezemolo, who ran Ferrari. Berger insists that Lauda wasn't being one of the Austrian mafia trying to hire him. 'Niki was 100 per cent on the side of Ferrari in all our discussions. He would deal against me, putting the best deal for Ferrari.'

Helmut Marko, friend, adviser and confidante, says, 'We had a discussion about what Gerhard should do. I was the one saying go to Ferrari because the aspect looks good having Barnard back there, having Lauda there. I didn't know that the Ferrari infrastructure was so bad. Nobody knew that. I had a big party in Graz and I said it was the right decision to go there, not only on the money side but because if he stayed he'd still be behind Senna — not as far as Michael Andretti is now, but still behind — and he couldn't stand that a fourth season. It was absolutely necessary. What he'd learnt from Senna and Mclaren was to work methodically, to go step by step, to learn about the car. Like Senna, everything has to be planned. You have the talent, you build on it, you work on it. What he had learnt would be important for Ferrari and, with a little bit of luck . . .'

This was an almost exact reversal of the theory which had taken Berger to McLaren: the way to beat Senna and thus become World Champion was to get your hands on the same equipment. Now the theory had become: the way to beat Senna is to get your hands on better equipment with another team, as Mansell was currently doing with the Canon Williams Renault. Berger himself, echoing Ron Dennis, has said with his usual candour that having Senna as a team-mate is the most difficult situation you can get.

'As Frank Williams always points out, in order to beat Senna you need to have very special machinery, meaning better machinery than Senna has,' Ramirez says. 'I don't think Gerhard could have taken a fourth year of it.'

A few days after Berger's visit to Bologna a Ferrari spokesman announced the dropping of Capelli for 1993 and added, 'Senna is our number one priority but we have told him we do not think we can win the Championship next year and we must work for 1994. If we do not get Senna we will have Gerhard Berger. That is the most probable thing.'

Just like Estoril in 1984 when the world watch Lauda, in Hungary the world watched Mansell. Who noticed Berger spin in qualifying? 'I lost downforce when I was running too close beyond Ayrton.' They'd noticed Berger in the race, all right.

The grid: Patrese, Mansell, Senna, Schumacher, Berger, Brundle.

At the green Patrese drew away from Mansell and angled across towards the first corner, a right-hander. In the rush to the mouth of the corner Patrese angled further across. Senna held mid-track three cars' length behind and, for a fraction of a second, Schumacher was ahead of Berger. They closed on the corner, Senna moving past Mansell, Berger level and then past Mansell. By lap two Patrese had gone from the McLarens' reach and Mansell moved up on them, increasing his pace so that after lap 4 he lay only 1.5 seconds behind Berger. At the end of the straight Mansell pressed the Williams hard, hard inside Berger. OK, you can go. At 24 laps:

Patrese	33:30.889
Senna	at 23.019
Mansell	at 23.660
Berger	at 24.406
Schumacher	at 25.357
Hakkinen	at 29.311

On lap 31 Mansell ran wide at the left-hander just before the pit lane entrance and Berger stole through. Mansell needed four laps to retake him — at the end of the straight again, Berger squeezing him for an instant before conceding. The race and the World Championship altered fundamentally when Patrese spun off on lap 39. Mansell settled behind Senna from laps 39 to 61 when, suspecting a puncture, he pitted and emerged sixth behind Senna, Berger, Schumacher, Brundle and Hakkinen.

Mansell came at them like the wind: Schumacher spun off, Mansell fled past Hakkinen on the straight, did the same to Brundle and did the same to Berger — 'When Nigel came up behind me he was going really quickly and I realized I had to give away second place.' Berger moved aside, no squeezing. OK, you can go.

Brundle, caught up in the momentum, attacked Berger. 'I had to work hard to keep the others behind me. I was touched by Brundle and when Schumacher spun behind me he almost hit me; but a nice race, very hard, a lot of pressure,'

Brundle says, 'Gerhard held me up for a long time in Hungary, a race I think I should have won although it doesn't stand out like that because I came only fifth. I just couldn't get past him. That Honda engine had some really serious grunt and anyway I'd lost sixth gear which didn't help. He'd lead down the straight and I'd catch him in the corners out the back. I had a big go at him and he moved over at the last moment and I ran into the back of him. There you go. He's a hard man, a hard man to pass and when he gets defensive you both end up going more slowly, that's the trouble.'

While the world celebrated Mansell, Berger spoke typically at the press conference. 'Firstly I would like to congratulate Nigel for winning the Championship. Although Ayrton knows what it is like to win it, I still want to know what it's like . . .'

As they sat waiting for the television interviews to begin Berger smiled, touched Senna on the arm and made what seemed to be a gentle joke. On the BBC Murray Walker said, 'Doesn't look as though Mansell's won the World Championship, does he? I suspect it is because he is extremely tired. You can see that Ayrton Senna looks pretty chipper and Gerhard Berger looks his usual underwhelmed self, seldom shows a great deal of emotion.'

When Mansell had the microphone he said, 'Gerhard drove great, very fair,' and Berger said, 'I saw Nigel was quicker in the corners so it would be too much risk to push him further to the side. (Smile.) I'd already done it a little bit so I said, OK I will be very happy with third place.' He smiled again when he said that, smiled on a day of many smiles.

On his thirty-third birthday, 27 August, and three days before the Belgian Grand Prix at Spa, Berger confirmed that he had signed for Ferrari. He'd been impressed with the way the negotiations had been conducted. 'We'd get back together on a specific point and they'd fix it. For me it was a new experience at Ferrari! Before, it was talk, let's eat, let's talk again. In the end I drew out two sheets of paper. On one I put down all the positive points for staying with McLaren. On the other I put the positive points for Ferrari. I drew a line between them and it ended up they were all the same. It seemed impossible to do the right thing.

'I knew quite early that my decision would be McLaren or Ferrari. Ferrari had the package together quicker and it was very clear to me that I would be the right person for Ferrari. I was getting really tired having to follow the politics of the driver market every day (Senna offering to drive for Williams for free, Prost not yet confirmed at Williams, Mansell in limbo). I hated that so I made my move first.' Moreover drivers were being offered *old* money, or rather Berger was being offered *old* money — you know, the multi-millions which had risen and risen over the years — but the global recession was at hand and he became the last to get the multi-millions.

Peter Collins makes a revealing observation. 'Gerhard wasn't really himself for two or three years, the sparkle that was Gerhard Berger disappeared from his driving and his personality. I really feel (paradoxically) that that was apparent at the end of 1992 when he knew he was leaving McLaren and he decided to become Gerhard Berger again, the sparkle came back and you saw a different driver. If you look at the points he scored . . .'

At Spa in a wet untimed Saturday session he had an enormous moment going down to Eau Rouge. The McLaren slithered sideways, struck the outside wall and was flung back across against the other wall. He emerged unhurt. The race proved to be no race at all for him. 'When I tried to select first gear at the start nothing happened so I tried to get neutral and still nothing. It felt like a clutch failure.'

At Monza in second qualifying, 'My last lap was going to be a very good one. There were cars in front of me as I came down to Parabolica but while the Ferrari moved over Alboreto (Footwork) obviously didn't want to get on the dirty line. As a professional driver he ought to have know better than that. I indicated my displeasure and did nothing else — then he drove into my car! I got upset and decided to play a little with him.'

The McLaren suffered engine failure on the grid so he started from the pit lane in the spare — 'only enough time to change the seat and pedals. I had to drive with Ayrton's settings and also the spare had a different engine specification to the race cars so under the circumstances I did the best I could.'

As the grid set off Berger nosed out of the pit lane and by the first chicane he'd caught the back of the pack. On that first lap he took Katayama (Venturi), Gugelmin (Jordan) and Naspetti (March). On the next lap he took Tarquini (Fondmetal) and this would be the story of his race: 'Hard overtaking all those cars.' At lap 10 he'd risen to thirteenth, at lap 20 to eleventh (after a pit stop because he'd worn his tyres so much), at 30 laps still eleventh before he rose and rose, unlapped himself three laps from the end and finished fourth.

Portugal contained moments of terror. After the pit stops Berger fended off a slogging assault from Patrese lasting 18 laps, cut and thrust, attack and defence, the cars always close. On lap 42 Berger rounded the right-hander to the main straight — the pit lane entrance not far down the straight — and 'positioned myself in the middle of the road to come into the pits'. He did not raise his arm, the universal signal indicating *I'm slowing* because 'you can't put your hand up coming through that fast right-hander'.

Patrese tried to flick left but the difference in relative speeds, Berger decelerating and Patrese accelerating, proved too great. Berger felt 'a bump and I saw him flying past me'. Patrese's front wheel rode over Berger's left, launching the Williams. As Berger peeled into the pit lane the Williams' front wheel hung limp as a severed limb, the car angled upwards and climbing, bits breaking off. Its rear wheels were now higher than Berger's car. The Williams angled leftwards in mid-air.

For a millisecond it seemed certain to flip, a millisecond later it surely was flipping, falling back over on itself. A millisecond after that it seemed to be travelling almost upside down. By some gravitational pull allied to its forward momentum the Williams righted itself so that when it landed after 100 m the left rear wheel acted as a pivot, softening the blow marginally. The Williams belly-flopped and straddled the track but the forward momentum twisted it against the pit lane wall. It ground along the wall flinging more debris with such force that bits reached the grass on the other side of the track. As it came its nose bored like a snout into the wall, the left rear wheel loose and bobbing wildly, the chassis digging a shower of yellowing sparks. And still it came, the nose bucking briefly from the wall before returning to it.

The Williams stopped half-way down the wall. Patrese freed the steering wheel and levered himself out. He stood in the cockpit, turned and looked back, clambered the pit lane wall. Ann Bradshaw, Canon's Press Relations lady, hurried to him. 'He looked like someone sleepwalking, he didn't know where he was or what was happening.' Andrew Marriott, interviewing for the American television channel ESPN, recorded Patrese as saying, 'I could have been killed. People should stay at home if they don't know the rules of the game. It is the behaviour of a killer.' Looking back on this now, Marriott strongly stresses that the words were spoken 'in the heat of the moment' and while Patrese was still in shock.

Later, and more calmly, Patrese said, 'I was lucky. He gave me no signal, the car went straight up and I saw the sky.'

Berger, visibly distressed, said, 'I really regret the incident with Riccardo which was the fault of neither of us. It was a misunderstanding.' As Berger had prepared to pit he'd thought Patrese 'would go round me on the left. I was really worried he might be hurt but I'm very pleased that he is OK. On some occasions in this sport there are situations where you can have misunderstandings and accidents like this. I don't want to say it was my mistake or his mistake, just something that went wrong. Thank God that nothing worse happened.'

The irony, if you can employ such a word about such an event, is that of all the drivers at Portugal on 27 September 1992, Gerhard Berger was arguably the least likely to do anything silly in any circumstances. His whole career stood as testament to that. How many drivers have been in 129 races, each with innumerable possibilities for drama and mayhem and the rest of it, and caused so few ripples?

His second place behind Mansell in the Portuguese Grand Prix became almost irrelevant. Williams protested Berger but the stewards rejected that on the grounds that it had been 'a racing accident' — based on the long accepted judgement that if you have a lot of cars doing a lot of races, every now and again circumstances will arise which go beyond rules, regulations and all safety precautions.

In Japan Berger pitted for tyres on lap 11. Well before he reached the pit lane entrance he made sure Schumacher, immediately behind, knew. He raised his right arm and waved it, then his left arm with a finger pointed to where he was going. He kept the arm aloft until he had moved into the pit lane entrance. Senna had gone, engine, and Berger emerged sixth. Schumacher dropped out, gearbox, Herbert dropped out, differential, and when Hakkinen pitted Berger lay third. Japanese television has a chronometrical device which shows the changing speed of cars as they lap Suzuka. The speeds change so quickly they flit-flicker-flit-flicker. The device tracked Berger and I include a segment of the times because while they are seemingly ordinary numerals if you study them you get both the range of speed and how fast the speed changes. The speeds are in km/h and please remember they're coming at you in the flit-flicker:

169 163 157 151 141 139 131 125 124 131 137 143 159 175 183 185 196 196 206 218 228 230 240 248 253 257 261 263 265 267 269 271 273 275 279 277 283 287 289 291 293 295 297 299 283 265 255 250 248 244 236 240 244 248 251 257 261 265 269 271 263 (braking for the chicane)

220 163 147 131 118 110 88 80 70 59 57 51 47 51 55 53 49 47 (exiting the chicane) 53 61 64 74 78 88 94 106 116 125 131 141 153 159 167 175 183 192 196 204 208 212 218 226 230 234 236 240 242 248 255 259 261 265 269 273 277 . . .

When Mansell dropped out with nine laps to go Berger inherited second place and ran there to the end.

In Australia, Berger's last race for Marlboro McLaren Honda and Honda's last race before withdrawing from Formula 1, he made a 'poor start', Alesi going outside him, clouting the kerb and moving in front, Schumacher crowding him on the other side. At the snaking left-right Mansell led from Senna, Patrese, Schumacher, Alesi, Berger. On the straight Berger thrust inside and took Alesi, a lap later did that to Schumacher at the same place. 'I had to work really hard to get past some cars, particularly Alesi's Ferrari.'

The race opened up when Senna bumped into the back of Mansell taking them both off. At 19 laps Patrese led Berger by 1.661 seconds, Schumacher third at 3.258. Berger took Patrese on the outside down the straight but his speed took him wide and Patrese nipped back through. Berger pitted for tyres and 'couldn't understand why Patrese didn't. I could pull up to him and I was closing when he dropped out (fuel pressure on lap 50).' By then Berger had taken Schumacher for second place. When Patrese went, the gap Berger to Schumacher stood at 25.517 seconds. Schumacher charged, cut it to 7.135 with four laps to go, Berger responded and won it.

If eras have to end, as they do, this was as good a way as any.

'When you have someone like Senna you need a team-mate who breaks up the seriousness, creates an atmosphere of good humour,' Ramirez says. 'It's good for a whole team and you miss it when it's not there. When Prost partnered Senna we had a few jokes but nothing like Gerhard! The best balance we had was Ayrton and Gerhard because they both respected each other. Gerhard admired Ayrton, got advice from Ayrton so it was always good.'

* * *

Conversational interlude
Hilton: 'How detailed would the information in debriefs be for Berger and Senna?'

Blundell: 'Pretty detailed. When Gerhard is serious he is serious. In analysing the car he was no different to Senna. In concentrating on what could be done he was as good anyone. Say I'd tested two days at Silverstone. Gerhard would go into it right down to the ride heights I'd run, springs, fuel loads, the balance of the car. We'd compare notes. Basically Gerhard had a slightly different set-up in a car to me, mine was closer to Ayrton's. I don't think Gerhard liked the car over-soft, he'd tend to set it up for an out and out lap. With his set-up he'd have to punish himself to do a race distance, the car hitting the floor, difficult to steer, while Ayrton's car was a lot more balanced, planned to be more comfortable, more relaxing over the race distance.'

Hilton: 'Is that why Berger is reputedly harder on tyres than Senna?

'Blundell: 'Possibly, possibly, but at the same time if that's the way he wants it, the way he can drive it the quickest, so be it. It's no disrespect to him. There is no right or wrong way to set up a car, it's what you feel is best and what you drive the best. That's the way he'd got to go. In any case, you put two blokes in the same cars and they probably have a different style. One throws the thing and one doesn't, one uses the throttle three or four times in a corner, the other only uses it once and then hits it. At the end of the day all these things apply.'

Hilton: 'All right, compare the driving styles of the two.'

Blundell: 'Gerhard's style is more aggressive, Ayrton's is a lot more finesse and flair. Gerhard is *arrive-point-turn-in*, take the corner by the scruff of the neck and get through — I don't mean badly, it's done with great skill and speed. Gerhard, after all, has produced some fantastic laps in his time. Ayrton uses the throttle a hell of a lot more than anyone else. If you look at his traces — the print-outs we get — you can see the amount of throttle opening, how many times he pumped at it and it's probably three or four times through a corner, others might do it twice, so he's stroking, stroking, stroking. As I said, it depends how you stick the car into the corner.'

Hilton: 'Could you be more specific?

Blundell: 'One driver might like to go in with understeer, another might like the front end to stick right in and worry about the rear later. If you look at my traces this year (1993) at Ligier and those of my team-mate Martin Brundle mine contain a lot more work with the accelerator foot, but what is interesting is that our speeds are virtually the same. That's right, you know, even over a whole lap.'

Hilton: 'This is a different kind of question. Senna regularly beat Berger. How did you observe Berger taking that.'

Blundell: 'Gerhard respected Ayrton for his abilities and knew that, at the end of the day, it was going to take an awful lot of work to get in front of him. He put that in and it brought rewards in qualifying laps and sheer speed on occasions. They had mutual respect although I suppose Gerhard looked at Ayrton and said to himself, "I am up against one of the all-time greats and if I get anywhere near him I'll know I'm doing pretty well." Sure he must have thought, "Bloody hell, why can't I get past him?" although he rationalized it, I am sure, by also saying, "I am with him, I have to make the best job of it and that is what I am trying to do."'

Hilton: 'No tension between them?'

Blundell: 'No, not to my knowledge. Gerhard is easy going and although I've only known him for 18 months everyone I speak to says he's always been the same. After testing we'd go out in the evening to have a bite to eat, one to one. I'd bounce a few thoughts off him or try to draw information out of him and he was helpful in that respect. He was kind in another respect too. I was coming to the end of my year's testing with McLaren and Gerhard was going to Ferrari. He'd ask me, "What are you doing next year? What are you doing next year?" He was concerned I wouldn't get a drive. (Blundell had not yet signed for Ligier.) He said, "Do you want me to try and talk with Ferrari, maybe for testing?" He didn't say it in passing, he meant it. He was a good guy, a good guy — a great guy.'

End of conversational interlude, end of an era.

***

10

Coming round again

Donington Park on the Thursday before the European Grand Prix, April 1993, was no place to have your faith in humanity restored. A slate grey sky tipped very English drizzle endlessly with sheets of heavy rain by way of variety. It brought an insidious damp, the kind which weaves itself into everything including human beings. A niggling wind tugged and plucked and the few people around the motor-homes rubbed their hands for warmth. The talk was of the weather for the Sunday and the race because the English invariably expect the weather to get worse. The forecast for Sunday: more of the same.

I'm sitting under the awning stretched from the Ferrari motorhome, fingers numb, influenza coming on hard. Eric Silbermann, who handles Berger's publicity, is as chirpy as usual and keeps smiling to try to neutralize the damnable cold.

We're waiting for Berger who's just been out in what they called Testing Practice, a session so drivers may introduce themselves to a new circuit, which in a sense Donington was. No Grand Prix had been held there since the War, although many of the field of '93 knew it from the lesser formulas and, in Berger's case, from European Touring Cars, too.

Some drivers, including Prost, previously said that Donington worried them, Prost using typically uncompromising language — so uncompromising that the Canon Williams Renault publicity machine sought to temper and soften the impact of them. Now Prost went quickest (again typically) with a lap of 1 minute 13.182 seconds, his team-mate Damon Hill next, then Berger, 1 minute 14.370, Senna 1 minute 14.481.

The drizzle dribbles, the slate grey of late afternoon closes like a clamp, and Berger is in a heavy debriefing in Ferrari's *other* motorhome next door, tinted glass and slightly forbidding. The debrief moves into its second hour, something not at all unusual; indeed perhaps the norm these days, and extremely understandable at a new track where each corner, each camber, each straight is a step into the unknown and must be dissected, just as the car's reaction to them must be probed, evaluated, studied.

He comes very suddenly, lean and with the ease of movement of the natural athlete, he sits and he's brought sunshine with him, a boyish grin, a chuckle and gurgle of a laugh, a merry twinkle. I spread the Alfa Romeo 'Ice and Snow' photographs across the small, white table and ask which car he's in. 'None! I rode a Ducati!' (See Chapter 2.) That makes him laugh, and me, and Silbermann, too, and it sets a tone.

Next he starts to recount how his career began and his English is racy, larded with certain Anglo-Saxon expressions which, dammit, spice the anecdotes perfectly, don't sully them in any way. Your granny would hardly have been offended and she'd have enjoyed the tales as much as I did.

The man running the Ferrari hospitality under this awning, a swarthy Italian who must be feeling the cold much, much worse than the natives, turns as we dissolve into more and more laughter — we're covering ground fast, truancy, the poker game of paying/not paying for his début in the Ford Escort, hilarious crashes — and as the swarthy Italian turns he shrugs as if to say, it's only Gerhard.

Berger needs to get back to his hotel in Nottingham (he has its name written on a piece of paper) but somehow his hire car is there, not here so I'm delegated to drive him the 10 miles and we'll chat along the way. One of the endearing characteristics of Berger is not just that he is easy in himself but he makes others feel that very quickly and, I am sure, not consciously. He just does it.

Normally, of course, Formula 1 drivers don't care to be driven and Michele Alboreto once confessed to me that he couldn't take taxis in Milan because the drivers looked at him and immediately tried to prove *they* were Formula 1 drivers. So: there we are in my Ford Sierra, which is not a rocket (let us say) but which is potentially as dangerous as any other modern saloon if you pull out to overtake and rush lorries head on. He clips up the safety belt and we thread our way out through the ebbing crowd, along past the museum and out on to the road towards the M1. He realizes very quickly that I'm not a lorry-rusher but he's at ease anyway, holding the tape recorder on his lap while we talk and letting the talking roam as it goes.

* * *

Conversational interlude

Hilton: 'What about Coloni and that air box in European Formula 3?'

Berger: 'I'm very upset about this. You know why? This hurts me.'

Hilton: 'What about Lauda?'

Berger: '(pause) Niki — of course when I grew up and did a little bit of racing he was the famous Niki Lauda. I didn't have any contact with him and honestly I met him the first time when I'd already been in Formula 1. He was nice because I remember I should have been making tests with Brabham and it was raining and raining and I couldn't. Martini did it, Danner did it, I should have done it at the end but it rained and I couldn't. But, before, I asked Piquet to show me the circuit, show me a little bit when to brake and things and he said yes, but he never did it.

'I asked him again and he said, "Yes, yes, yes, a little bit later" and three days long he just never did it. Suddenly, Lauda came. He said, "If you need something, if I should show you something just tell me" and that was very nice. He went round the circuit with me, he told me a little bit and that was my first real contact with him.

'And then of course I went into Formula 1 and he went out. For him, you know, when he stopped everything was more important to him than Formula 1, so he wasn't very involved. We knew each other but we weren't friends, we were not close, we didn't really have much to do with each other. We'd say, "How are you?"

'It was not that he was in Vienna and I was in Worgl (at the other end of Austria), no, it was more a feeling. That is to say, I didn't have a great feeling for him, he didn't have a great feeling for me. And now everything changes with Ferrari, because he comes to me and he says, "Listen, we want Senna or we want you and we are working on both." I was very careful in what I said. Then we did the deal slowly, and after the deal more and more we get together and more and more I find respect for him and I think the same happened with him. (Chuckle.)

'Suddenly we get on very well together. I find out that the guy has very, very high qualities, very clear directions, and that he's a brilliant guy. Before, he was three times World Champion and you're not three times World Champion if you're not clever. Still, my respect for him now is much higher than it was five, six years ago. He's a great guy and we are friends, we are phoning, we are speaking and we have a close relationship. He speaks logically, clear, short, he knows what he wants.'

Hilton: 'The first time in a Formula 1 car, what's it like?'

Berger: 'I just remember one thing, especially with the turbos you had in those days — you were talking a thousand horsepower — you went on to the straight at Zandvoort and then Zeltweg and the bloody car never stopped to push. You're going already 175, 185 mph (282, 298 km/h) and you're pushing forward. The straight goes on and the car is still push, push, push and you say, (expletive) this thing will go on for ever. Honestly the car was driving me, I wasn't driving car. I did everything by reflex rather than by brain, you know. But it was OK (grin).'

Hilton: 'People say you have a natural talent. For example Alan Rees (see Chapter 5) says that in your first year you made mistakes, spins and so on, but you had the talent to get out of trouble whereas someone who lacks it and had got here by sheer hard work wouldn't.'

Berger: 'Yes, that is 100 per cent true but you have one disadvantage with this kind of high natural talent and that is you are not used to working hard. And then you go to a level where you're going to fight with Senna — a level where you meet people with very high natural talent who also spend 24 hours working on it. That was my big change in McLaren, because until McLaren I did everything on natural talent. I didn't work for it. Everything just came naturally from myself.'

Hilton: 'And then you come up against Senna . . .'

Berger: 'Yes, and then I saw there was another step to do on top of my talent and that was to work a lot to catch up, because those other days I just drove the car.'

Hilton: 'Now with Senna you're the only team-mate who has survived.'

Berger: 'It looks like it (chuckle).'

Hilton: 'You go through the list . . .'

Berger: 'And I finished last year one point behind him in the Championship. He had three wins, I had two wins. OK?'

Hilton: 'How did you get on with him?'

Berger: 'Good, I got on well with him. I am easy going. If somebody doesn't try to (expletive) me I'm fine, you know. I can get into difficult personalities if they are difficult with me, but I could get on quite well with Senna and he got on well with me.'

Hilton: 'He told us once that you went on holiday together, you went swimming and he said he'd done that with Elio de Angelis a little bit at the beginning but then stopped and not done it with anyone else.'

Berger: 'He's a great bloke. First, I have high respect for his performance. He is a similar age to me, he went the same way, Formula 3 at the same time. I still get on well with him.'

Hilton: 'What about Benetton?'

Berger: 'Ah, Benetton was a great year for me but and I tell you what, that year I could have won three Grands Prix already. I was really unlucky. I won the Mexican Grand Prix, I could have won the Austrian Grand Prix very, very easily. Half distance I was leading by

I think nearly one lap. I went into the pit stop just to change tyres, bloody battery broken. It was me and Teo (Fabi) on the front row, Teo over-revved the engine and I was leading, just miles in front. This race hurts me a lot. Another race where I could have won was Monza but something broke on the front — and Spa was good. OK, I crashed on the first corner but the practice was good. I just lost the pole to Piquet. So Benetton was a good year. Unfortunately I didn't have enough experience to use the car to the full.'

Hilton: 'When you got to Mexico, who decided to run with no tyre stop?'

Berger: 'Me, and I remember that I was the only one who used different tyres to all the other Pirelli drivers — different compounds. At the start they still tried to convince me to change it and I said, "OK, maybe you are right" and they said, "No, no, it's too late! We have no time any more" (chuckle), so I said, "OK, then let's go and do it (chuckle.)'

Hilton: 'There were moments in that race when there was a lot of pressure on you.'

Berger: 'In those days I could live very well with pressure.'

Hilton: 'Just talk to me a little about that, because you're now going to win your first Grand Prix, the world has gone to see Mansell become World Champion, he gets the start wrong, then we have a pressure race from a lot of other drivers. Then you're about 17 seconds in front and really not making a mistake.'

Berger: 'I could handle pressure because I was young, I didn't actually have the pressure of winning because nobody was expecting me to. Today you have much more pressure because people are going to expect you to win the Championship, you know. Look back to Mansell. The thing turns. If you do it when you're young, you take so much pressure away from yourself, it makes life so much easier and you make less mistakes.'

Hilton: 'Maurice Hamilton of *The Observer* did an interview with you last summer which was very interesting about the pressure of being a top driver, the expectations. At Benetton you win and everybody says great, at McLaren people say you should win every race.'

Berger: 'That's one of the worst, most difficult things to handle. That makes so much more pressure it's just unbelievable. I tell you, our McLaren car was always a difficult car to drive. Senna was really great in how he could manage it, but I think a lot of the time I did a very good job, too. In fact we worked well together and did a good job and that was the reason why we had success together with a very good team — McLaren — yes. But believe me it was not always easy, especially not for me and even not for Senna although he won a lot.'

Hilton: 'Turning to lighter topics, what about skiing?'

Berger: 'When I was at school I always knew there were two things I was going to do, either ski racing or car racing, but I preferred car racing much more so I said, "OK, let's stay on the skis until you have a licence and just play at skiing." I was quite good.'

Hilton: 'Did you see yourself as a downhill racer?'

Berger: 'Of course (chuckle). Where I come from everybody wants to be a downhill racer. Usually when I was six, seven years old we went skiing all day long. We all took skating boots, walked to the rink and played ice hockey without any proper dress. We ended up with blue knees and things. I kept going at ice hockey and I still do it now.'

Hilton: 'You still play?'

Berger: 'Yes, I still play.'

Hilton: 'Dangerous . . .'

Berger: 'No, not dangerous, it's very good sport. The professionals are mad, yes, but you can do it another way.'

Hilton: 'I spoke to Michele Alboreto, who's a nice guy . . .'

Berger: 'He can be quite difficult . . .'

Hilton: ' . . . about how he heard when Enzo Ferrari had died. And you?'

Berger: 'How did I hear when Enzo died? I knew he was seriously ill, but I don't remember any more how I heard, if I'm honest.'

Hilton: 'Monza and the Italian Grand Prix was a very strange occasion because you have the McLarens who should win, all of Italy wants Ferrari to win if only because of Enzo.'

Berger: 'Yes, that was the first race (in Italy) after his death. It was his race, it was the perfect race to win.'

Hilton: 'How did you approach that?'

Berger: 'I didn't think about the win. The problem is the moment you think about the win you don't get it. I thought, "OK, let's do the race as well as possible", then I saw that Senna had a little bit of trouble with fuel consumption or whatever because he slows down and I said, "OK, let's push to be sure whether he's really in trouble or not" and it was just the perfect thing to do. And he made a mistake.'

Hilton: 'Was it emotional afterwards?'

Berger: 'Yes, the most that I ever had. To stand on the podium in Monza with a Ferrari — you cannot believe it and then after Enzo's death, that was a great feeling to have done it. It was one of those days when a lot of factors come together.'

Hilton: 'How did you get on with Enzo?'

Berger: 'Good, very good. I didn't speak the language, but you know he liked to speak about girls, I liked to speak about girls, so (chuckle, deepening into a laugh) it went well. I know Niki had problems with him but I didn't. I never had any problems with him, not one.'

Hilton: 'What about driving for Ferrari, because it is a big thing.'

Berger: 'It's still a big thing, especially when the team gets well again, you know, and I believe it will. I have two challenges now: the first to win again with Ferrari, and the second challenge is to help them to come back. We're going to do it.'

Hilton: 'Tell me about the practical jokes. Why?'

Berger: 'I mean, I am a happy person and that's still my most important thing. Maybe you find people who say, "The most important thing for me is to win everything," but for me the most important thing is still my life. To win, it makes me happy but some other things make me happy so I follow all the things which make me happy.'

Hilton: 'I want to call the book *The Human Face of Formula 1* because it seems that something terrible has happened to so many of the other people, namely they become enclosed in Formula 1. They don't think there's another world outside and it's very easy for it to happen but I've never had that feeling about you at all.'

Berger: 'Yes I'm happy so long as everything goes well. Of course, I take my job very seriously and when I do it I do it seriously, but that does not mean that I cannot laugh, that I have to go around with a long face all day long. I don't think there is any reason why I should. Did you speak with Charley Lamm? I liked him the most from all the racing people that I've met. Charley was like a brother, I mean it was unbelievable. When I was racing for Schnitzer, he was the guy I felt the most for.'

Hilton: 'Why did you drive the Touring Cars?'

Berger: 'I had fun and I would still like to do it. I know it's difficult after Formula 1 because it's a step down but I love to drive these kind of cars so much, especially the 635 where I did a lot of development work with BMW and in the end the car handled exactly as I wanted. Nobody could do the same times as me in a 635. The car was perfect for my driving style. We won the Spa 24-hour race twice — well, the second time we were leading by three laps until the last half an hour when something broke and we finished second. But we had a lot of success, Ravaglia and myself, in that car.'

Hilton: 'Did you enjoy the contrast between Formula 1 and the Touring Cars?'

Berger: 'Those days I took Formula 1 very easy. It was similar, you see, in that Benetton was an easy group, I was easy, Peter Collins was very good and easy. I like Peter Collins a lot — but if I think back now Schnitzer and BMW was the best time of all my times. Mind you they were very hard races with good people, Schlesser, Tom Walkinshaw, Stuck. We had a lot of fights and I was competitive.'

Hilton: 'I think it was Ravaglia who said it's very unusual to find a team-mate like you and you worked as a team. If he was faster somewhere and you were faster somewhere else that was fine, didn't matter because you were a team.'

Berger: 'No it didn't . . .'

Hilton: ' . . . but he said you didn't like it if Stuck went quicker.'

Berger: 'First I looked after my car and I know if I'm quicker I have to tell my team-mate how he gets quicker so we get the maximum out of the weekend. It worked the other way round, too. You know, those days Stuckie was the quickest saloon car driver in the rain and in the dry, very, very spectacular. I was a young coming driver and it put Stuckie under pressure, so of course for me it was a big challenge. It was the reason why I always tried to beat Stuckie. Those and Formula 3 were the happy times, everyone racing hard and enjoying themselves. You don't have it in Formula 1 now because Formula 1 is too hard to have that kind of life. You have to respect it when you get a lot of money, and so it's another life.'

Hilton: 'But look at Schumacher, who's only 24. If he races for another 10 years he'll have known nothing else.'

Berger: 'But don't forget in other sports you spend six or seven years reaching a professional life like this, too. Look at the Olympics and how people are pushed for them. In athletics they're pushing people when they're 12, 13 years old. You look at gymnastics. They're training from six years old every day from early morning. They have nothing else, no childhood, nothing.'

Hilton: 'Taking an overall view, you've never tried to be what other people might have wanted you to be, you've always been yourself and you are also extremely popular.'

Berger: 'The only thing is, I would love to be World Champion once but it's going to be difficult (chuckle). I'm still going to try. It's difficult anywhere, even more difficult with Ferrari, but three years ago people said Mansell was never going to do it and today he's the big hero, so . . .'

End of conversational interlude

* * *

Berger had tested the car at Estoril in January and said during the testing, 'Our main problem is the lack of experience with the active suspension, so we have to analyze every part of it to accumulate data. At the moment the car is not at all balanced. We are getting nearer to solving the problem and we now have a clearer picture than yesterday, and we have gained experience with the active system.

'We were not at all interested in our lap times, we just got on with the work. Of course it would be nice to put up some good times but until we fix the balance of the car this won't be possible. We will be working on this tomorrow when we will also try a new specification engine. Over the past two days we have come up with a list of things that we can improve but we have a long way to go and not much time.

'The fact that my contractual commitment from last year prevented me from driving the Ferrari until now has not held us back. I could not physically fit into last year's Ferrari anyway. The new car was finished between Christmas and the New Year. The car is brand new and the bench testing of the active system only finished last week. Everything is running to the planned time schedule and once we have sorted out the active suspension and found the right balance we will make significant progress. We also have to make improvements to the gearbox and engine.

'Under these conditions I do not think that the car will be competitive in time for the first race, but at least this new car has potential and we can make a big step forward. I am under no pressure from the team to try for a time, which is a good thing because this would really disrupt our work.

'I am sure if we ran the car with passive suspension we could go quicker today because we have plenty of experience with springs and roll bars and so forth, but it is better to start now with the active car which has the potential to perform much better. I know this is a long job. I first drove an active Marlboro McLaren two years ago and it is still not working properly now. It is extremely complicated but once it works and you understand it, it gives a big advantage. As a driver the two systems feel much the same, but with the active one you have far more possibilities to work with and this is what makes it difficult.

'Our other problem is the engine. We need to find more power and I am looking forward to trying the new specification. We need more power but power is not the only solution. If an engine has a wider power band this can significantly reduce the lap times. Even though the team has a long way to go I am still optimistic.'

This was candid enough and relayed by Marlboro's publicity machine. To journalists Berger said, 'The car is virtually impossible to drive — its cornering is very unpredictable. On the one hand it's tempting to try for a good lap time but on the other it's dangerous as you don't know what the car will do. It's obvious we can't fix the problem here: we need a new software program. On the engine side Ferrari has some good people but they don't have the same working methods as the Honda engineers and I'm trying to give them the benefit of my experience. The engineers here have a great deal of potential to improve.'

Of this Barnard says, 'To be fair to Gerhard, he is more astute today than we was before. He has done all the testing this year for

Ferrari (my interview with Barnard was late May 1993), well, the effective testing, let's say. On the engine side his feedback in various areas is a marked change since he came from working with Honda, yes very marked. He is always looking for different performances. As he said, "Before I worked for Honda I just thought, well, engine all right, it is not missing, it's going and that's it. OK, maybe it doesn't have much power but end of story."

'Now he is picking out where the engine is working, where it is not working, where it is strong, where it responds, the whole thing. So yes, yes he learnt a lot with Honda. Initially he has done all the work this season and what has happened? Jean Alesi being Jean Alesi and being bloody quick, Jean tends to get given a set-up based a lot on Gerhard's work, goes out and goes bloody quick. Gerhard is left saying, "Ah, ah, ah, I need to go forward but I'm not quite sure I need this!" (Laughter.)'

It didn't matter at Estoril — particularly since Berger wasn't looking for lap times — that Prost, now with Canon Williams Renault, went quickest with 1 minute 13.42 seconds, Alesi ninth with 1 minute 18.53, Berger tenth with 1 minute 18.98. What did matter was that the first race, South Africa, lay only six weeks away and in testing at Imola just before South Africa the problems seemed to mount. South Africa would throw these problems into the open for the global audience to see.

At Kyalami Berger's worst fears came true, fourteenth after the first day's qualifying, fifteenth after the second. Ferrari took two kinds of active suspension, an 'old' one initially intended for Alesi and a 'new' one for Berger. 'The old one had less potential,' Berger says, 'so we decided I'd try and develop the new, which had to be the way forward. Unfortunately, though, we struggled all the way through. On the Friday we fitted a new type of actuator which we had only tried the previous week. It was better but less reliable and for qualifying we returned to the old one.

'Partly because we were unable to work on the set-up and partly because I had a hydraulic failure I couldn't do a decent time on Friday. On Saturday I did my quick lap with no pressure in the system. The car was out of balance and difficult to drive, but developing within the pressure of a race weekend helped us a lot.'

At the green Andretti stalled. Alliott, behind, pulled between the two columns of cars; Fittipaldi behind Alliott followed. Berger was *already* out and clear at the other side, two wheels on the thin strip of concrete in front of the pit lane wall. As Fittipaldi turned his Minardi to straight ahead, Berger was *already* virtually past the stationary Andretti and coming back full on to the track in front of him. It gave him a clear channel on the left, handy for turn one — a right-left — and he surged up it. Damon Hill (partnering Prost at Williams) spun and at that instant Berger lay tenth, a gain of five places from the grid. He rode there for five laps.

Senna led, Schumacher behind, Prost third, then the Saubers of Wendlinger (the son!) and Lehto, then Alesi holding back the Ligiers of Blundell and Brundle, then pressure from Alliott and Hill who'd recovered strongly. Hill vanished when Zanardi punted him. Berger ran ninth until lap 24 when he moved up briefly to eighth during the pit stops but sank to twelfth after his own.

On lap 31 Berger was lapped and dark cloud gathered, seemed to be moving towards the circuit. Berger paced himself and as others dropped out he moved into the points on lap 40, moved up to fifth when Patrese spun on lap 47. The rain began, Berger tucking in and following Prost although a lap down, of course. Warwick, a lap behind Berger, flirted with a pass, the Footwork twitched and War- wick tried again. Berger hugged the kerbing. OK, you can go.

Last lap: the rain fell harder and harder and a shaft of lightning flicked across the circuit. The track resembled an ice hockey rink, slick tyres casting palls of spray. Berger stopped, parked it on the sodden grass and handed the steering wheel to a marshal. The engine had overheated. By one of those quirks which make motor racing so difficult for outsiders to understand, Warwick crossed the line in front of Prost but still almost two laps behind him and so had to complete another lap to finish the race. On that lap his Foot- work slithered off, moving Berger up to sixth. Yes, I've tried to explain to people how two cars can swap positions when neither is actually moving and it's not easy.

Blundell came third behind Prost and Senna. 'You know,' Blundell says, 'the weekend at Kyalami was nice. On the podium Ayrton came up and gave me a hug and said, "Look, well done," and I sup- pose that in the background he knew I'd done a lot of work last year and was pleased for me being up there after I'd left McLaren.' It mirrored the happy atmosphere there had been between him, Senna and Berger, as well as McLaren.

At Interlagos in Brazil, Berger had a major shunt in the Friday untimed session. The active suspension betrayed him in a left- hander, he struck a tyre wall backwards and that pitched the Fer- rari full across into the barrier at the other side. Afterwards Berger said, "When it's 30° outside and you are still shivering, you know your body is telling you something" — that it's just had a very unpleasant surprise. 'The car just got away from me.' The position- ing of the grid is important: Prost, Hill, Senna, Schumacher, Andret- ti, Patrese, Lehto, Alesi, Wendlinger, Blundell, Alliott, Herbert, Berger, Barichello.

At the green Lehto came close to jumping the start and flung his Sauber between the twin columns, potentially a superb move. He exploited it, moving cleanly past Andretti. Wendlinger came strong- ly too, and as they reached towards turn one they were three abreast: Wendlinger, then Andretti and Berger.

Distorted images: Andretti struck Berger, Andretti's McLaren twisted full in front of Berger and locked in a bizarre embrace. They moved across the grass, Andretti now uncoupled from the embrace and travelling backwards. Berger's Ferrari slewed on the grass trying to turn away from Andretti but broadside. Andretti struck the red and white painted tyre wall — eight tyres high — and Berger helplessly rammed the front of the McLaren. The McLaren, airborne, rotated twice a long, long way from the ground.

Andretti was taken to hospital with a painful back. Wendlinger said, 'Michael was on my right, trying to go outside me but I held my line. I didn't hit him and I didn't change my line, he just went to the right when he braked and went straight into Gerhard.'

There is no doubt that Wendlinger came a long way to the right, no matter that a millisecond later he had the Sauber straight again.

At the start of a race a driver's senses are heightened, his reflexes sharp and poised and pumping. They need to be. Andretti, in that heightened state, reacted. 'I was forced to the right and Berger who was coming up behind me did not have any room to manoeuvre. It was a hell of a knock.' Berger said, 'I don't understand how something like this can happen. Andretti moved so violently I had no time to react. I could not brake because Michael was too near. After the first impact the McLaren flew over my car, hitting the roll bar and the engine cover. It was a miracle no one was hurt.'

To be fair Andretti had been nurtured on rolling starts in Indy Car racing, demanding the same sort of reflexes but rarely, by definition, so much bunching and jostling. A rolling start stretches the grid, not compresses it. When he saw Wendlinger he *had* to react.

The miracle of deliverance is fully revealed by studying the slow motion. As Andretti struck the tyre wall the McLaren lifted. Berger, striking it, increased its lift and Berger passed completely underneath. Andretti corkscrewed in the air and as he rose a complete section of the tyre wall rose with him. The McLaren angled on to its side, the front two wheels *over* the tyre wall and its impetus turned it through 180°. Its rear struck the tyre wall as its nose dipped on to the grass, stabbing that grass. The rotation continued when it landed, the nose spearing the tyre wall. The McLaren lay shattered, debris in a swathe back towards the track.

Berger walked the short distance to the pits, helmet in hand, tucked the helmet under his arm and gave an interview. On his face: shock more than anger.

In qualifying at Donington the active suspension lacked consistency again. 'Same expletive, different place,' he was reported as saying. The forecast proved right and in a wet race he ran seventh until he pitted for tyres on lap 14, worked his way back up until lap 19. 'I felt fluid dropping on to my legs right from the start. The car became more and more difficult to drive because there was a fault in the left front actuator and we decided to stop.'

Deep into the race at Imola a haunting thing happened. Young Alessandro Zanardi, with Lotus — run by Peter Collins — found himself pursuing Lehto and, 'I could see him getting nervous and making a few mistakes. I was much quicker. Then he braked early in the last corner and to avoid him I got two wheels on the grass and spun. Unfortunately I hit the wall and damaged a wheel. I could see the car was on fire and you know how you think really quickly sometimes. I remembered Berger's 1989 accident and knew that the marshals at Tamburello are very efficient so that's where I went. Seriously.' Berger himself? He ran fifth until the gearbox failed, lap 9.

At Barcelona he could qualify only on the sixth row but mounted a late assault and nipped sixth place from Blundell. He was, however, two laps behind the winner, Prost. Two days later Ferrari announced that Jean Todt would become their director of sporting operations, assuming his post in June after the Le Mans 24-hour race. Todt, long director of Peugeot's sporting activities and a man with a reputation for winning — in June he'd be overseeing Peugeot's defence of Le Mans, hence the short delay in going to Maranello — said candidly that Ferrari remained the most famous name in motor racing and had the greatest potential. The problem was to realise it.

It represented a new beginning, not least for Berger and Alesi, and suddenly they had time. Alesi agreed to stay until 1995, Berger to 1994 and, with a further option, perhaps to 1995. While the future is dangerous to predict, particularly in Formula 1, what might Todt and Barnard do? Give Berger a Championship-winning car?

At Monaco that process seemed to be beginning. Prost nibbled the start and got a 10 second penalty, stalled trying to get out of the pits after the penalty leaving Schumacher easily in the lead. A hydraulic failure stopped him. Senna led, Berger running fourth. Berger pitted for tyres and flew, overtaking Alesi and catching Hill with giant strides. With only eight laps he'd drawn tight behind Hill *and could see Senna, leading, just up ahead*. He thought, 'I can win Monaco.'

It's easy to criticize, particularly if you're not a driver and you haven't done 70 hot and sticky laps within the compression of the street circuit of Monte Carlo; and it's easy to miss the context, the frustrations of early season and suddenly, all at once, you feel you're within striking distance of grasping the most famous Grand Prix and perhaps the most famous race of any kind in the world, including the Indy 500, and passing *Senna* to get it. At the Loews hairpin, a tight downhill snakeback snakebite, he tried to dive inside Hill who, following the racing line, turned into him. *Thump.* Hill somehow resumed, Berger got out and stayed, head bowed, contemplating it.

'On the Sunday night,' Jo Ramirez says, 'I met him in a restaurant in Monaco and I gave him a bollocking. I said, "If you ever want to drive a McLaren car again you must write on a piece of paper a thousand times *I must not attempt to pass at the Loews hairpin, I must not attempt to pass at the Loews hairpin . . .*'

Moreover it wasn't Senna that Berger had seen but Andretti.

After Monaco someone said, 'You'll have to reinvent motor racing to beat Senna, come at it from another direction.' So what did you do, quit or back yourself against him, believe you're better? Always with Senna he gave you uncomfortable questions and you had to answer them because you knew he would be answering them. Could Todt and Barnard and Berger find the answer? Moving towards the mid-season of 1993 they seemed to at least have time.

And, in time, Berger would say that 'Todt has made a lot of difference because first he's a hard worker and second he knows how to structure a company: so he comes, he brings new people in, he tries to improve morale.'

In Canada, two weeks after Monaco, Berger finished fourth but a lap behind the winner, Prost. In France his good humour was tested to the extreme. *Autosport* summed it up neatly and cryptically, so neatly that expansion isn't necessary.

'Gerhard had all manner of problems in qualifying, with steering trouble and terrible handling on Friday which left him eighteenth overnight. Saturday was not much better as he went off in the morning and lost a lot of setting-up time. In the afternoon, he improved to fourteenth on the grid. Ran across a gravel-trap in the warm-up. Had trouble with his active suspension in the race and had to pit three times for new tyres. Finished fourteenth.'

These active suspensions, shortly to be banned, were damnably tricky, and at the British Grand Prix at Silverstone Berger retired after ten laps.

'The car wouldn't go round left-hand corners and eventually I gave up. It was simply too dangerous to carry on. It's depressing. I can't ever remember working harder on a car than I have recently and there is so little to show for it. Nine races, five points.'

Rare it is for a driver to confess that his car has become too dangerous; many other reasons for stopping can be advanced. It is a measure of Berger's candour as well as a measure of the state of the Ferrari that he simply spoke the truth. It did not diminish him. To the contrary, it enhanced his stature. Motor racing is dangerous enough if your car is working perfectly, as Hockenheim would demonstrate.

In qualifying there, Berger clipped a kerb at the third chicane and hammered into the protective barrier at immense speed, the Ferrari badly damaged, Berger badly shaken. He qualified on the fifth row. In the race he worked his way up to fourth and was in combative, *racing* mood. Senna, on a vast charge after a spin, did what he was always going to do. He cut past everything so that, from 24th after the opening lap, he reached Berger in eighth place on lap 11. Perhaps a mark of true friendship is that it is constructed on an unstated understanding. On the track, we *race* each other as hard as we know how. Senna probed and searched, darted and looked, and each time Berger stayed firmly on the racing line — even, once, forcing Senna into error at a chicane so that he had to scrabble back onto the track. 'After my spin,' Senna said, 'I had nothing to lose. The car went very well on the corners but it lacked straight line speed. That is why I couldn't pass Gerhard.' Senna made a tactical decision: rather than go on like this he pitted for tyres.

Blundell (Ligier) reached the same problem at mid-point in the race, although he reached it in reverse order; namely, he had just pitted for tyres and now, travelling extremely quickly, challenged Berger for fourth place. Blundell drew up hard and close and his Ligier had the Renault engine, giving him — in theory — great power, perhaps 5 mph more than Berger. They fled out of the Stadium section nose-to-tail, fled towards the wooded countryside which is Hockenheim. In Turn One Berger ran wide, which allowed Blundell to close up even further, squeezing him. On the long rush to the first chicane, Blundell flicked out to the right and they ran abreast until Berger danced the Ferrari towards mid-track, forcing Blundell to respond by a nervy flick away from him.

On the long curve to the chicane, Blundell held the inside line and it became suddenly simple. Whoever braked later seized the entry to the chicane. Blundell did that. Inside the twist-wrench of the chicane, Berger thrust the Ferrari to Blundell's outside: more theatrical than productive because in the compression of a chicane you can't overtake on the outside. You're a captive of geometry. Too narrow.

They fled into the long rush round the curve towards the second chicane, Berger up hard and close but directly behind Blundell; might have been trying to deceive him, might have been saying *you're the man with the power, I'm just following you doing the best I can, nothing else I can do.* The curve tightened, Blundell obediently on the racing line — that theoretical line that now took Blundell angling towards mid-track for the chicane. At that instant Berger sprang out from behind and had the Ferrari's front wheel level with the Ligier's rear wheel. Berger was going for it. Blundell angling across, Berger had to put two wheels onto the white boundary line of the track, almost onto the grass beyond. He did not lift off — no, he kept his foot ferociously down.

They were abreast, the mouth of the chicane opening to them. Berger danced towards mid-track himself so that the Ferrari pointed *into* the flank of the Ligier. Instantaneously Berger corrected that, pointed the Ferrari forward again. Instantaneously, too, Blundell responded with another nervy flick away from him. The cars that had threatened to bore and butt stabbed apart, far apart, Blundell to the right, Berger to the left. Berger, foot still ferociously down, took the lead.

They fled through the second chicane, bouncing the kerbs. Blundell, blood up, tracked him and along the straight before the third chicane drew up closer, closer, closer. They bounced through this third chicane. Out of it Blundell pitched the Ligier far to the left, but Berger covered that. Approaching the Stadium section Berger held mid-track so that, to take him, Blundell had to go to put two wheels onto the white boundary line of the track.

Blundell made it through and set off into the distance. By the chequered flag — and in third place — he'd have pulled out some 34 seconds over Berger, sixth, but he lost no time in expressing his displeasure with Berger.

'I honestly don't know what Gerhard was playing at. This wasn't four or five laps from the end, it was the middle of the race. I passed him once and he came by again weaving all over the place. Finally I overtook him for good with two wheels almost on the grass. At 200 mph, that wasn't fun at all.'

Berger mounted this defence: 'It was a good fight. With the professionalism of drivers like Mark, you can do this without having to worry for your safety.' I wonder if he was grinning his impish, naughty-boy grin while he was saying that . . .

Only a few days before Hungary, Berger had an operation on his left elbow because, although doctors couldn't diagnose why, fluid had built up there causing him 'agony'. He felt it must have been the result of being knocked around so much in racing cars for so many years. He had only minor surgery — enough to enable him to run in Hungary, although he missed a testing session the week before — with the intention of having major surgery to cure the problem after Hungary.

He came to the Hungaroring in pain. He came to a circuit that is all braking and tight corners, up hill and down dale and no respite anywhere, particularly on the only bit that really wasn't a corner: the long start-finish straight. There, you'd either be making attacks or repulsing them. He'd explain that he'd had treatment with antibiotics as the elbow worsened but he progressively lost mobility in it; hence the minor operation. The wound had been left to heal naturally, which meant no stitches. He did have a protective plaster on it but the confines of the Ferrari cockpit were so precise that he wouldn't be able to wear it while he was driving. A leading

French surgeon, Professor Gerard Saillant, had been flown in to minister to him and watch over him during the weekend. That did not dilute the central question: how long could he possibly drive for? A few laps, surely, but not more before the pain defeated him.

On the Friday in untimed practice he covered 23 laps (tenth quickest) and in first qualifying covered 11 laps (eighth) and grinned and quipped. 'It wasn't painful while I was driving, but it was when I stopped!' Then, more seriously, he confessed that 'the real problem, though, is the effect of the antibiotics. I've had the occasional general anaesthetic, as you know, but this time I feel listless and weak and my blood pressure is low.'

On the Saturday he felt better and moved up to sixth quickest.

Clearly he couldn't last the race, not the full 77 laps, not the full 1 hour 40-odd minutes. Could he? To the observer, when the green light blinked on Berger seemed to be making a statement. *I might not get far before I have to stop but I'll show them a thing or two. No surrender 'til my ammunition's spent.*

This start, intuitively quick on the draw, demands to be examined in detail. Prost stalled before the parade lap and was now at the back of the field, giving this grid:

(Vacant)

Hill

Schumacher

Senna

Patrese

Berger

At the green light Berger went diagonally to mid-track aiming for the gap between Senna and Schumacher, but Senna angled across, too. For an eye-blink Berger appeared to be sandwiched between Senna and Patrese, who was pounding up with gathering power. These three drivers twitched their wheels in a communion of thought (or self-preservation) to prise the sandwich open. The short, sharp lunge from the grid to Turn One, a spooning right, habitually resembles an onslaught because you can gain more places in the few seconds it takes you to get there than in the whole of the rest of the race. Those damned corners, remember, rationed any overtaking.

The sandwich open, the grid only just shed and Turn One looming in the near distance, this is how it was: Hill clearly in the lead, Schumacher second and in mid-track with Senna tucked behind, Berger to the extreme left and slightly ahead of Senna, Patrese behind Berger. Habitually it sharpens precisely now, the places to be gained here. Berger kept the power on and drew level with Schumacher, Senna carving across to the inside.

Picture it. The width of a track which, some 30 metres ahead, coils in that tightening spoon to the right, virtually out of sight. They turned in: Hill clear, Schumacher now fully ahead of Senna and Berger. *As* they turned in, Senna hugging the kerbing to the inside, Schumacher a little wide on the left, Berger thrust the Ferrari *between* them. It was outrageous and wonderful and the essence of the racer all distilled into the frantic mosaic of movement — but Senna was good at that, too. He stayed clamped to the inside, making Berger run round the outside of him, and now Berger was held prisoner of *this* geometry. Turn One uncoiled on and on, right-right-right, *so* tight that the long way round — the outside — couldn't be quicker than the shortest way round — the inside — to two cars moving at essentially the same speed. Exiting onto the tiny downhill 'straight' to the next left, Senna had moved in front of Berger. It did not inhibit Berger from saying that overall 'I enjoyed that!' Order: Hill, Senna, Berger, Schumacher.

This remained unchanged until lap 18 when Senna went out, throttle. Berger pitted immediately for tyres after a lively battle with Schumacher — Schumacher outgunned him on the outside of Turn One and defeated the geometry by doing that early, at the mouth of it, so that he retained enough momentum to go the long way round; but shortly after he spun. Berger's pit stop pressed him back to 12th and it might have been a good time to say the ammunition was all spent now; 12th is a hopeless position to be in on a circuit like this and I'll give the elbow a rest in the motorhome.

No.

Berger launched himself on a long pursuit and handled this so effectively that it brought him to third place by lap 31 of the 77. On lap 52 he made a second stop for tyres, which pressed him back to sixth. He launched himself again and dealt swiftly with Pierluigi Martini (Minardi), moved on Brundle. Out at the back of the circuit, in a left loop, Berger dived to the inside and clouted Brundle's Ligier. It was a *racing* moment, perhaps, a time-honoured thing: two cars want to occupy the same piece of road. Now Warwick (Footwork) up ahead. Berger got a 'tow' down the start-finish straight and gunned through into Turn One, a move almost as outrageous and wonderful in its lateness and its execution as the one he'd made at the beginning.

'In general,' Warwick says, 'Turn One is not a real problem. It's a third gear corner, it's a very long, sweeping 180 degrees, it's very fast in but there's a big run-off area. There are several lines in. It's not really an horrific corner at all. It's virtually the only overtaking place, but you've got to remember also he was on new tyres, I was on used tyres. It was my first points finish and he was on a mission. I think he would have stopped at nothing to get by me and I chose to let him go by rather than not finish myself. If you both want Turn One badly enough then obviously it can end in tears, but generally what happens is people are weaker because of speed or the situation or loss of concentration, and those sort of things can pan out one way or the other way. We were both mature men, we both knew the other wasn't going to do anything silly.'

Berger was third and stayed there to the end. Hill, poised to win his first Grand Prix and touring prudently to be sure he did that, allowed Berger to unlap himself.

I don't know how you measure outright bravery, a raw wound of an elbow jostling and rubbing in those G forces for 77 laps and 1 hour 48 minutes 57.140 seconds, but it must look something like the Hungaroring, 15 August 1993.

Irony upon irony. Approaching the next race, the Belgian at Spa, Berger said, 'Before you come here it makes you happy to think about Eau Rouge because you think of the challenge of going through fast.' He'd always delighted in that, measuring himself against it; and it was the way the world was. Irony? There'd be one early. Breasting the top of Eau Rouge on the Friday morning, Alessandro Zanardi's Lotus broke out of control and beat itself to pieces against the armco in a shocking spasm of destruction and devastation. His very survival — Zanardi suffered concussion and a broken foot, nothing more — restated the comparative sanctuary of the cockpit. You could, as it seemed, rend these cars with massive forces, fling them at metal barriers at near 200 mph, and if you did break a bone you'd count that unlucky.

We must have been fools to think it, and deep down we were.

There'd be a further irony grouped around Eau Rouge, but that wouldn't come until 1994 when the world had changed for ever. In the race, 1993, Berger started from the pit lane with a suspension problem and would get as high as sixth after another long pursuit before he collided with Blundell on the last lap.

Monza, of course, stirred all the old hopes and emotions of the *tifosi*, who are uninterested in logic and only partially dismayed by such cold facts as Prost leading Senna 81–53 for the Championship, Berger eighth on 10 points, Alesi 12th on 4. The *tifosi* believe they can make their Chosen Sons' Ferraris go decisively to victory by willpower, not to mention the belief that Ferrari always hold something back for Monza. This cosy thinking was broken apart in the closing moments of the second qualifying session. Alesi had just hammered a time good enough for third position on the grid, which, in context, came from the realms of faith and willpower. The chequered flag to end the session had been waved and Alesi circled to the acclamation of the *tifosi*. Berger, however, was still on a flyer — as he was entitled to be. When the chequered flag is waved at the start-finish line, some cars will be out on the circuit beyond it and can finish their lap at whatever pace the driver selects, including completing the flyer.

Berger, making the Ferrari yearn as he tried to improve on his sixth place, came upon Alesi in the dip towards the Ascari chicane, which is some two-thirds of the way round the circuit. 'I saw Gerhard in my mirrors and I decided to let him pass on the right. I moved to the left,' Alesi says. It was the rational decision of an aware man and, in Alesi's favour, it must be said that at this point in a qualifying session — when to all intents and purposes it's over — you could be forgiven for permitting the rejoicing to substitute itself for keeping your eyes firmly in the mirrors and your wits sharp. You should always keep your eyes firmly in the mirrors and your wits sharp, of course, but not all of them do that. Never mind. Alesi did.

Berger's closing speed was simply too immense and he was already committed to going past on the left. He assumed — and at these closing speeds there is no time for anything but assumption — that Alesi would stay over the other side. Berger was presented with Alesi there in front of him like a metallic screen. He twisted the Ferrari away from Alesi, pitching it in a stabbing motion over the narrow, grassy verge and into the armco. He'd been doing 203 mph.

The impact and speed pitched Berger into a series of furious rotations down the verge, the Ferrari's front wheels buckled and useless. These rotations sent it spinning on towards the chicane and over the kerbing there in a bound; sent it — still spinning — directly across Alesi who was reaching the chicane himself; sent it — still spinning — across the gravel trap on the other side of the chicane. It battered against a tyre wall, its speed dissipated but enough remaining to lift it onto its side, airborne, at the impact there. It belly-flopped down again. Photographers, grouped behind the barrier on the far side of the tyre wall, were already fleeing for their lives.

Typically Berger made light of it. 'If I'd hit Jean, I'd have flown to Milan.' Milan, incidentally, is 15 kilometres from Monza. That did not prevent some from musing that it had been this way in 1982 at Zolder and the final moments of the second session for the Belgian Grand Prix, Gilles Villeneuve on a flyer in a Ferrari and a car in front making a rational decision but *pulling over to where Villeneuve was aimed*. The closing speed had been too great and Villeneuve had flown, flown to his death; but that was 1982, that was the way the world was and was no more. Wasn't it?

Berger raced, of course. At the green light and from the third row he ran fourth, but retired on lap 16 when the active suspension failed. Not even the willpower of the scores of thousands grouped around the circuit could overcome the mysteries and modulations and maddening quirks of active suspension.

In Portugal he qualified on the fourth row and ran as high as fifth. He pitted for tyres on lap 35, an ordinary, unremarkable pit stop lasting 6.44 seconds. The back of the car, however, was lower than it ought to have been. The software controlling the active suspension evidently wasn't working properly. Worse, the Ferrari pit happened to be at the far end of the sloping, bumpy pit lane, giving Berger a lengthy run back towards the track and, with no speed limit operating then as it would in 1994, he'd reach a high speed — perhaps 150 miles an hour — at the moment he rejoined the track.

As he accelerated from the stationary position a crocodile of cars was coming down the elongated runway which is the start-finish straight at full bore, straining up to whatever their cars would give them: Erik Comas (Larrousse), then a short gap to Warwick, then JJ Lehto (Sauber) in Warwick's slipstream.

The active suspension on Berger's Ferrari was thinking entirely for itself. The software, already dubious, might have done it or a bump on the pit lane might have deranged the active suspension. The car was uncontrollable. It went across the track *at right-angles*, boring into that short, short gap between Comas and Warwick. From nowhere, nowhere, Warwick was presented with the full width of the Ferrari spread broadside just in front of him. Fantastically — not a word used carelessly here — Warwick was able to react, trying to wrench the Footwork right-right-right away from Berger.

'I suppose we' — the three cars in the crocodile — 'would have been doing 180 miles an hour,' Warwick says. 'I had no warning at all, absolutely none. I reacted and it is absolutely instantaneous. You know, you subconsciously weigh up what's going to happen and with that subconscious you make a move left or right, and I weighed up the situation that I was going to miss him — but I was very aware that if he hit the barrier he would bounce back out. All this you're working out in literally thousandths of a second. It's amazing how the brain works so quickly, actually. How far was I from him? We were close — we were (Warwick's voice slows for emphasis) v-e-r-y, v-e-r-y close. It could have been one of the most horrific accidents ever. I'd have hit him side on virtually at the cockpit. It could have been horrendous, but it was one of those things which was just, well, lucky.'

The Ferrari kept on across Warwick and did punt the armco, did bounce back onto the track, but by then Warwick and Lehto had gone safely by. Berger wrestled it, two wheels destroyed, into a little escape area.

* * *

Conversational interlude
Hilton: 'If that happens to a normal motorist, a terrible sort of twitch goes through them, a shock, a shiver.'
Warwick: 'Quite.'
Hilton: 'What happens to you?'
Warwick: 'That shiver that the normal motorist feels, we're

already up there. Our adrenalin is already pumping up around that shiver area, so therefore you don't get a sudden rush because your heart is already beating at, I don't know, 180 a minute. Your *pressure* is already up. The only reaction that I, or we — meaning other Formula 1 drivers — would get is the fact that you then start to lose concentration. You think what could have happened and you try and work out what did happen. (Was that really a car that went across me? Warwick said at the time that he was deep into Turn One before he *realised*.) It had all happened so fast, you see; and then you end up losing a bit of time that lap, you maybe drop off a second or two that lap just because you lose concentration.'

And a word from Berger, reflecting generally a year later after active suspension, among other electronic driver aids, had been banished.

'I had a lot of accidents in 1993, many of them through car failures, and it just shows what a difference the rules make, because this year until now (July) I haven't even had a spin. Some people, including certain ex-drivers, say "active was more safe". Jesus! Think of the teams with no money trying to develop an active system. I hated all that technology and I was glad to see it go.'

Berger would add, more privately, that some people thought he'd made a crass and elementary error at Estoril and simply lost control of the car. That offended him.

End of conversational interlude

* * *

In Japan Berger ran fourth early on but retired, engine; in Australia he crashed heavily in the Friday untimed session, escaped unscathed, ran fifth early on and after two tyre stops finished fifth but a lap behind the winner, Senna. As the Grand Prix fraternity dispersed from Adelaide on 7 November, nobody could know that this was Ayrton Senna's final victory. The communal thinking concentrated more on Senna's unlimited future. Mansell had won the 1992 World Championship at a canter (relatively speaking, of course) in the Williams Renault, and Prost had duplicated that at a canter (relatively speaking again, of course) in 1993. Senna was departing Marlboro McLaren for Williams. What would he do when he got his delicate hands on the Williams for the first race of next season, Brazil, 27 March?

Beyond that, a perennial question lurked, the one that is asked as every old season melts into memory and every new season seems to rear so close. Will *this* be the year Ferrari get it right?

Anyway, the fraternity dispersing, Prost 99 points and retiring, Senna 73, Hill 69, Schumacher 52, Patrese 20, Alesi 16, Brundle 13, Berger 12.

11

Light and darkness

On a late January day at Silverstone the Finnish driver JJ Lehto, who'd newly joined Benetton, plunged off at Stowe at some 140 miles an hour and thundered the tyre wall. He was knocked out and had a broken bone in his neck. He might have been paralysed but wasn't. He might have missed the Brazilian Grand Prix, but the fight to get him fit for that had already begun. This seemed an entirely normal situation moving into 1994.

The new Ferrari, bearing a working designation 645, was unveiled at Maranello in early February and would start the season with a 65-degree V12 engine but was anticipated to move to a new 75-degree configuration. At the unveiling, a sumptuous occasion beautifully choreographed, Berger said that 'it's a nice-looking car and you can see the signs of John Barnard in the detail work. It's important to me that he's had time to look into details. Niki Lauda is impressed by the new car, but for the Championship he thinks Senna and Williams will win. He is not as optimistic as me. We still have a long way to go to be really competitive, but this is a new start. At the end of the day we have to be competitive with Williams. It is easy to dream, but we have the potential to win races. When I was testing in Spain I was quickest, or had the same time as the quickest, because I know what to do with this bloody suspension. It was different with the active system . . .'

Perhaps an accurate way to gauge the importance of the perennial question is to consider that *Autosport*, which is after all a British magazine, devoted eight pages to the presentation of this new Ferrari and covered it in such detail that the section needed its own mini-editor. One of the quotes in it proclaimed that 'The car's most dramatic aspect is its aerodynamics, described (in Italy) as being "like a stone smoothed by the sea".'

250

Ah, but Italians talk like that. In testing at Barcelona soon after, Berger had four days of engine problems, handling problems and gearbox problems which made him spin a couple of times. Never mind the eternal sea smoothing stones, this was reality. Barnard soon got to work on that and, just before Brazil, Berger agreed to stay with Ferrari through 1995. Thence to Brazil, where reality wouldn't go away. In first qualifying he covered but two laps before the gearbox went naughty and, because it rained in second qualifying, he was only 15th fastest. In the Sunday morning warm-up he suffered engine problems and the engine had to be changed. That failed, too, and in the race — when he was eighth — the third engine failed. Schumacher won from Hill, Alesi third. Senna spun off. There'd been a massive crash during the race involving Eddie Irvine (Jordan), Brundle (McLaren), Jos Verstappen (Benetton, deputising for Lehto) and Eric Bernard (Ligier), but they all walked away, of course.

In testing at Mugello between Brazil and the second race of 1994, the Pacific Grand Prix at Aida, Japan, Alesi crashed so heavily that he knocked himself out and had no feeling in his left arm. 'Afterwards I was terrified of being paralysed.' He wasn't. He might have to miss a couple of races but he'd be back for Monaco. Nicola Larini would deputise in Japan. At Aida, a new circuit to Formula 1, Berger qualified fifth and finished second to Schumacher (Schumacher 1 hr 46 min 01.693 sec, Berger 1 hr 47 min 16.993 sec), Senna punted out at the very start by Mika Hakkinen (McLaren) and Larini. Some statistical thoughts: Berger had not been as high as second since Japan, 1992, and Schumacher led Senna for the Championship 20–0. (Meanwhile there had been rumblings that Ferrari were using a now illegal form of traction control — called popularly a 'power reduction' device — but Ferrari made soothing noises to the FIA and another mini-storm in Formula 1 blew itself out over the eternal sea.)

So Senna landed at Forli for the San Marino Grand Prix and Berger landed at Bologna. On the evening of 1 May, when Berger had been to the Maggiore Hospital and returned to Bologna, he could not help seeing Senna's plane waiting for the man who would never come back to it (Senna's British Aerospace jet had been taken from Forli to Bologna in case it was needed). The world had been driven headlong into change because two good men drove into walls that should never, never, never, never, never, never have been there. One of the two men was a great man.

RIP.

And Roland, too.

The Grand Prix Drivers Association was reformed, headed by Lauda, Berger, Schumacher and Christian Fittipaldi. That alone stirred a further conflict within Berger, who told Nigel Roebuck: 'All through my life I've been a bit . . . risky, you know? Even when I was a child I was always looking for experiments, let's say, which had nothing to do with safety. So it doesn't really fit my character, but, again, maybe I have the most experience, especially in accidents. Maybe I can help to improve things, I don't know, but one thing I want to get over very clearly: we, the drivers, can only give some input. Everything must be actually run by Bernie Ecclestone and Max Mosley. Some of the drivers are very aggressive, threatening to strike all the time, but that's not the solution. What we must do is explain to Bernie and Max why we want something, and then they're going to do it by themselves. They're not stupid. Safety and money should not mix up, you know, but at the same time we should never forget what we earn. Look at the motorbike guys. They have much more risk than us, and what do they earn compared to us? Nothing. So we should say thank you to guys like Bernie, who have built up Formula 1, and not try every day to threaten this or that.'

At Monaco Berger bared his soul at the Press Conference and, as we have seen, drove as bravely as any man after Wendlinger's crash on the Thursday morning. 'That first morning in the car at Monte Carlo was very important. I knew I wanted to go on racing, but perhaps there would be something inside now that said *be careful*. I was immediately quick and I knew within two laps that everything was all right. That was just as well, because I wasn't prepared for what would happen if I didn't feel that way.' He qualified third, ran second behind Schumacher, lost that when he spun on oil and finished third. 'I saw a yellow flag and then, just as I put the brakes on, an oil flag. Too late, of course.'

The drivers did threaten to strike if a chicane wasn't added in Spain, and it was, two tyre walls with a gap in the middle and so tight that Berger missed it altogether a couple of times, sailing clean by its side. In the race the gearbox failed. On the Ile Notre Dame he qualified third (Schumacher pole, then Alesi), and ran third early on, finished fourth in the Canadian Grand Prix. In the terrible turmoil of 1994 he lay third in the Championship: Schumacher 56 points, Hill 23, Berger and Alesi 13. Berger added a third place at Magny-Cours in the French Grand Prix.

He had regained his good humour by Silverstone, if indeed he'd ever lost it, despite Imola. I know because I was wandering along near the Ferrari motorhome and from deep within the awning on the motorhome's flank came a roaring noise. It was Berger calling me over. He's sitting at a table chatting with Austrian journalist Helmut Zwickl of the *Kurier*, Vienna.

'How's the book selling? How's the book doing?' Berger begins.

I'm a sucker for a kind word; if you want to buy me you don't need money — a strategically placed compliment will do — but it's nothing like that now. Berger is genuinely curious, and anyway he really is one of the easiest people to speak to. Zwickl is intrigued about the book and I start to recount the tales of frogs and snakes and bare breasts (coming along in this chapter, any moment now), and Zwickl, eyebrows raised, murmurs 'you put *that* in?' and then 'you put *that* in?'. Berger, sitting back completely relaxed, chortles the whole way through, delighting in it.

Later I'm lurking with Roebuck beyond the motorhome because — and this is the way it goes at Silverstone, the temporary torment of tasks to be completed — Roebuck has to get Berger to autograph a postcard of Berger in order that a friend can give it to the owner of an Italian restaurant, who's a supporter. Berger emerges and, looming in the background, is a $10,000 dollar fine because he's exceeded the mandatory speed limit in the pit lane. Ferrari had a new version of their speed-limiting device on the car, which should have made it impossible for Berger to do that, but it hadn't worked. Berger signs his autograph on the postcard and strides off towards second qualifying. 'Gerhard,' Roebuck calls, 'what about the fine?'

Berger halts, turns and a great big smile envelops his whole face. 'I'll tell you who won't be paying it. Me!' Then he strides off again. In that second qualifying he held provisional pole, although eventually he'd be elbowed back to third behind Hill and Schumacher. Coming out of the pit lane *towards* the track to begin his last run, he made an astonishing error and hit the wall! Nobody had ever seen this before and we may have to wait many years to see it again. The consensus of uninformed opinion (which is all too frequently how a Press Room has to operate) was that — Silverstone being hot and British young *gels* not as inhibited as their mothers — Berger had glimpsed some lovely limbs in a brief bikini in the crowd and momentarily found them more compelling than pointing the multi-million dollar Ferrari straight ahead. I mentioned this theory to John Barnard and *he* started chortling . . .

Berger ran third in the race and led for four laps during the pit stops, went down to fifth when he made his and the engine let go after 32 laps.

Schumacher led the World Championship, and while this is no place to explore the traumas, tumults and ultimate triumph of his season, he generated colossal fervour at Hockenheim and the German Grand Prix. For Friday qualifying some 61,000 spectators came to the snaking concrete grandstands that make the Stadium section such an unusual sight; for Saturday qualifying that increased to 75,000. They came to celebrate Schumacher and his Benetton, came to savour the pole position he would surely take. Berger could scarcely be expected to threaten that, a notion sharpened when in the Friday morning untimed session his engine caught fire. *Motoring News* reported it like this: 'Shortly before the end of free practice, Berger's Ferrari blew its older E4 V12 in spectacular style, going past the pits spewing oil, smoke and flame that would have done credit to any Peugeot V10 (almost an in-joke, that, referring to Peugeot's troubled first season in Formula 1, with McLaren) before spinning on its own Agip going into Turn One. During the lunchbreak, Ferrari switched perforce to the E5A 94 V12 that it had intended to keep for Saturday, Jean Todt feeling obliged to keep Alesi up to par with Berger and insisting that his car should get the same treatment, too.' In other words, they had to change Berger's car to the new specification engine and decided to do the same for Alesi.

In the afternoon Berger got to within 0.59 seconds of Hill in a session that someone has described as 'charged' — the vast crowd waved German flags and sent off firecrackers whenever Schumacher appeared, hooted whenever they glimpsed Hill and the Williams. Berger and Alesi set their times before the final rush at session's end: in that final rush Berger felt something amiss with the engine and preferred caution than the risk of blowing it, and Alesi ran out of fuel.

Hill	1:44.026
Berger	1:44.616
Schumacher	1:44.875
Alesi	1:45.272

The Saturday was hot in all senses. Alesi did a 1:44.138, improved marginally then went thunderously fast with 1:44.012, which might conceivably have been good enough for the first pole position of his career. He appeared to be travelling even faster on the next lap, but the engine cover blew off. Berger began more circumspectly — 1:44.511 — but shortly after Alesi's problem he carved a smooth-looking 1:43.582, a time nobody would beat. It was Ferrari's first pole since the Portuguese Grand Prix in 1990 (Mansell) and, with Alesi alongside, the first all-Ferrari front row since Portugal 1990, too (Mansell, Prost).

'I was pushing like hell on that lap!' Berger said. 'I went wide in one corner because I braked too late and I lost a little time there. Otherwise it was a perfect lap. Sometimes you can get these things together. Well, this was one of the days when you can get everything together.

'At the beginning of the year, we did not have the step-by-step strategy that I was used to at McLaren. Now I have the feeling that we are working in a similar way to what happened with Honda at McLaren. Every race we have something new, and even though it isn't always an improvement, at least it's something to work on. We owe a lot of this to Jean Todt, who is very strong on details. When I arrived at Ferrari in 1993, there was no structure, there was no team. Now it's a team, it's a good atmosphere and the people understand high technology, people understand what it means to win a race, so it's going in the right direction.'

A vision of the pit lane wall during that second qualifying as Ferrari watched what the other cars were doing: Alesi, overalls done up, looks stern, prepossessed; Berger, overalls folded down to bare his tee-shirt, is chuckling about something, shakes his head, chuckles on.

Berger	1:43.582
Alesi	1:44.012
Hill	1:44.131
Schumacher	1:44.268

The start detonated. At the green light Berger pressed on the power and took the Ferrari over to the left, already clearly ahead of Alesi, over to the right. Far behind him de Cesaris (Sauber) struck the rear of Zanardi's Lotus and both Minardis became involved. That was four cars out and they would not be alone in that for long. Hakkinen made a bold thrust down the right, running alongside the pit lane wall, and nearing the mouth of Turn One clipped the front wheel of young David Coulthard's Williams. That threw Hakkinen's McLaren completely off balance and it screamed across the pack. Blundell reacted as fast as Warwick had done at Estoril — but braked because he had no chance to try and swerve. Barrichello could do nothing but ram him. In the chaos both Jordans went off, Blundell was out and so was Heinz-Harald Frentzen (Sauber). The race was not stopped.

Berger stretched his lead into the country. He'd been hoping for support from Alesi to keep Schumacher and Hill at bay, but Alesi was already slowing. The electrics had failed. Berger couldn't see Hill in his mirrors, but he could see Schumacher all right. Berger murmured to himself '(expletive), he's here already.' The Ferrari mechanics, assuming that the race would be stopped, instantly began to make ready the spare car for Alesi and the re-start; but coming through to complete the first lap — Schumacher now hustling Berger — the drivers were given only the yellow flags being waved: *great danger . . . slow down . . . be prepared to stop . . . no overtaking.*

Berger and Schumacher held an elongated lead from Ukyo Katayama (Tyrrell), Hill into the pits for repairs. He had had contact with the Tyrrell. Schumacher moved hard on Berger who threw the Ferrari over the kerbing of the chicanes, squeezed power on the straights. Crossing the line to complete lap 2, the Stadium section resembled a flag-waving festival, the black-red-yellow of Germany carving the air on every tier of the mighty grandstands, the yellows being waved from beside the pit lane: *still great danger . . .*

Out into the country again, Schumacher moved the Benetton as close as physically possible to the Ferrari without actually touching it. The weight of Germany, the weight of the thousands at Hockenheim was upon him. Germany, so strong in car manufacturing, had never had a World Champion before and here would be Schumacher's next move towards becoming that. He had irresistible momentum. Or did he? 'In the first part of the race, I was dancing right on the limit,' Berger said. On lap 7 at a chicane Schumacher went for the inside but Berger stayed resolutely on the racing line.

'He was almost alongside me but I managed to discourage him.' Schumacher swung wide, edging towards the grass, came on again, threatening, re-applying the pressure. Berger accepted it and resisted it so that, on lap 12, Schumacher pitted for fuel and tyres, a strategic decision to — perhaps — give him a touch more speed when he reached Berger again.

Schumacher charged from 22.973 seconds adrift. Could he get close enough to Berger that, when Berger pitted, he'd have the lead for himself? While this was unfolding, Schumacher's team-mate Verstappen came in for his stop and the fuel pump malfunctioned. You could see the fuel in a spray all over the Benetton, and when it touched the hot engine Verstappen and the mechanics changing the wheels disappeared into a wild, sheer sheet of molten flame. There had not been a spectre of fire as appalling as this since Imola, 23 April 1989. Mercifully no one received more than minor burns.

By lap 17 Schumacher had only cut the gap to 21.256 and, just then, whisps of smoke ebbed from his engine. He toured in, his race over.

* * *

Conversational interlude

Hilton: 'What was your thinking, Gerhard, in the early stages?'

Berger: 'An early pit stop is Benetton's usual strategy anyway, so maybe this would have been Michael's only one. I was sure he'd have an early stop, but I was still trying everything to keep in front. I was right on the limit. While he was pushing on his new tyres, I was doing the same on my old ones, and I kept checking the gap to see how much time he was making. For sure he was closing, but not as much as I expected. I knew if he made two stops it wouldn't be a problem for me — but if he was only going to have the early one he would make up time on me and maybe I'd come out behind him when I made mine. Then I'd have had to do something special in the last five laps.'

Hilton: 'In those 12 laps of such pressure, you were driving like a mature man.'

Berger: 'What does that mean?'

Hilton: 'It means I've done this before, I know exactly what I'm doing, everything is under control. After all, he was coming at you like a train.'

Berger: 'I had no problems. I knew he wanted to overtake me and I didn't want him to overtake me so I just positioned my car where he couldn't do it. I wasn't blocking him, I stayed on the racing line and, well, he couldn't get past. It became a question for me of not making a mistake.'

Hilton: 'But the pressure is mental as well as physical at that close range.'

Berger: 'Mentally it wasn't a problem either, wasn't a problem.'

Hilton: 'This may seem a rude question, but with his strength and his willpower, were you not frightened of him?'

Berger: 'I'm not! I think many of them are not frightened of him. He did a good job in 1994, especially for his age. He's quick, physically he's all right and he and the car were a good combination. He was also quite lucky in a way because he never really had direct pressure on him except the last race — and then he had pressure and then he made a mistake. But in general he brought everything finely together and he used it. He brings everything together by luck and hard work, but he uses it with his talent. That's it.'

Hilton: 'At Hockenheim you had the big pressure — a win for Ferrari, but he wants the win so much because he's a German in Germany — and you didn't make a mistake, nothing like a mistake.'

Berger: 'No, no, no, I didn't, but it's a big difference if you're fighting for a race or you're fighting for the Championship. It's a pressure ten times bigger if it's the last race, it's for the Championship and someone is "under your gearbox" (as Hill was, threatening and pressuring Schumacher at Adelaide, the 1994 showdown). It becomes this question: whether you are going to win the Championship or not. Mistakes always happen. Look at me at Adelaide. I had pressure and I positioned my wheel on the kerb and I went off, you know. I could have won the race and I made a mistake. Other drivers make mistakes, too . . .'

End of conversational interlude

* * *

At Hockenheim Berger pitted nice and gently on lap 20, stationary for 16.3 seconds, and after a brief flurry of checking on the rear wing he eased out again. Olivier Panis (Ligier) was second, and although the Frenchman was relatively close — 2.705 seconds, which at Hockenheim is visual all the way round the circuit — Berger needed to do no more than run to the end. It became a question of whether the Ferrari could do that. It could. He shed Panis who fell further and further behind, long out of sight.

Touchingly, Alesi spent the race among the Ferrari personnel on the pit lane wall *willing* Berger to win it. When Berger had crossed the finishing line to give Ferrari their first victory since Spain in 1990 (Prost), Alesi said 'I have also been waiting four years for this day and I feel reborn. This injection of faith for the team makes me sure that with so many races still remaining we will be competitive for the rest of the season. Gerhard is fantastic and together we will be able to satisfy our incomparable supporters again.'

Berger, relaxed and maybe just a little tired, said softly, 'I think if we keep going like this, we have a good chance to be strong on other circuits, and I tell you it makes it really fun again to drive in these circumstances — that you know you can go in *bold*, that you know you have a chance to win. I'm just laughing because at the last race Schumacher and Hill were joking. Schumacher said, "OK, I'll let you win here at Silverstone and you let me win at Hockenheim", and I said, "Hey, don't forget me because *I'm* going to win at Hockenheim" (big grin), so really it's just perfect.' He was in his best jovial mood. Someone asked who he'd like to dedicate the race to and he replied 'To me, if that's all right with you . . .'

The mood hardly lasted. He did well to qualify fourth at the Hungaroring, because the handling of the Ferrari didn't like the twists and turns there, ran fourth early on, rose to third, went off, was halted with a mechanical problem when he ran fifth towards the end. The Ferrari might like Spa, although Eau Rouge of such majesty and memory had been truncated. The descent remained unaltered but ahead lay a run-off area and now red and white kerbing directed the cars hard left, then hard right as the ascent up the hill beyond began. Eau Rouge, which — in the old days, because that is what they were now — some risked flat out if their nerve held and some didn't, and of which Senna himself once said *trying to take it flat you can only believe so much*, had become an everyday chicane.

'It was a great place,' Berger says, 'but the decision to alter it was the right one. I hope it can be like it was before but with proper run-off areas.'

He spun on the Friday morning and in first qualifying had another spin, had an oil leak and a fire, leaving him 11th. Nothing could be done to improve that because it rained on the Saturday. It also gave pole to Barrichello, his first and the Jordan team's first. This had no direct relevance to Berger, but I mention it because, well, dammit it was so good it deserves a mention. At the start of the race Berger got round La Source hairpin in midpack, and did so with full awareness of the possibilities of bumping and boring from any direction. Somehow, in the compression of cars squeezing La Source, he created space for himself to get safely round. He gave Brundle, bustling his Marlboro McLaren along on the inside, a wide berth, ceding a place. Berger was thinking clearly. If you're this far back one place doesn't matter much but a crash does. No criticism of Brundle, incidentally. He didn't do anything wrong; in fact he did it right.

By lap 11 Berger was sixth when his engine let go at the Bus Stop. The geography proved important: there's a right curve and then the Bus Stop snaps left-straight bit-right, but at the entry to the Bus Stop the road also continues straight ahead. This is the way to the pits. If you're racing you snap left, if you're pitting you steam directly on. Between the Bus Stop and the road to the pits lies a broad segment of grass.

Berger snapped left and the engine blew, billows of smoke. He couldn't very well park it in the Bus Stop because the action is habitually lively there, cars flicking through fast and furious. He raised his arm to tell anyone behind *I'm slowing, I'm in trouble* and turned onto the grass, ran bumpety-bumpety-bump over the grass, arm still raised, with the intention of joining the road to the pits — these pits where he would park it if he could get that far. As he rejoined it, up steamed Brundle en route to an ordinary pit stop. Brundle found Berger slithering across his front but so slowly that he passed by before the snout of the Ferrari reached him.

For this Berger was given a suspended one race ban. 'I'd indicated what I was doing by putting my hand in the air, but I hadn't realised Martin was close behind. At that angle it was difficult to see him in my mirrors. I admit it was dangerous but I did it with good intentions.'

Alesi took pole at Monza, Berger within 0.13 (on the Saturday, Alesi 1:23.844, Berger 1:23.978) which stirred the *tifosi* nicely. Quali-fying done, Berger and Alesi clambered on to the pit lane wall and stirred the fervour up another degree or two, waving imperiously and affectionately to the crowd. *You're with us and we're with you.* At the Press Conference Alesi, in a wonderful growling French accent, did say 'I very 'appy to beat my team-mate (gestures towards Berger, who's just arriving) because he did his maximum and I'm quicker.' Berger's response? The lovely grin.

He was not grinning after the Sunday morning warm-up and few others were, either (although he did inevitably find humour within the aftermath of what happened). He was reaching up to some 186 mph on the approach to the Variante della Roggia, a left-right kink before the sweeping Lesmo curve out at the back. The Ferrari got away from him, went onto the grass and spun, clipped the armco and spun on into a gravel trap before thumping a tyre wall back-wards. This was a big impact, the whole tyre wall shuddering in alarm. Marshals took him from the cockpit and laid him down on *the racing side* of the armco. Cars kept coming so close to where these marshals, as utterly vulnerable as he, tried to tend him. The session was not halted: only a yellow flag waved. The notion of one of the cars losing control or having brake failure at virtually full speed and ploughing the group crouching over Berger reared from your night-mares. They tended him for 8 minutes, the cars keeping on coming.

'You wouldn't believe it,' Berger said. 'You cannot leave some-body there with cars doing 180 miles an hour. And the guys taking my helmet off, they didn't know how to do it.' This could have been important. Berger's neck has screws in it from his road crash of 1984. The session was stopped to let the ambulance journey round to collect him and he was taken to the medical centre. 'You go in and there are 25 doctors. One pushes you this way, the other that way. One says we need to X-ray this, another says X-ray that.'

* * *

259

Conversational interlude

Member of medical centre: 'Now we are finished but you have to wait 10 minutes for the X-ray pictures to take them back with you.'

Berger: 'Please, do me a favour. Can you send someone back with the pictures? I have to go back to work on the set-up of my car because at three o'clock I have a race and it is already one o'clock.'

Member of medical centre: 'No, you cannot go. First you have to sign that you don't want your brain pictures.'

Berger: 'OK, I don't want them. Where do I sign? Now I go, OK?'

Exit Berger to ambulance.

Berger: 'Please take me back to the track.'

Ambulanceman: 'No, you must wait 5 minutes until the doctor comes.'

Berger: 'I don't need a doctor any more. I want to go to the track, otherwise I miss the race.'

Exit Berger from ambulance, advances on policeman.

Berger: 'Please take me back to the track.'

Policeman: 'No, you must go in the ambulance.'

Berger: 'OK, I have enough of this. I walk.'

Berger sets off and after a few paces feels the strong grip of an officer of the law.

Policeman: 'No, no, you have to go back in the ambulance!'

End of conversational interlude

* * *

Nothing, including the above which Berger recounted with a certain undisguised relish, should obscure the potential horror of what might have been and, like a concrete wall at Tamburello, it must never, never, never, never, never, never be permitted again.

In the race Alesi led, Berger second and, when Alesi dropped out, gearbox — he demonstrated visible rage — Berger led. A slow pit stop cast him back to fourth but he rose to third, and on the final lap, in the final corner, Coulthard up ahead ran out of fuel. Berger finished second. While the winner, Hill, spoke solemnly at the Press Conference, Hakkinen (third) leaned over behind Hill's back, tapped Berger and pointed to something funny he'd noticed. And there it was, the big, impish grin. Berger would say, 'I had to go in the spare car because my race car was destroyed this morning, so my best engine was gone. It was a little down on power and altogether it was just not enough. Otherwise I think I could have fought more with Damon, although that would have been difficult. I wasn't expecting after this morning that I was going to be sitting here in the first three.'

He took pole in Portugal and led for seven laps, then the gearbox failed. A pity, he'd say, because the car felt great. He qualified sixth for the European Grand Prix at Jerez and finished fifth. In Japan he qualified 11th and the car lasted until lap 10 when the electrics

failed. In Adelaide, the world preparing to watch Hill get his Rothmans Williams up the gearbox of Schumacher's Benetton, Berger
qualified 11th, worked his way up . . . and up. Schumacher and Hill
crashed, of course. Mansell led and Berger, second, pressured him;
after the pit stops Berger led and Mansell pressured him. Strong
stuff, it was, but clean, fair, *mature.*

On lap 64 Berger made the mistake he mentioned earlier in this
chapter. He ran wide going into a right-hander and went straight on
into a deep run-off area, gathered it up, returned. 'Mature? It was a
bit different in Adelaide from Hockenheim. I did not have everything
under control. I saw Mansell was quicker into the corner onto the
straight and I also saw he had a good chance to overtake me at the
end of the straight. At Hockenheim I was coming out of the corners
quickly, I was clear provided I didn't make a mistake and I knew
Schumacher wasn't going to overtake me. At Adelaide I was saying
to myself "Even if I don't make a mistake Mansell has a good chance
to overtake me", so it was a different kind of thing altogether.'

He tracked Mansell to the end and occupied himself during this
Press Conference by calculating the combined age of the first
three, Mansell (born 8 August 1953), himself (27 August 1959) and
Brundle (1 June 1959), and thought it must be 'about 120'. He also,
as Mansell recounted, congratulated him — Mansell — by saying
'Well done, you old bastard!'. Mansell enjoyed that. Berger enjoyed
that. Everybody enjoyed that.

Reasons to be cheerful in spite of everything? The Human Face?
Yes, and surely more reasons at Ferrari now, but, whatever, you've
better quality of life if you don't worship the winning as everything
and feel meaningless without it.

'Gerhard still has a lot of little boy in him,' Barnard says. 'There
used to be a time in motor racing when the practical joking was a
hell of a lot more than it is today. It's all the pressures of big, big
business and the super-clinical teams that have washed it away.
Even when I started, some of the stuff that went on was amazing.
Slowly but surely it has been leeched out of the system to achieve
the super-clinical, this technical perfection that teams are always
striving for. So when you still get a little bit of it — which is what
Gerhard is all about, he still likes a joke and so on — it's nice.'

All sport has become a Very Serious Matter and grown into
something it was never intended to be; too often a greedy and love-
less spectacle of self-importance enacted in the enclaves (golf,
tennis and motor racing particularly) but relayed globally by television, giving the illusion there are no enclaves but something so
open it embraces the globe. Serious? One year Boris Becker,
defending Wimbledon champion, was knocked out in an early
round and at the (mandatory) Press Conference journalists ques-

tioned him in phrases more suited to thermo-nuclear warfare.

'I don't see the problem,' Becker said. 'Nobody died.'

They didn't. It was a tennis match played on grass with a soft ball demanding many human qualities, but in the end only another tennis match. The way their world was. Since then Monica Seles has been stabbed on court by the supporter of the girl she happened to be playing, Steffi Graf.

People do die in motor racing, as 1994 so mercilessly underscored, and that's a total difference. The successful driver earns massively, but the risk always runs at his elbow and cumulatively over a career it can become a bitch of a thing, the enclosing into Formula 1, the ceaseless technology and travel, the pressures that don't go away and putting your life on the line 16 times a year — not to mention testing, where you're just as vulnerable.

Helmut Marko says, 'Gerhard is a natural driver and you can always see that in his style in fast corners. At quick circuits he was always good. The tighter the corner, the slower the corner, the more problems he had. One thing he's developed very, very much is his sense of money. I think at the moment he's the best paid driver and always in comparison to his results he was well paid. The only change that really happened to him is that in the old days he'd buy you a cup of coffee. That money was in his pocket and he'd pay for the coffee. Nowadays that's impossible. You discuss half an hour before he buys you a coffee. That's just some sort of *sport* not to spend a penny — that you can live without spending anything. That's his *sport* nowadays. No, no, no, it's not that he's mean because he is not — it's *sport*.'

This is a very human way of coping with being a millionaire many, many times over, of living beyond the enclave, of mischievously passing ordinary moments; a vignette of the man.

'I just know from watching Gerhard on television over the last few years since he's been in Formula 1, listening to his interviews, reading his comments, that he's the same Gerhard and he didn't change a bit,' Tommy Byrne says. 'That's why I like him best. The rest of them get there, they're all stick-in-the-muds. Jesus, I had a laugh, you know. You win the race, you win the Championship, you go out on the town, you don't win the race, you don't win the Championship, you go out on the town.'

Or, as Gunter Schmid says, 'What is interesting is that Gerhard hasn't changed, he's still a nice guy. I talked to him on the phone last week and he's the same, for me always the same. From the very beginning on he never changed and I don't think he ever will. And don't ever forget he's very intelligent, too.'

Sometimes the sense of humour is executed with a deft, delicate, delightful touch, unless you're the victim, and Ayrton Senna proved an irresistible target. One time in Mexico City Berger was driving along in a hire car with a passenger who wondered what the over-powering smell from the boot might be. Mexico City itself has, as I've said, an overpowering smell of its own, so whatever it was in the boot had to be very, very pungent indeed.

'It's fish,' Berger said.

Evidently he'd bought it some time before and allowed it to steam in the smog until rancid. Up to Senna's bedroom tiptoe, fish hidden everywhere: in and under the bed, behind the wardrobe, in the bathroom. Senna, so the story goes, spent a long time finding it, got into bed, sniffed, got out and started the search again, found more, got into bed, sniffed . . .

No doubt he uttered a single word.

Berger!

Not forgetting Berger dropping Senna's briefcase from a helicopter at Monza just because it seemed like a good idea at the time. Initial reports suggested it exploded on hitting the ground, but Ayrton Senna corrected this. 'We were to land at Monza in 1991. It fell on the landing area. I was lucky because it was grass and extremely fortunately the briefcase did not open. But to give you an idea, the briefcase had cost £2,500 and now cost £300 to repair. The only reason Gerhard did not throw it out when the helicopter was over Lake Como, coming from the hotel where we were staying, is that Ron Dennis's wife Lisa would not let him. Can you believe it? In the lake!

'I have everything in there, passport, credit cards, documents . . . everything. He is completely mad — and dangerous, though in a good way of course. He is totally irresponsible when it comes to the jokes (Senna laughed), no limits. He does the most absurd things as though they were normal. It was the only side of Gerhard I was careful about. It was just impossible to imagine what was coming next.'

Ramirez waited 'near the helipad. I didn't see the briefcase come down. Someone picked it up and ran towards the helipad to give it back. Ayrton was really upset. Gerhard said, "Well, you're lucky. I opened one catch on the briefcase and if I could have opened the other I'd have thrown everything out." He would have done it. Gerhard also said, "Why do you buy such expensive briefcases? You buy a cheap one like mine and you won't have a problem."

'No limits to Gerhard's jokes? On his boat at Monaco people would take their shoes off and he'd throw them into the harbour. However, I remember going into a car park in Belgium on a very windy day. Ayrton got Gerhard's address book, took all the pages out and threw them into the air. Gerhard had to go round trying to pick them up. After races, when they went to put their clothes on, they'd have cut trouser legs off or shirt sleeves off. Yes, you miss that when it's not there any more.'

But, Mr Ramirez, did Berger ever give you the treatment? 'Not exactly, but he is always pinching my girlfriends. We seem to have the same taste . . .'

Not forgetting dubious tales of 'superglue' in the night in hotels (Berger doing it to Senna or Senna doing it to Berger), so that when the victim awakes he discovers his wallet and anything else stickable firmly stuck to a table. Not forgetting dubious tales of itching powder in tee-shirts before races (Berger doing it to Senna and Senna doing it to Berger), or poor old Ayrton's briefcase being filled with talcum powder — although the jury is out on that one and it may well not have been Berger.

And definitely not forgetting a certain incident at Cairns, Australia, where Berger hired two locals to catch frogs. They caught 26, which were secreted in Senna's bedroom. Senna came down, face black as thunder according to one witness, and said — part statement, part accusation -

Berger!

Berger wondered how many frogs Senna had found, Senna said 16 and Berger said, 'There are another 10 and, oh, Ayrton, did I mention the snakes?'

Senna's revenge? 'It was in Port Douglas, Australia, where we went on holiday between the Japanese and Australian Grands Prix of 1991. He was with his girlfriend Anna. One day I managed to get a spare key for his room and went into it. The chambermaid was making the room up so I walked in as if it was my room, looked around for a while and picked up a newspaper that was on the table. I thought it would all seem as if I had come back for it. As I did that I couldn't believe my eyes or my luck. He'd left his "card" key for the door there.

'That evening I met Gerhard and Anna at a reception. They were going out for dinner. I thought *this is my chance*. With my cousin Fabio we went into his room and turned it upside down. We filled his jacuzzi and threw all the bed sheets, towels, clothes, Anna's clothes too, and even a big frog right in the middle of the jacuzzi. We hung some of his underwear and her underwear in the ceiling fan and turned it on. He had two Filofaxes, the kind you can open to put more pages in. I took all the pages out and threw them around the room. The place was covered with paper. We carried the bed to the bathroom, too.

'The most amazing thing was that the next day he did not mention a thing. It was as though nothing had happened. At one point we simply could not resist asking him if everything had been OK in his room when he got back to it. With a straight face he said "Yes, OK". He is mad.'

Distorted images. In the dear, dear old days of the Touring Cars, when Dieter Quester didn't want to be the driving instructor, Quester's career, as Charley Lamm says, 'was nearly over. Gerhard enjoyed the difference in their attitudes. Quester was very, very careful when it came to food, he did regular fitness and only later did Gerhard see the importance of this. Gerhard would eat a special Bavarian-Tyrolean dish of pork whenever he wanted, drink a beer. Quester took care about when he went to bed, what he ate for breakfast. People laughed at him. At one stage Quester started to have a special tea, which he prepared with some ceremony. Gerhard got some oil we used on the cars (!) and put it into the water that Quester would need to make the tea.

'Quester came down to breakfast and he had one of those small bags that women put their toiletries in, full of special things to prepare the tea. He went through the ceremony of preparing it; poured the water and said "This looks strange". Bubbles from the oil were rising. Gerhard could hardly contain himself from laughing out loud. Quester took two mouthfuls and said he didn't want any more. He never did find out.'

And Quester suffered The Passport Ploy. 'One time in Italy,' Lamm says, 'Quester handed his passport in at the hotel reception because that is what you have to do. Gerhard came in, noticed it there, said to the receptionist "I need my passport" and pointed to Quester's. He took it and drew on Quester's photograph a moustache and sunglasses. Obviously when Quester checked out he didn't look at the passport, but when he reached the Austrian customs and they looked at it . . .'

The Schnapps Ploy attracts Berger enormously. Alex Lichine's *Encyclopedia of Wines and Spirits* describes schnapps thus: 'In Germany and Holland, any strong, dry spirit, in Scandinavia usually aquavit. An aromatic schnapps is made from a base of Dutch-style gin flavoured with herbs.' It is strong and burns all the way to the pit of your stomach. Dieter Stappert became (almost) a victim of The Ploy.

'Practical jokes? He didn't pull any in the early days because I think he had too much respect for me. Later not much practical joking either, because I was always very cautious. Gerhard is the guy who would tear a page out of your passport or put a picture of some bare-breasted woman on top of your passport photograph.' *Your* means Senna's.

I must interrupt Strappert's tale for Senna, who said that 'to get even after what I'd done to his bedroom he tore two pages out of my passport. At the time I had a standard passport and a diplomatic one. Not content with tearing the pages out — the ones with my personal detail and photograph — he also stuck pictures of naked women in a very indiscreet position there. I did not notice.

'The Australian Grand Prix was over. I left Australia on a once-a-week flight from Adelaide to Buenos Aires, where I was to be picked up and taken to Brazil. Well, they let me out of Australia no problem and I don't know how. When I arrived in Buenos Aires I gave my passport to the VIP assistant and went to the VIP lounge to wait for it. It took ages and I was there for a good half-hour wondering what was going on. Next thing, the bloke came back and said to me, "Sorry to keep you waiting, sir, but we are having some problems with your passport. There are some pages missing." He opened them and straight away I knew it had been . . .'

Berger!

'The bloke showed me the naked women pictures. I knew who'd done it. They ended up letting me out, but can you imagine if I'd had problems in Adelaide, with the flight only once a week. I'd probably have had to spend another week stuck there! He is completely irresponsible (laughter).'

Now, back to Dieter Stappert. 'When I became a television commentator I flew back to Innsbruck from one Grand Prix with Paul Rosche and Gerhard. We rented a car and drove to Worgl. Gerhard said, "Come, it's a festival". They'd stopped the traffic, plenty of beer and music. What amazed me all the time was that whenever Gerhard went back he always felt at home. For the people there he was still the Gerhard they had always known. He was famous in Formula 1, rich, but nobody made a fuss. People passed by and said, "Ah Gerhard, why did you retire from the race yesterday?" They talked to him normally and I never thought a guy so famous could be regarded so normally. Nobody stopped him and asked for his autograph — well maybe a tourist from Frankfurt who happened to recognise him! But the locals couldn't care less.

'We arrived late and no space left to sit outside on a beautiful summer's evening. I blamed him. I said, "You knew there would be no space." He said, "Don't worry." He walked inside the pub and started carrying out tables and chairs from the restaurant and arranged them, everything on the pavement. In the end the whole restaurant was outside! We sat there, Paul next to me. Gerhard said we must have schnapps. Paul said, "No, we have to go." We sat there for an hour, perhaps two, talking and then Gerhard started to order the small, clear stuff — schnapps. I said, "I have to go, I have business to do in the morning." Gerhard said, "You stay here and Paul, you stay here too." Each time Gerhard said that, Paul dug me in the ribs and said "We must go." We knew if we stayed half an hour longer we'd never make it home, not after three or four more schnapps.

'I always carried little notebooks with me to the races. I tend to forget things easily and so I wrote a lot of information in them for my commentaries. I had my notebook in my back pocket. He took it out and said, "Stay here or you don't get your book again." I thought if I didn't get it back I'd screw up at the next Grand Prix. By now Paul was on the edge of trying to persuade himself and myself to stay. I was happy because I had my passport in the back pocket and Gerhard didn't notice it. The lovely bastard that he is, he gave the notebook back . . . at the end of the season!'

The Schnapps Ploy was used to maximum effect on Peter Collins at Suzuka in 1992, Berger's last race for Marlboro McLaren. It happened on familiar ground (to Berger), the Camel hospitality unit. Collins is virtually teetotal. 'I hadn't ever had schnapps before. Gerhard said, "You do it like this" — straight down the hatch. I did that and he said, "Ah now you have started you must have four more and then you can go, OK?"'

Distorted images. Collins vaguely remembers Berger 'sitting there with a cigar in his mouth and a cap on the back of his head drinking, enjoying himself. I thought, this is the real Gerhard Berger again. Then someone said Ron Dennis is coming up the stairs and Gerhard said expletive Ron Dennis! Laughter everywhere.' When Collins departed scarcely vertical, he moved past a journalist and mumbled at him. The journalist, knowing Collins to be a good man and a sober one, wondered and wondered and didn't stop wondering until six months later when I told him what Berger had done.

Derek Warwick was forewarned and forearmed. 'We were at Willi Dungl's doing training and fitness stuff and we had adjoining rooms with an adjoining door. You are always aware that Berger is going to try something on you sometime. I went to bed, lay there but didn't go to sleep. I heard a lot of giggling next door, which would have woken me up but, as I say, I was awake anyway. He'd obviously gone to reception and picked up the key because the adjoining door opened. He came through it with a big white sheet over his head like some sort of ghost, came over to the bed and jumped on it. I was behind him and I jumped on him so hard I frightened the life out of *him*! I thought it was all absolutely perfect. I thought also that the significant aspect wasn't my anticipating the practical joke — because that was obviously going to happen — but the fact that, as he was doing it, he couldn't stop himself giggling like a schoolboy.'

Reasons to be cheerful in spite of everything? Oh yes.

You remember Roberto Ravaglia, the hire car, the ignition key thrown out, the steering locking, the halting just in front of a tree. All unknowing, Senna took revenge for Ravaglia many years later.

'We were leaving a test at Monza,' Senna said, 'in Gerhard's Ferrari. Joseph Leberer, the team's physiotherapist, was with us. Imagine three in a Ferrari. Late in the evening on the autostrada I took out the main key — like a racing car, Ferraris have a main switch that turns everything off — and threw it out of the window. Gerhard went mad. He braked hard, stopped, rushed out of the car and started to look for it. The key is plastic and if it had broken . . .

'He came back with it a few minutes later and began to pull me out of the car. I clutched my briefcase (!) hard. What a spectacle! Me holding my briefcase with both hands and being dragged out of a Ferrari in the middle of the night on an autostrada. Two mentally retarded people! The perfect definition of Gerhard is "lunatic Austrian". I call him that and he doesn't mind. He *laughs*. He recognises that he is raving lunatic. A great guy!'

'He's very funny guy,' Marko says, 'who is — how do you say it? — playing all sorts of jokes every second of every minute. You should have been at my birthday party at Graz last weekend (May 1993) where all these jokes were recounted. Niki was there, and Wendlinger (the father) and Paddy McNally, people from the old days. I was so drunk I must say I can't remember the stories, but it was always action with Berger.

'He was absolutely mad in traffic on the road, you know. He drove on the motorway in snow in fifth gear, 125 mph (200 km/h), things like that. He spun through an accident that had happened ahead without hitting anything, immediately first gear, second, third, fourth, fifth. You know where his house is? Up in the mountains along a very small road. I sat in the passenger seat, my son in the back. In front of us was a German, driving normally for these sort of conditions, and Gerhard was already driving crazy. My son said "I am getting old".

'I got into position (bracing himself) prepared for anything. The car left the road and started rolling — I don't know how many times — until we were suspended between two trees. Gerhard was hanging down on me and I worried that one of the trees, a small one, might not be strong enough to hold us and if it broke we'd roll another 200 metres. I could see how small the tree was from my position. I was down, Gerhard was up, both of us in seat belts. The discussion went like this. *I* said I should get out first because I was nearer to the earth. *He* opened his seat belt and bang, fell on *me*. Then *he* climbed — climbed — out and complained about *me*!'

We might contrast this levity with the words of Warwick, because we see another Berger when we do. 'In 1994 Gerhard was the bravest driver in Grand Prix racing — bravest because he lost two of his friends and almost lost three, two of whom were Austrian. Ayrton was a partner he drove with for many years and they were close. I think in 1994 Gerhard showed not only enormous courage but respect, he showed everything one expects from a great sportsman.'

A central question must be faced. Is it possible to win the World Championship without total surrender to achieving that? The enclave has tentacles that can choke, however you try and organize yourself to live within it. Thus, before a Brazilian Grand Prix, Berger tested in Italy, flew to Argentina to do some promotional work, flew back to Italy for testing, then flew to Interlagos. Another random example. In 1988 he said, 'You know I have been home for one day in the last four weeks and when I leave Imola (after testing) I am going to Vienna for a couple of days to see Willi Dungl and then I fly to Rio. My family will come to Vienna to see me. It gets more and more difficult and it makes me think a lot about my private life. I cannot see any easy solution.'

If all that isn't enough — and mercifully testing has been curtailed — the growth of the debrief swallows the driver every race weekend. The trend is for the driver to arrive at the circuit the day before qualifying, chat, see what's going on. Five years ago you might have wandered the pits the day before and seen, say, only Senna, now they all drift in.

Take any race weekend. Friday: untimed practice from 9.30 to 11 with a debrief after that, flowing on to the first qualifying session, 1.00 to 2.00. The debrief after that may last well into the evening when the driver returns to his hotel to sleep. He'll be up early on the Saturday to reach the circuit for the untimed session, then a debrief, then second qualifying, then another long debrief, the hotel and sleep. He'll be up early on the Sunday for the warm-up session from 9.30 to 10.00, then a debrief because the car has been running in race trim. Plenty to talk about there. That flows into the starting routine for the race. Almost every waking moment from Thursday until late afternoon Sunday the driver has been travelling to reach the car, discussing it or driving it with short interludes for food and sleep. As the man says, 'I cannot see any easy solution'.

Moreover, as the complexities of the car grow there's always more to discuss, eyes scanning page after page of computer printouts. One year testing at Imola Senna was there until 10 at night scanning them, understanding them, wringing meanings from them.

One year in the mid-1960s, Jim Clark came to Monaco very late from Indianapolis, arrived while first qualifying was going on, changed into his overalls, popped the Lotus on pole and vanished to his hotel. You could do that then. Not now. In 1993 Senna came to Imola very late from Brazil (5 minutes to spare before the untimed Friday session of the San Marino Grand Prix), covered 11 laps and spun. Jet lag? The modern car makes such demands that you must approach it in peak condition.

Nor does the enclave set its frontiers there. As long ago as 1988 in an interview with Nigel Roebuck, Berger remembers something Niki Lauda said to him years before: 'Formula 1 is full of people who think they're so important. I can't stand the people in this paddock any longer.' Berger didn't understand that then. 'I was just starting and I thought he was crazy! Look at the girls, and the people giving you money everywhere, you get the best hotels, eat the best food. What more could you want? Now, though, I have to say I don't find these things important. Niki was right. I just come to the track, race and afterwards I go back to the hotel where I like to be alone or with friends who have nothing to do with Formula 1. What I still really like about Formula 1 is to sit in the car and drive.'

The central question returns. What happens if you can't envelop yourself? It is a personal question directly involving what you want, how much you want it and how much of yourself you judge you'll lose getting it. Alan Rees of Footwork gives a large part of the answer, expanding on what he had to say in Chapter 6.

Hilton: 'What sort of chap was Gerhard when you got to know him?'

Rees: 'He was Gerhard, you know, always laid back really, and I think it has probably been evident all the time in his career.'

Hilton: 'When you say laid back, do you mean entirely laid back?'

Rees: 'Yes, perhaps not quite professional enough. He enjoys life, enjoys things, enjoys racing, enjoys life (Rees repeated this) but a very good driver. Perhaps he was slightly laid back and that took the edge off him.'

Hilton: 'It's unusual in a young Formula 1 driver — they are a lot of things but not laid back.'

Rees: 'That's right. I think that is the overall impression I got. I mean, he had all the talent and all the determination, but at the end there was just a little bit of the fact that he was laid back. That didn't take the edge off his driving but maybe off his overall performance — only a little bit, only a fraction.'

Hilton: 'He's won Grands Prix and a stack of points . . .'

Rees: '. . . but if you compare him with Senna or Prost they were just that little bit more professional in their whole attitude out of the car. In the car Gerhard is fine, that's right. Where he might have lost very slightly to somebody like Senna or somebody like Prost was in preparation, practice.'

(To be fair to Rees, he was reaching towards something and wasn't really criticizing. Later in the interview he said pointedly that he didn't want it blown out of proportion. It remains, however, central to the question of what you want, how much you want it and how much of yourself you judge you'll lose getting it.)

Hans Stuck says, 'Gerhard had the same talent as Senna and Prost but my problem and his problem was that I don't think we took it seriously enough. We stayed the nice guys who came down from the mountains' — Stuck from Garmisch, a winter sport centre south of Munich — 'not typical computer-drivers like Senna or Prost. We took the driving seriously, of course, but we enjoyed it. I had good times and bad times, but I haven't wanted to miss a single day of my 24 years as a driver.' (To be fair to Stuck, he was reaching towards something and wondered if this was the right way to phrase it. Like Rees, he's talking about degrees of seriousness, not a lack of seriousness itself.)

When I broached the notion to Berger that the world outside Austria had only heard of four Austrian sportsmen — Rindt, Lauda, Klammer and himself — he accepted the notion modestly enough, accepted it as a fact rather than an opinion.

Where does Berger fit among them? That's another central question because Rindt became World Champion, albeit posthumously, Lauda became World Champion three times. The dynasty, therefore, is not a cosy domestic Austrian matter, but a matter of worldwide significance.

'In many ways Jochen was like Gerhard in driving styles and behaviour,' Marko says. 'Jochen also moved around like he didn't have any straight bones in his body. Same in skiing. I think, incidentally, the chances of Gerhard having an accident in skiing are much bigger than in motor racing. Gerhard goes where you wouldn't believe, where nobody else has been before, avalanches and things like that.

'As drivers, for sure they were the two most similar of all the Austrians because they liked to go flat out and let a car really fly — like Jochen at Silverstone, rear end out. Gerhard did the same thing at Zeltweg with the BMW turbo engine, all out, full throttle. Their personalties? Jochen became more mature and during his racing career he changed a lot. Gerhard is always thinking what naughty things he can do next. After their first years in Formula 1, Jochen changed and Gerhard didn't. Remember Gerhard at Hockenheim overtaking on the grass, sixth gear, a ridiculous move! Gerhard changed slowly after his crash at Imola. He began to think a little bit more.

'Jochen became serious, he was interested in business, which Gerhard is also, but Jochen thought of big business. When Gerhard buys a Ferrari he calculates how much he can earn when he sells it again!

'Jochen got scared when he was at Lotus. I met him 14 days before his death and he was scared. Always before he'd said, "I don't care, it's just life, let's go." Jochen was convinced by Colin Chapman that the new Lotus would allow him to reduce the risks by 20 per cent and still win — and as World Champion he'd get double as much money as before. That was the reason why he wanted to keep on. He had a very successful motor show running in Austria and he wanted to expand it all over Europe. He wanted me to go into a Formula 2 team that he would set up with Bernie Ecclestone to keep interest in motor racing alive in Austria until someone came along after he'd retired. Jochen was already thinking like that.'

John Miles, once a Lotus driver, explores Rindt, and I include his observations for several reasons that I hope will be self-evident. 'I don't think Rindt was any different than other prodigiously talented racing drivers in recent history. The obvious person is Clark, you can say Nuvolari, you can say Ronnie Peterson, Senna, those drivers who are incredibly fast, have a way with a car, a touch with a car. It's more than just a talent, it's some sort of brilliance. If you like, it's the difference between an actor who has an enormous stage presence and another actor, technically just as good, but who doesn't have that stage presence. Rindt was clearly one of the former.

'He actively disliked testing, disliked wasting his time doing it because he had the confidence that, given a reasonable car he was comfortable with he could be competitive. I can't say I knew him well and I can't say how many people did know him well. He had certain character traits that were quite clear and that you saw off the track. Someone once described him as having this inner dynamo. He had a sort of power in him once he was in a car, an enormous aggression — no, not exactly that, it was aggressive but not in the sense of crashing a lot, aggressive in the sense that he could somehow extract from the car extraordinary things.

'He could be a pretty aggressive character off he track. He was blunt. Chapman often talked of his bluntness and they didn't immediately hit it off at all. It's the old thing. Rindt was cruel but fair, one of these characters who was very straight talking, a very honest man in his approach to people and in his business dealings.

'He admired people who were rash, who took risks, and I didn't take to that. He'd bought an aeroplane and was looking for a pilot, he found one and employed him on the basis that the pilot flew into an airfield when it was closed by snow and he didn't have the full licence. It was deemed rather a plus-point that this particular pilot was prepared to take risks. There was that element to Rindt, and it's no good saying there wasn't, an urgency about him that forced him to take risks. It was almost important to take risks.'

But what is the ability to make cars go so fast? 'In one or two races I felt totally confident, only one or two, but I felt that no matter who was driving the car they could not have driven it faster. Something had taken over. It's not like an out-of-body experience, it's that all the good forces combine on that day in that race to produce a performance. Now the thing with exceptional racing drivers is that, first, they have a confidence in their ability that is undiminished regardless of whether, say, Rindt drove a Cooper half-way down the field or a Lotus 72 at the front. The confidence is always there, tremendous confidence. Secondly, like for example all the great actors or jazz musicians, they can turn on a performance. Miles Davis, when he was dying, did the Antibes jazz festival and he played magically.

'All external influences go once the driver is in the car. Jackie Stewart was very articulate, very, very sensitive out of the car, in it a mask of remoteness, in a sense a machine. This ability, and the ability to turn on a performance that takes the car to its limits, may be allied to understanding the car, getting into the car's personality instinctively. It's not something you can explain to anybody. It's something you know how to do. You're born with it. There are some people who can extract the ultimate from the capabilities of the car every time they get in it, and other people who have off-days or maybe only have one or two *on*-days in their entire career . . .'

Alan Rees also worked at Lotus. 'Jochen was World Champion in

1970, but he could have been any year — but to do that he would have had to make up his mind to do it. He wasn't the sort of driver like Senna who would go out every race every year and drive flat out. Jochen had to have the feeling he had a chance. If he felt that, nobody was going to beat him. That is what happened in 1970. He realised during a certain part of the year that he had a car that could win the World Championship and that was it.

'If he thought he didn't have the right equipment he didn't bother, and that was the trouble with Jochen. He didn't have a career long enough. If he had been able to go on longer he might have had a bigger reputation today, but from the point of view of natural ability there was no one quicker, absolutely no one in his day, just like there was no one quicker than Jimmy Clark in his day, no one quicker than Senna.

'Jochen had a great sense of humour, but he was a very, very ruthless person. Whatever he wanted he would get, and whatever he wanted to do he would do if he made his mind up to do it. He was very hard from that point of view. I got on well with him because you could make fun of him and you'd laugh and he'd laugh, which is a great advantage — like Berger, that's right.'

Now we have a dynasty of Austrians: Rindt, Lauda, Berger.

'Lauda? Very professional, not so much natural ability but super, super professional. That is why he won three World Championships: absolute dedication to what he was doing, 100 per cent, and he worked it all out. Jochen didn't do that. Jochen got in the car and bang. "If I have a car that will win the World Championship, I will win the World Championship, if I don't I could win this race but I'm not interested in the race, forget it." Mind you, it didn't happen all the time, say 20 per cent. Jochen could do anything with the car, absolutely anything. Amazing. He could throw it all over the place and not get into trouble. Very few have that ability. Maybe the fact that they live in or near mountains, always snow, makes them, like the Scandinavians, develop a certain amount of natural talent.'

How do you acquire balance? Are you born with it? Either way, growing up in the Alps actively promotes it. Years ago I was in Alpbach, a homely little old resort just up the road from Worgl, and in the morning I saw a horde of schoolkids, satchels strapped to their backs, pouring down a long, snow-clad field on short skis to reach the school bus. They had balance: unconscious adjustment to the contours of the snow, letting the skis run smoothly and quickly, and never falling down, of course. (I was covering the British Junior Championships and one morning a waitress asked what was going on because you could see the racing from the hotel. I explained and she expressed incredulity. 'Those are national championships? We've half a dozen young skiers better than that in this village.')

It is this balance that allows a man like Berger to take pole position in the stone-clad corridors of Phoenix and the broad sweep of Silverstone, the jabbering bumps of Mexico and the street corners of Adelaide. It is this balance that allows you to out-qualify Senna a time or two when the equipment is the same, no advantage to either man — and rarely be much slower than Senna when you don't out-qualify him, a genuine feat in itself. In three years with Senna at Marlboro McLaren, Berger took four pole positions. In two years with Senna at Malboro McLaren, Prost took . . . four pole positions.

'The way Gerhard skis is something special,' Charley Lamm says. 'At the end of 1986 he said, "Come on, we'll go skiing." We went to Sestriere, all the Formula 1 drivers around. We skied and then he said, "I'd like to look for a more exciting slope." Stefan Johansson was there and a ski instructor who said, "Well, maybe I can help you. We can go to the other side of the valley." We reached the top over there and the instructor said the first section was a normal downhill piste. We covered that but Gerhard said the snow wasn't right and we went off-piste. At one point the instructor feared for his own legs, stopped and took his skis off!

'Gerhard, me following, went into a forest, in between the trees, and we went over rock on just a little bit of snow. We got down although I must say it was tough for me. He put his arm round my shoulder and said, "This is pure enjoyment for me, I get not only pleasure but satisfaction out of it." Speaking of balance, he could take a natural route down a mountain even if it did go through trees and over rocks.

'He found a mogul field (moguls are large snow-clad humps that lie in profusion) and you have to balance to go between them. You need to be accurate to within a hundredth of a second from one moment to the next, decide which path to take. It's an exercise in concentration, split-second decision and never putting the ski wrong.

'The Hahnenkamm is the most demanding downhill and I asked him once about it, and he said he'd been down it on occasions, but "My problem now is that I'm in Formula 1 and if I did it again I'd go down and not see the danger and that could be dangerous if I hurt my legs".

'This is basically the same sort of balance as in a racing car. You think about lines, you think about the critical balance, although obviously you see that more in a downhiller because the whole body has got to move. But again, physical balance is also required in a racing car — you have to feel the car, so there are many similarities. I am sure you learn it by skiing from a very early age, and it can be applied to anything, cars, dancing, virtually all sports.' Like ice hockey . . .

The point of all this is not that you need to be a *wunderkind* skier, but that it can only help.

The fact that you go looking for life after Grands Prix, and see the debrief as a debrief rather than an addition to the Ten Commandments, scarcely diminishes you in the big world, which is where we all live, even the ones so deep into Formula 1 that they are no longer aware of it. Gerhard Berger remains aware.

'Lauda and Berger were very, very different,' Jo Ramirez says, 'but more similar than Senna and Berger as men. Forget the fact that you're talking about racing drivers. They enjoyed more or less the same thing, although Gerhard was much more extrovert and Lauda always an introvert. I worked for Lauda for a few years and I never really understood him, never really got close to him as I have with Prost and Senna and Berger and everyone else. Lauda was a very enigmatic person, difficult to get deep into. I learned more about him when he'd retired and I read his autobiography (*To Hell and Back*). I wish I could have worked with him after I'd read it!

'He was a tremendous driver, not very good in qualifying, not very good testing, but a good race driver once he got in there because he was very much a tactician, he used psychology to beat a lot of the people he raced. Senna thought a lot of Lauda — Prost was at the top, Prost was the man to beat, but Senna learned from Lauda. Gerhard has the speed, much more speed than Lauda ever had. The biggest problem with Gerhard is the total concentration. He hasn't got it, he can't master the concentration.'

It leads to the central question again. Can the man with The Human Face become World Champion? It's December 1994 now, he's in London for the *Autosport* annual awards and also for talks on safety. At the award ceremony he gets very excited because Rowan Atkinson is the star turn and Berger babbles like a schoolboy, 'Mr Bean is coming, *the* Mr Bean?' Yes, Mr Bean is coming and is very funny and perceptive — evidently he's a Formula 1 follower.

Berger, meanwhile, hears the latest news on the Formula 1 front: that Williams are supposed to have an option on the brilliant young Scotsman David Coulthard, but Marlboro McLaren have signed him; the matter is subject to an inquiry and that has supposedly thwarted the intention of Ron Dennis to announce to the assembled host that his new driver is Coulthard. Berger has to make a speech himself and says only, 'Sorry Ron, I hear the lawyers got there first.' A moment of silence, then the place erupted.

Next day I'm due to meet Berger in the Dorchester, all arranged for two o'clock. He has the safety meeting first, which means he'll be late, and I've taken along a book, *Enzo Ferrari, The man and the machine* by Brock Yates, to pass the time. No deliberate choice of it. I just happened to be reading it at the time. The tea room in the Dorchester is timeless, decorous, dignified and not, let us say, cheap. I order a small pot of coffee (£3.10) and, as the wait extends, another. I'm £6.20 down *but* they need to set my table for high tea and ask me, with exquisite politeness, if I'd mind moving to another table. No problem at all. Because they have asked this, they won't let me pay for the coffee. Company policy, evidently. I'm £6.20 up again. Yippee.

Berger arrives at high speed wearing a chic embroidered sweater that somehow, even among all the American tourist ladies weighed down with their finery and the Japanese businessmen who seem to have been pressed into dark suits, looks appropriate. We shake hands and he says 'back in a minute' and sets off again at equally high speed. (This is the way it is with Formula 1 people. Hell is sitting still.) He returns, sits and thumbs urgently through the book concentrating on the pictures. We'd like pots of tea — he orders fruit tea, 'any kind' — but the petite waitress explains with the same exquisite politeness that at this hour they only serve the full high tea and it's £8 a head. We only want a pot each and no muffins, crumpets, sandwiches or whatever else they have, and I volunteer to pay. I'm £16 down again, not to mention the tip.

We talk. How frustrating has it been for you over the last two seasons knowing that you were capable of winning regularly but the car really wasn't?

'I tell you, I wasn't too frustrated because when I signed for Ferrari I knew what was going to happen. But I still signed because I saw it as a long-term project. Maybe that's the wrong thinking for a Formula 1 driver, maybe you shouldn't think long-term because you are limited in the years you have. Usually you see everything in the short term. Maybe that was a mistake in my thinking, but on the other hand I liked to go to Ferrari. I knew what the conditions were, I knew what I'd have to go through but now, finally, I'm ending up where I thought I'd end up. We are competitive — or quite competitive — so I'm all right. We are certainly close to being competitive.

'The final thing is still to do, and that is not just be competitive but be competitive enough to win a World Championship. To win one race or two races is one thing, to win races consistently is another thing. We are far away from that. There has been a big improvement in 1994 but we don't know if next year will be the year — it's a question mark again, and if you go into a season with a question mark it's not very good.'

Candour, you see, and more candour upcoming because I wonder if he'll talk about his team-mate, Jean Alesi.

'Sure.'

I venture that Alesi worries me.

'Why?'

Because he drives like people do when they're 17, fearless and florid and frantic. Berger smiles.

'I was very careful with him in the beginning, I was careful to check what kind of character he had because I'd heard different opinions, I'd heard different messages. So I checked it out myself and I have to say he's a good guy. A funny guy. He likes to laugh and if you get friends with him you realise that. My experience with him has been fine, and frankly I enjoy having him as a team-mate. He's very quick so he's pushing. Of course he makes some mistakes, but for me it's a good push. He's *bloody* quick, yes. Whether he can put a Championship together I don't know, but he's certainly quick enough to win races.' The central question, of course, and also applicable to Gerhard Berger himself.

Next day, as luck would have it, the American *Forbes* magazine publishes a table of the world's highest-paid sportsmen in millions of dollars.

		Salary	*Endorse-ments*	*Total*
1.	Michael Jordan (US) Basketball	0.01	30.0	30.01
2.	Shaquille O'Neal (US) Basketball	4.2	12.5	16.7
3.	Jack Nicklaus (US) Golf	0.3	14.5	14.8
4.	Arnold Palmer (US) Golf	0.1	13.5	13.6
5.	Gerhard Berger (Austria) F1	12.0	1.5	13.5
6.	Wayne Gretzky (Canada) Ice Hockey	9.0	4.5	13.5
7.	Michael Moorer (US) Boxing	12.0	0.1	12.1
8.	Evander Holyfield (US) Boxing	10.0	2.0	12.0
9.	Andre Agassi (US) Tennis	1.9	9.5	11.4
10.	Nigel Mansell (GB) F1/Indy	9.3	2.0	11.3

And I volunteered to pay for the tea . . .

The notion that keeps tickling my fancy is that Berger can become World Champion and would make a champion to reverse the flow of time and take us back to where we really want to be — while at the same time bringing to Formula 1 what it needs most of all: approachability, normality, schnapps, monkey masks, honesty, naked breasts protruding in unlikely places, acceptable expletives. We'll never see him again, or anyone else, through the old Eau Rouge flat, an immense sight and proving that you can have a joke or two before and a joke or two after, but when the business is to be done, let's do the business. We will see him again, I trust, show-ing a certain grace in victory and defeat, which is how it should always be in any sport, see great, great high-grade racing, which is what it's really about, anyway.

Behind it, as Barnard implies, a little bit of the boy will remain in the man and a little bit of the boy should remain in every sports-man. We grow old and wise and withdrawn too soon, we lose the perspective, the simple purity of the pursuit of pleasure. Peter Collins distils the whole of our story. 'He loves, he loves life. At Suzuka I was drunk but I remember it as funny when he kept giving me the schnapps. I said, "I am going to get you for this", and he said, "Sit down, have a drink, tomorrow you could be dead." That really sums him up. Live for today.'

12

Statistics

Gerhard Berger's career in single-seater racing, but including European Touring cars.

R = retired   P = pole   FL = fastest lap   ET = European Touring cars

1982
German Formula 3

27/28 March	Nurburgring 300 km	Martini-Alfa	Heat 1	8
			Final	16
3 April	Hockenheim	Martini-Alfa		6
23 May	Salzburg	Martini-Alfa		4
6 June	Wunstorf	Martini-Alfa		3
20 June	Hockenheim F2000	Martini-Alfa		R
4 July	Erding	Martini-Alfa		5
18 July	Nurburgring	Martini-Alfa		R
1 August	Diepholz	Martini-Alfa		10
22 August	Zolder	Martini-Alfa		3
26 September	Nurburgring	Martini-Alfa		4
3 October	Kassel-Calden	Martini-Alfa		9

J. Nielsen 140 points, B. Eichmann 110, G. Berger 83.

1983
European Formula 3

17 April	Zolder	Ralt-Alfa	3
1 May	Magny-Cours	Ralt-Alfa	6
22 May	Osterreichring	Ralt-Alfa	2
12 June	Silverstone	Ralt-Alfa	13

26 June	Monza	Ralt-Alfa	R
10 July	Misano	Ralt-Alfa	7
31 July	Zandvoort	Ralt-Alfa	11
7 August	Knutstorp	Ralt-Alfa	2
13 August	Osterreichring	Ralt-Alfa	4
4 September	Nogaro	Ralt-Alfa	R
11 September	Jarama	Ralt-Alfa	R
25 September	Imola	Ralt-Alfa	6
20 November	Macau GP	Ralt-Alfa	3

P. Martini 66 points, J. Nielsen 62, E. Pirro 52, G. Berger (7th) 18

1984
European Formula 3

25 March	Donington	Ralt-Alfa	4
1 April	Monza ET	BMW 635CSi	R
8 April	Vallelunga ET	BMW 635CSi	R
15 April	Zolder	Ralt-Alfa	4
1 May	Magny-Cours	Ralt-Alfa	7
13 May	La Chatre	Ralt-Alfa	3
27 May	Osterreichring	Ralt-Alfa	1
2 June	Monaco	Ralt-Alfa	2
10 June	Silverstone	Ralt-Alfa	4
17 June	Nurburgring	Ralt-Alfa	3
24 June	Monza	Ralt-Alfa	1
1 July	Salzburgring	BMW 635CSi	8
8 July	Enna	Ralt-Alfa	3
15 July	Mugello	Ralt-Alfa	2
28/29 July	Spa ET	BMW 635CSi	R
19 August	Austrian GP, Osterreichring	ATS	12
9 September	Italian GP, Monza	ATS	6
16 September	Nogaro	Ralt-Alfa	3
23 September	Zolder ET	BMW 635CSi	R
7 October	European GP, Nurburgring	ATS	R
21 October	Portuguese GP, Estoril	ATS	13

European Formula 3: I. Capelli 60 points, J. Dumfries 54,
G. Berger 49.

1985

31 March	Monza ET	BMW 635CSi	R
7 April	Brazilian GP, Rio	Arrows A8	R
21 April	Portuguese GP, Estoril	Arrows A8	R
5 May	San Marino GP, Imola	Arrows A8	R

19 May	Monaco GP, Monte Carlo	Arrows A8	R
9 June	Brno ET	BMW 635CSi	3
16 June	Canadian GP, Montreal	Arrows A8	13
23 June	US GP, Detroit	Arrows A8	11
30 June	Salzburg ET	BMW 635CSi	8
7 July	French GP, Ricard	Arrows A8	R
21 July	British GP, Silverstone	Arrows A8	8
27/28 July	Spa ET	BMW 635CSi	1
4 August	German GP, Nurburgring	Arrows A8	7
18 August	Austrian GP, Osterreichring	Arrows A8	R
25 August	Dutch GP, Zandvoort	Arrows A8	9
8 September	Italian GP, Monza	Arrows A8	R
15 September	Belgian GP, Spa	Arrows A8	7
29 September	Zolder ET	BMW 635CSi	4
6 October	European GP, Brands Hatch	Arrows A8	10
13 October	Estoril ET	BMW 635CSi	3
19 October	South African GP, Kyalami	Arrows A8	5
3 November	Australian GP, Adelaide	Arrows A8	6

1986

23 March	Brazilian GP, Rio	Benetton B186	6
6 April	Donington ET	BMW 635CSi	2
13 April	Spanish GP, Jerez	Benetton B186	6
27 April	San Marino GP, Imola	Benetton B186	3
4 May	Misano ET	BMW 635CSi	1
11 May	Monaco GP, Monte Carlo	Benetton B186	R
18 May	Anderstorp ET	BMW 635CSi	R
25 May	Belgian GP, Spa	Benetton 186	10
8 June	Brno ET	BMW 635CSi	6
15 June	Canadian GP, Montreal	Benetton B186	R
22 June	US GP, Detroit	Benetton B186	R
6 July	French GP, Ricard	Benetton B186	R
13 July	British GP, Brands Hatch	Benetton B186	R
27 July	German GP, Hockenheim	Benetton B186	10/FL
2/3 August	Spa ET	BMW 635CSi	3
10 August	Hungarian GP, Budapest	Benetton B186	R
17 August	Austrian GP, Osterreichring	Benetton B186	7/FL
7 September	Italian GP, Monza	Benetton B186	5
14 September	Nogaro ET	BMW 635CSi	1
21 September	Portuguese GP, Estoril	Benetton B186	R
28 September	Zolder ET	BMW 635CSi	2
12 October	Mexican GP, Mexico City	Benetton B186	1
26 October	Australian GP, Adelaide	Benetton B186	R

1987

12 April	Brazilian GP, Rio	Ferrari F1/87	4
3 May	San Marino GP, Imola	Ferrari F1/87	R
17 May	Belgian GP, Spa	Ferrari F1/87	R
31 May	Monaco GP, Monte Carlo	Ferrari F1/87	4
21 June	US GP, Detroit	Ferrari F1/87	4
5 July	French GP, Ricard	Ferrari F1/87	R
12 July	British GP, Silverstone	Ferrari F1/87	R
26 July	German GP, Hockenheim	Ferrari F1/87	R
9 August	Hungarian GP, Budapest	Ferrari F1/87	R
16 August	Austrian GP, Osterreichring	Ferrari F1/87	R
6 September	Italian GP, Monza	Ferrari F1/87	4
20 September	Portuguese GP, Estoril	Ferrari F1/87	2/P/FL
27 September	Spanish GP, Jerez	Ferrari F1/87	R/FL
18 October	Mexican GP, Mexico City	Ferrari F1/87	R
1 November	Japanese GP, Suzuka	Ferrari F1/87	1/P
15 November	Australian GP, Adelaide	Ferrari F1/87	1/P/FL

1988

3 April	Brazilian GP, Rio	Ferrari F1/87/88-C	2/FL
1 May	San Marino GP, Imola	Ferrari F1/87/88-C	5
15 May	Monaco GP, Monte Carlo	Ferrari F1/87/88-C	2
29 May	Mexican GP, Mexico City	Ferrari F1/87/88-C	3
12 June	Canadian GP, Montreal	Ferrari F1/87/88-C	R
19 June	US GP, Detroit	Ferrari F1/87/88-C	R
3 July	French GP, Ricard	Ferrari F1/87/88-C	4
10 July	British GP, Silverstone	Ferrari F1/87/88-C	9/P
24 July	German GP, Hockenheim	Ferrari F1/87/88-C	3
7 August	Hungarian GP, Budapest	Ferrari F1/87/88-C	4
28 August	Belgian GP, Spa	Ferrari F1/87/88-C	R/FL
11 September	Italian GP, Monza	Ferrari F1/87/88-C	1
25 September	Portuguese GP, Estoril	Ferrari F1/87/88-C	R/FL
2 October	Spanish GP, Jerez	Ferrari F1/87/88-C	6
30 October	Japanese GP, Suzuka	Ferrari F1/87/88-C	4
13 November	Australian GP, Adelaide	Ferrari F1/87/88-C	R

Senna 90 (94) points, Prost 87 (105), Berger 41.

1989

26 March	Brazilian GP, Rio	Ferrari 640	R
23 April	San Marino GP, Imola	Ferrari 640	R
28 May	Mexican GP, Mexico City	Ferrari 640	R
4 June	US GP, Phoenix	Ferrari 640	R

18 June	Canadian GP, Montreal	Ferrari 640	R
9 July	French GP, Ricard	Ferrari 640	R
16 July	British GP, Silverstone	Ferrari 640	R
30 July	German GP, Hockenheim	Ferrari 640	R
13 August	Hungarian GP, Budapest	Ferrari 640	R
27 August	Belgian GP, Spa	Ferrari 640	R
11 September	Italian GP, Monza	Ferrari 640	2
24 September	Portuguese GP, Estoril	Ferrari 640	1/FL
1 October	Spanish GP, Jerez	Ferrari 640	2
22 October	Japanese GP, Suzuka	Ferrari 640	R
5 November	Australian GP, Adelaide	Ferrari 640	R

Prost 76 (81) points, Senna 60, Patrese 40, Mansell 38, Boutsen 37, Nannini 32, Berger 21.

1990

11 March	US GP, Phoenix	McLaren MP4/5B	R/P/FL
25 March	Brazilian GP, Interlagos	McLaren MP4/5B	2/FL
13 May	San Marino GP, Imola	McLaren MP4/5B	2
27 May	Monaco GP, Monte Carlo	McLaren MP4/5B	3
10 June	Canadian GP, Montreal	McLaren MP4/5B	4/FL
24 June	Mexican GP, Mexico City	McLaren MP4/5B	3/P
8 July	French GP, Ricard	McLaren MP4/5B	5
15 July	British GP, Silverstone	McLaren MP4/5B	14
29 July	German GP, Hockenheim	McLaren MP4/5B	3
12 August	Hungarian GP, Budapest	McLaren MP4/5B	16
26 August	Belgian GP, Spa	McLaren MP4/5B	3
9 September	Italian GP, Monza	McLaren MP4/5B	3
23 September	Portuguese GP, Estoril	McLaren MP4/5B	4
30 September	Spanish GP, Jerez	McLaren MP4/5B	R
21 October	Japanese GP, Suzuka	McLaren MP4/5B	R
4 November	Australian GP, Adelaide	McLaren MP4/5B	4

Senna 78 points, Prost 71 (73), Piquet 43 (44), Berger 43.

1991

10 March	US GP, Phoenix	McLaren MP4/6	R
24 March	Brazilian GP, Interlagos	McLaren MP4/6	3
28 April	San Marino GP, Imola	McLaren MP4/6	2/FL
12 May	Monaco GP, Monte Carlo	McLaren MP4/6	R
2 June	Canadian GP, Montreal	McLaren MP4/6	R
16 June	Mexican GP, Mexico City	McLaren MP4/6	R
7 July	French GP, Magny-Cours	McLaren MP4/6	R
14 July	British GP, Silverstone	McLaren MP4/6	2

28 July	German GP, Hockenheim	McLaren MP4/6	4
11 August	Hungarian GP, Budapest	McLaren MP4/6	4
25 August	Belgian GP, Spa	McLaren MP4/6	2
8 September	Italian GP, Monza	McLaren MP4/6	4
22 September	Portuguese GP, Estoril	McLaren MP4/6	R
29 September	Spanish GP, Barcelona	McLaren MP4/6	R/P
20 October	Japanese GP, Suzuka	McLaren MP4/6	1/P
3 November	Australian GP, Adelaide	McLaren MP4/6	3/FL

Senna 96 points, Mansell 72, Patrese 53, Berger 43.

1992

1 March	South African GP, Kyalami	McLaren MP4/6B	5
22 March	Mexican GP, Mexico City	McLaren MP4/6B	4/FL
5 April	Brazilian GP, Interlagos	McLaren MP4/7	R
3 May	Spanish GP, Barcelona	McLaren MP4/7	4
17 May	San Marino GP, Imola	McLaren MP4/7	R
31 May	Monaco GP, Monte Carlo	McLaren MP4/7	R
14 June	Canadian GP, Montreal	McLaren MP4/7	1/FL
5 July	French GP, Magny-Cours	McLaren MP4/7	R
12 July	British GP, Silverstone	McLaren MP4/7	5
26 July	German GP, Hockenheim	McLaren MP4/7	R
16 August	Hungarian GP, Budapest	McLaren MP4/7	3
30 August	Belgian GP, Spa	McLaren MP4/7	R
13 September	Italian GP, Monza	McLaren MP4/7	4
27 September	Portuguese GP, Estoril	McLaren MP4/7	2
25 October	Japanese GP, Suzuka	McLaren MP4/7	2
8 November	Australian GP, Adelaide	McLaren MP4/7	1

Mansell 108 points, Patrese 56, Schumacher 53, Senna 50, Berger 49.

1993

14 March	South African GP, Kyalami	Ferrari V12	6
28 March	Brazilian GP, Interlagos	Ferrari V12	R
11 April	European GP, Donington	Ferrari V12	R
25 April	San Marino GP, Imola	Ferrari V12	R
9 May	Spanish GP, Barcelona	Ferrari V12	6
23 May	Monaco GP, Monte Carlo	Ferrari V12	R
13 June	Canadian GP, Montreal	Ferrari V12	4
4 July	French GP, Magny-Cours	Ferrari V12	14
11 July	British GP, Silverstone	Ferrari V12	R
25 July	German GP, Hockenheim	Ferrari V12	6
15 August	Hungarian GP, Budapest	Ferrari V12	3
29 August	Belgian GP, Spa	Ferrari V12	10

12 September	Italian GP, Monza	Ferrari V12	R
26 September	Portuguese GP, Estoril	Ferrari V12	R
24 October	Japanese GP, Suzuka	Ferrari V12	R
7 November	Australian GP, Adelaide	Ferrari V12	5

Prost 99 points, Senna 73, Hill 69, Schumacher 52, Patrese 20, Alesi 16, Brundle 13, Berger 12.

1994

27 March	Brazilian GP, Interlagos	Ferrari V12	R
17 April	Pacific GP, Aida	Ferrari V12	2
1 May	San Marino GP, Imola	Ferrari V12	R
15 May	Monaco GP, Monte Carlo	Ferrari V12	3
29 May	Spanish GP, Barcelona	Ferrari V12	R
12 June	Canadian GP, Montreal	Ferrari V12	4
3 July	French GP, Magny-Cours	Ferrari V12	3
10 July	British GP, Silverstone	Ferrari V12	R
31 July	German GP, Hockenheim	Ferrari V12	1/P
14 August	Hungarian GP, Budapest	Ferrari V12	12
28 August	Belgium GP, Spa	Ferrari V12	R
11 September	Italian GP, Monza	Ferrari V12	2
25 September	Portuguese GP, Estoril	Ferrari V12	R/P
16 October	European GP, Jerez	Ferrari V12	5
6 November	Japanese GP, Suzuka	Ferrari V12	R
13 November	Australian GP, Adelaide	Ferrari V12	2

Schumacher 92 points, Hill 91, Berger 41.

Index